Globalizing Human Resource Management

The role of international HR professionals is coming to the fore as new information and communication technologies transform both organizational structures and geographic boundaries. As a result of these changes, businesses are increasingly realizing that without attention to foreign markets and competitors their prosperity and survival may be at stake.

Globalizing Human Resource Management serves to establish the agenda for global HR as seen through the eyes of HR professionals themselves. The text is at once a broad, coherent overview of the field of IHRM and a detailed, practical analysis of what is needed to be successful in this crucial area of modern management. A number of key questions are addressed:

- Does IHRM drive the business agenda more than domestic HRM?
- What is the impact of IHRM on organizational effectiveness?
- What are the keys to success in IHRM?

Drawing upon current research conducted as part of the Chartered Institute of Personnel and Development's *Globalization Research Project* the text includes data from surveys of HR professionals and company practice as well as longitudinal case studies. These case studies cover diverse organizations, including industrial, consumer, online recruitment and non-profit firms.

Essential reading for all students of Human Resource Management and International Business as well as for practicing HR professionals.

Paul Sparrow is Ford Professor of International HRM at Manchester Business School.
Chris Brewster is Professor of International HRM at Henley Management College.
Hilary Harris is Director of the Center for Research into the Management of Expatriation at Cranfield Management School.

Routledge Global Human Resource Management Series

Edited by Randall S. Schuler, Susan E. Jackson, Paul Sparrow and Michael Poole

Routledge Global Human Resource Management is an important new series that examines human resources in its global context. The series is organized into three strands: content and issues in global human resource management (HRM); specific HR functions in a global context; and comparative HRM. Authored by some of the world's leading authorities on HRM, each book in the series aims to give readers comprehensive, in-depth and accessible texts that combine essential theory and best practice. Topics covered include cross-border alliances, global leadership, global legal systems, HRM in Asia, Africa and the Americas, industrial relations and global staffing.

Managing Human Resources in Cross-Border Alliances
Randall S. Schuler, Susan E. Jackson and Yadong Luo

Managing Human Resources in Africa
Edited by Ken N. Kamoche, Yaw A. Debrah, Frank M. Horwitz and Gerry Nkombo

Globalizing Human Resource Management
Paul Sparrow, Chris Brewster and Hilary Harris

Managing Human Resources in Asia-Pacific
Edited by Pawan S. Budhwar

Globalizing Human Resource Management

Paul Sparrow, Chris Brewster and
Hilary Harris

LONDON AND NEW YORK

First published 2004 by Routledge
11 New Fetter Lane, London EC4P 4EE

Simultaneously published in the USA and Canada
by Routledge
29 West 35th Street, New York, NY 10001

Routledge is an imprint of the Taylor & Francis Group

Typeset in Times New Roman
by Keystroke, Jacaranda Lodge, Wolverhampton
Printed and bound in Great Britain
by TJ International Ltd, Padstow, Cornwall

British Library Cataloguing in Publication Data
A catalogue record for this book is available from the British Library

Library of Congress Cataloging in Publication Data
Sparrow, Paul.
    Globalizing human resource management / Paul Sparrow, Chris Brewster
and Hilary Harris. – 1st ed.
        p. cm. – (Routledge global human resource management series; 3)
Includes bibliographical references and index.
1. International business enterprises–Personnel management. I. Brewster, Chris.
II. Harris, Hilary. III. Title. IV. Series.
HF5549.5.E45S63 2004
658.3–dc22   2003019890

ISBN 0–415–30552–7 (hbk)
ISBN 0–415–30553–5 (pbk)

Contents

Illustrations

Figures

Tables

Boxes

About the authors

Paul Sparrow is the Ford Professor of International Human Resource Management at Manchester Business School. He was Editor of the *Journal of Occupational and Organisational Psychology* 1998–2003 and is or has been on the Editorial Boards of *British Journal of Management*, *Journal of Management Studies*; *European Management Review* and *Journal of World Business*. He returned to Manchester Business School in 2001 and took up the Ford Chair in 2002. He has co-written and edited a number of books including *European human resource management in transition*, *Designing and achieving competency*, *Human resource management: the new agenda*, *The competent organization: a psychological analysis of the strategic management process*, *The new workplace*, *The employment relationship: key challenges for HR*, and *International HRM*. He has also published over thirty journal articles and forty book chapters and consulted with a number of major multinationals.

Chris Brewster is Professor of International Human Resource Management at Henley Management College in the UK. Previously he held the same title at Cranfield and at South Bank Universities. He had substantial experience in trade unions, Government, specialist journals, personnel management in construction and air transport, and consultancy, before becoming an academic almost twenty years ago. He has conducted extensive research in the field of international and comparative HRM; and published some twenty books and over a hundred articles. In 2002 Chris Brewster was awarded the Georges Petitpas Memorial Award by the practitioner body, the World Federation of Personnel Management Associations, in recognition of his outstanding contribution to international human resource management.

Hilary Harris is Director of the Center for Research into the Management of Expatriation (CREME) at Cranfield School of Management. Dr Harris has had extensive experience as an HR practitioner and has undertaken consultancy with a broad range of organizations in the public and private sectors. Her specialist areas of interest are international HRM, expatriate management, cross-cultural management and women in management. She teaches, consults and writes extensively in these areas.

Foreword

Global Human Resource Management is a series of books edited and authored by some of the best and most well-known researchers in the field of human resource management. This series is aimed at offering students and practitioners accessible, coordinated and comprehensive books in global HRM. To be used individually or together, these books cover the main bases of comparative and international HRM. Taking an expert look at an increasingly important and complex area of global business, this is a ground-breaking new series that answers a real need for serious textbooks on global HRM.

Several books in this Routledge series are devoted to human resource management policies and practices in multinational enterprises. Some books focus on specific areas of HRM policies and practices, such as global leadership, global compensation, global staffing and global labor relations. Other books address special topics that arise in multinational enterprises such as managing HR in cross-border alliances and managing legal systems for multinational enterprises. This book, *Globalizing Human Resource Management* by Paul Sparrow, Chris Brewster and Hilary Harris, does a superb job of describing the roles of the HR function, the HR professional and the HR profession in multinational enterprises. The authors provide a wealth of company examples to illustrate their discussions of such topics as measuring the contribution of the HR function, knowledge management in multinational enterprises and developing global HR professionals.

In addition to books on various HRM topics in multinational enterprises, several other books in the series adopt a comparative approach to understanding human resource management. These books on comparative human resource management describe the HRM policies and practices found at the local level in selected countries in several regions of the world. The comparative books utilize a common framework that makes it easier for the reader to systematically understand the rationale for the existence of various human resource management activities in different countries and easier to compare these activities across countries.

This Routledge series, Global Human Resource Management, is intended to serve the growing market of global scholars and practitioners who are seeking a deeper and broader understanding of the role and importance of human resource management in companies as they operate throughout the world. With this in mind, all books in the series provide a thorough review of existing research and numerous examples of companies around the world. Mini-company stories and examples are found throughout the chapters. In addition, many of the books in the series include at least one detailed case description that serves as a convenient practical illustration of topics discussed in the book.

Because a significant number of scholars and practitioners throughout the world are involved in researching and practicing the topics examined in this series of books, the authorship of the books and the experiences of companies cited in the books reflect a vast global representation. The authors in the series bring with them exceptional knowledge of the human resource management topics they address, and in many cases the authors have been the pioneers for their topics. So we feel fortunate to have the involvement of such a distinguished group of academics in this series.

The publisher and editor also have played a major role in making this series possible. Routledge has provided its global production, marketing and reputation to make this series feasible and affordable to academics and practitioners throughout the world. In addition, Routledge has provided its own highly qualified professionals to make this series a reality. In particular we want to indicate our deep appreciation for the work of our series editor, Francesca Poynter. She and her predecessor, Catriona King, have been behind the series from the very beginning and have been invaluable in providing the needed support and encouragement to us and to the many authors in the series. She, along with her staff, has helped make the process of completing this series an enjoyable one. For everything they have done, we thank them all.

Randall S. Schuler, Rutgers University/GSBA Zurich
Paul Sparrow, Manchester University
Susan E. Jackson, Rutgers University/GSBA Zurich
Michael Poole, Cardiff University

Preface

This book is intended to combine insights from the latest theoretical thinking in the area of internal human resource management (IHRM) and strategic human resource management (SHRM) – two fields that are rapidly converging in their focus – with our own research data. The concept for the book can be traced back to a research call from the UK/Irish CIPD (Chartered Institute of Personnel and Development). They appreciated that a growing number of HR practitioners were now operating in an international context and wanted to understand what the impact of globalization was on the role of these professionals. Was the activity of HR practitioners at the international level any more strategic than the corporate activity that they carried out at the domestic level? What models and frameworks should be used to guide their activity in this area? There were a number of competing bids of which two came to the fore. One of these bids concentrated on the insights that should be gleaned by looking at the activities of the international HR function and the conduct of quantitative comparative surveys. The other concentrated on the conduct of longitudinal case-study analysis to track the evolving role of HR practitioners as they worked on the global stage within their organizations. In their wisdom, the CIPD saw the merits of both proposals and asked if we could not combine our resources and methods and design a study that would help inform the HR community about this important aspect of their work. Thereby began a collaboration that has taught us all much about the field of IHRM. We set about this task in the knowledge that we needed to marshal both a wide range of theory, academic and practitioner writing whilst also building up a picture of the emerging role of HR practitioners that would be accessible and useful to them in their everyday work. The final structure of this book says much about the way that practitioners now see and explain their role.

We begin the book as always by explaining the important messages that emerge when we consider the context for the work of international HR. These messages in effect represent the usual caveats and "health warnings" that one must signal before moving on to describe some of the more advanced and innovative practices that can be found. The first important aspect of context is the process of globalization itself. This is an ongoing process, tied up in the strands of history, economic imperatives, institutional constraints and ultimately very much dependent on the actions of organizations and the perceptions of individuals. We outline the competing sources of data or evidence that protagonists and detractors use to position organizations today in Chapter 2 and consider some of the different ways in which one might judge that an industry or the firm is internal in Chapter 3. Globalization is rather like floating in what feels like competing incoming tides and outgoing eddies. In this current of events, there are dangerous rocks that might bring any particular organization's journey to an end, becalming periods when everything seems to be in the doldrums, and sudden maelstroms that require all hands to be on deck whether they agree with the destination or not. The front cover depicts a sailing ship about to set out to trade globally. The technology might have changed but the experience has not. We cannot think of a better metaphor for this book and congratulate the cover designers.

Throughout this book there is a clear message that globalization represents one of those "uncoupling" forces that is making the currently highly nationalistic systems of HRM more receptive to change. It is leading to – sometimes voluntarily sometimes not – an increased transfer of knowledge and insight into different national systems of management. It is leading to a higher-level and more strategic agenda to which HR practitioners can contribute. However, here lies the second important contextual message that concerns the global convergence thesis. Although much of this book concerns emerging consensus of better (we should never say "best") practice, the reality is that national conceptions of best practice and HR effectiveness are still dominant. What is meant by words such as standardization and optimization, or centralization and decentralization is actually very important to practitioners for they have the task of executing the HR strategy, not just formulating it.

Nonetheless, a series of pressures are driving HR practitioners towards more constructive and innovative ways of working across national borders. Our research concentrates on a series of these pressures – the pursuit of organizational capability on a global scale, the development of centers of excellence alongside more routine and transactional types of HR work, the e-enablement of many HR processes, and the opportunities for newly designed HR networks and forum. Together this impact of technology and strategic drivers has brought the effectiveness of global expertise networks and knowledge transfer mechanisms to the fore. We pay particular attention to the nature of HR knowledge that practitioners and their organizations have to transfer.

We also tease out the most important global themes that HR practitioners are using to help coordinate and control their activity on a global basis. This includes integrating their national operations around core strategic competencies or capabilities, managing organizational values and building the equivalent to a brand for the organization and competing for talent in ever wider geographic markets. These sorts of initiatives bring both a sense of coherence across national operations but also involve their own unique implementation challenges when executed across a range of different geographies. They also are carried out hand in hand with the activities more familiar to the field of IHRM – managing international mobility and the global assignment cycle.

Finally, we give some attention to the issue of evaluation and the question of whether we should consider IHRM as a profession. The question of evaluation is critical. HR practitioners – no different to many other management functions – are under the critical gaze of corporate headquarters and line managers alike. They have to prove their worth and we examine some of the main mechanisms and processes through which they do so, ranging from balanced scorecards to service-level agreements. In order to continue to respond to this evaluation and ensure their own relevance, IHR practitioners have to be developed themselves. We end by looking at what makes them professionals and examining some of the key competencies that they can bring to bear to help keep their organizational ship in charted waters.

Acknowledgments

We would like to acknowledge the UK/Irish Chartered Institute of Personnel and Development for sponsoring this research. In particular, our thanks go to Fran Wilson, Bob Morton, Peter Squire, John Campbell and Duncan Brown for their support of this project.

Understanding the impact of globalization on the role of IHR professionals

1

Introduction

Why should we reconsider the international element to the role of HR professionals when so much current research has reaffirmed that HRM is constructed within strong national boundaries? The role of international HR professionals is coming to the fore as firms continue to globalize at a pace. Information and communication technologies are transforming organizational structures and business processes, breaking down organizational and geographic boundaries. Businesses, whether large or small, are finding competition increasing at rapid rates as more and more competitors enter traditional markets through the use of technology that were once the preserve of national companies/enterprises. Businesses have realized that without attention to foreign markets and competitors their prosperity and very survival may be at stake.

As we look to the near future, the advent of the Internet and e-commerce is further increasing the international flow of goods and services and therefore the pace at which internationalization will impact on the HR role is likely to accelerate. Expansion of the Web is now beginning to affect organizational structures, business processes and global trade patterns. Some believe that the impact of e-commerce in the twenty-first century will be as significant as the introduction of mass production methods in the twentieth century. Certainly, it is already opening up new opportunities for the delivery of international HR services (Sparrow, 2001, Harris *et al.*, 2003).

In this context, managing internationally mobile employees is in many cases the least of the worries on the mind of an international HR manager. An underlying shift in global thinking can be seen in the actions of several leading multinational and domestic organizations. They are being driven by the need to remain innovative in what may be contracting and rationalizing markets, or markets that are being shaken up by new entrants and new competitive behavior. Initiatives aimed at improving temporal, functional or financial flexibility are being introduced side by side with integrated programs intended to link work practices to the need to deliver radical cost improvements. In increasing flexibility, firms also want to change employee identification and their sense of involvement, and this changed identity knows few national borders. Partnership employee relations are being considered on a pan-regional basis, the skills and competencies of middle managers and supervisors are being reprofiled internationally (challenging some national vocational and education training systems). New and more entrepreneurial forms of wealth distribution are being pursued. Firms are then pursuing several different models of IHR organization (Harris *et al.*, 2003).

IHRM in the literature

However, much of the early literature on international HRM (IHRM) tended not to focus on this central issue. Instead, we saw much written about the management of expatriates (see, for example, early work by Ivancevich, 1969; Tung, 1981; Torbiorn, 1982; Mendenhall and Oddou, 1985) as well as significant streams of research into either cross-cultural issues (Hofstede, 1980, 1993: Laurent, 1986) or the more recent comparative HRM (Pieper, 1990; Sparrow and Hiltrop, 1994; Brewster *et al.*, 1996). In line with a growing literature on international business strategy (Porter, 1986a; Prahalad and Doz, 1987; Bartlett and Ghoshal, 1989), most interest was shown in the issues of managing people in international organizations.

Early models in the field of IHRM focused on the role of MNCs and argued that finding and nurturing the people able to implement international strategy is critical for such firms. IHRM was considered to have the same main dimensions as HRM in a national context but to operate on a larger scale, with more complex strategic considerations, more complex coordination and control demands and some additional HR functions. Additional HR functions were considered necessary to accommodate the need for greater operating unit diversity, more external stakeholder influence, higher levels of risk exposure and more personal insight into employee's lives and family situation (Dowling *et al.*, 1999). The research focused on understanding those HR functions that changed when the firm went international. The research also began to identify important contingencies that influenced the HR function to be internationalized, such as the country that the MNC operated in, the size and life-cycle stage of the firm and the type of employee.

Looking back on the development of international management research, it can be divided into three categories:

1 Studies that look at the management of firms in a multinational context, that is, the international aspects of management that do not exist in domestic firms, such as the internationalization process, entry mode decisions, foreign subsidiary management and expatriate management;

2 comparisons of management practices across different cultures (cross-cultural studies) and nations (cross-national studies); and

3 studies that look at management in specific (single) countries (in order to overcome the bias of existing work on a North American perspective) within the domain of international management.

Werner (2002) recently carried out a very useful analysis of the research that gets published in the top US journals in the field of international management. This provides us with a clear picture of the field as traditionally defined (see Figure 1.1). He concentrated his analysis on the first category of research outlined above that looks at the management of firms in a multinational context by analyzing systematically research published in the top US journals, that is, the discourse that is important within the US (and increasingly non-US) academic promotion system (lists have been developed by Gomez-Mejia and Balkin, 1992; Johnson and Podsakoff, 1994; Van Fleet *et al.*, 2000). The 271 articles published from 1996 to 2000 represented 5.5 percent of total content, up from 1.8 percent of content over the previous 20 years – so international management is still a small focus of study but an increasingly important one in the academic field. The field as defined by these 271 articles can be broken down into twelve domains:

- *Global business environment:* threats and opportunities of global economy, global markets, political and regulatory environments and international risk.
- *Internationalization:* descriptions and measurement of internationalization as a process, its antecedents and consequences.
- *Entry mode decisions:* predictors of entry mode choices, equity ownership levels and consequences of entry mode decisions.
- *International joint ventures:* partner selection, partner relations and consequences of IJVs.
- *Foreign direct investment (FDI):* timing, motivation, location and firm and host country consequences of FDI.
- *International exchange:* international exchange, determinants of exporting, export intermediaries and consequences of exporting.
- *Transfer of knowledge:* antecedents of knowledge transfer, processes and consequences of transfer.
- *Strategic alliances and networks:* alliance relationships, networks and outcomes of strategic alliances.
- *Multinational enterprises (MNEs)/multinational corporations (MNCs):* multinational enterprise strategies and policies, models of MNEs.
- *Subsidiary-HQ relations:* subsidiary role, strategies and typologies, subsidiary control and performance.
- *Subsidiary and multinational team management:* sudsidiary HRM practices, subsidiary behaviors, multinational negotiations and multinational team management.
- *Expatriate management:* expatriate management, issues for expatriates, expatriate and repatriate reactions.

As the field advanced, two developments occurred. First, there began to be some convergence of interests between the fields of IHRM and comparative HRM and second, more attention was given to the strategic nature of IHRM activity.

Boxall (1995) highlighted the distinction between comparative HRM and IHRM. The comparative HRM field tends to cover the second and third categories of international management research, that is, comparisons of management practices across

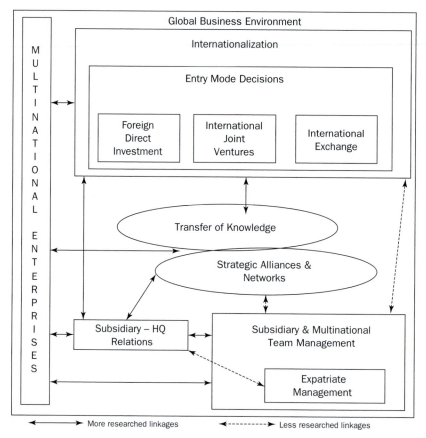

Figure 1.1 Current themes in international management research
Source: Werner (2002)

different cultures and nations and studies that look at management in specific (single) countries. It concentrates on how people are managed differently in different countries by analyzing practices within firms of different national origin in the same country or comparing practices between different nations or regions (Pieper, 1990). IHRM, in contrast, focuses on how different organizations manage their people across national borders. It addresses the added complexity created by managing people (the most nationally specific resource) across a diversity of national contexts of operation and the inclusion of different national categories of workers (Tung, 1993). Although originally comparative and international HRM were distinct fields of study, the increasing reliance on strategic partnerships and joint ventures, coupled with a trend towards localization, has made the need to understand how HRM is delivered in different country contexts more important. Consequently, there has been a degree of convergence in thinking within the comparative and international HRM fields (Budhwar and Sparrow, 2002).

More recent research into IHRM has also acknowledged the importance of linking HR policies and practices to organizational strategy, resulting in a body of literature on strategic IHRM – called SIHRM (see, for example, Schuler *et al.*, 1993; De Cieri and Dowling, 1998). The ways in which MNCs organize their operations globally has been the subject of extensive research by international management scholars (see, for example, Prahalad and Doz, 1987; Bartlett and Ghoshal, 1989: Porter, 1990). Recurring themes in this literature have been as follows:

- the link between strategy-structure configuration in MNCs and the competing demands for global integration (see, for example, Levitt, 1983; Hamel and Prahalad, 1985; Bartlett and Ghoshal, 1989; Adler and Ghader, 1990b; Hu, 1992; Sera, 1992; Yip, 1992; Ashkenas *et al.*, 1995; Birkinshaw and Morrison, 1995; Evans *et al.*, 2002); and
- as against the need for local responsiveness (see, for example, Whitley, 1992; Rosenzweig and Nohria, 1994; Sparrow and Hiltrop, 1994).

An element of both is required in most organizations (Evans *et al.*, 2002) but where global integration and coordination is important, subsidiaries need to be globally integrated with other parts of the organization or/and strategically coordinated by the parent. In contrast, where local responsiveness is important, subsidiaries will have far greater autonomy and there is less need for integration. The key debates in the literature relate to the following *four* issues:

1 *The strategy-structure configurations of international organizations* has been explored by authors such as Perlmutter (1969), Hedlund (1986), Doz and Prahalad (1986), Bartlett and Ghoshal (1997), Ghoshal and Nohria (1993) and Birkinshaw and Morrison (1995). In general, these typologies denote a move away from hierarchical structures towards network or heterarchical structures.

2 *The differences between domestic and international HRM* have been key issues for authors such as Morgan (1986), Dowling (1988), Adler and Bartholomew (1992) and Sundaram and Black (1992). These texts generally indicate the greater complexity and strategic importance of the international role.

3 *How MNCs approach the staffing and management of their subsidiaries.* Thus, Perlmutter (1969) and Heenan and Perlmutter (1979) developed a typology of organizations based upon the dominance of HQ thinking. Though not without their critics (see, for example, Mayrhofer and Brewster, 1996; Myloni, 2002; Rosenzweig and Nohria, 1994; Scholz, 1993) these classifications provide indicators for defining the predominant approach to IHRM within an international organization and have been reflected in other typologies (Adler and Ghadar, 1990).

4 *The role of organizational factors in determining the extent of internal consistency or local isomorphism.* These include the degree to which an affiliate is embedded in the local environment; the strength of the flow of resources such as capital, information and people between the parent and the affiliate; the characteristics of the parent, such as the culture of the home country, with a high degree of distance between cultures being predicated to lead to more internal consistency (Rosenzweig and Nohria, 1994; Taylor *et al.*, 1996).

There have also been attempts to offer an integrative framework for the study and understanding of SIHRM that include exogenous and endogenous factors (Schuler *et al.*, 1993). The exogenous factors include industry characteristics and technology, the nature of competitors and the extent of change; and country/regional characteristics such as political, economic and socio-cultural conditions and legal requirements Endogenous factors are the structure of international operations, the international orientation of the organization's headquarters, the competitive strategy being used and the MNC's experience in managing international operations. Taylor *et al.* (1996) applied the resource-based theory of the firm to SIHRM and identified three international HRM orientations – the adaptive, exportive and integrative – to corporate, affiliate and employee group level HR issues, functions, policies and practices.

These models demonstrate the complexity of HR decisions in the international sphere and the broad scope of its remit. By attempting to adopt these SIHRM perspectives, HR practitioners in international organizations would be engaging in every aspect of international business strategy and adopting HR policies and practices aimed at the most effective use of the human resource in the firm. Even these integrative models, however, do not fully answer some of the criticisms that have been leveled against the fields of IHRM and SIHRM. These include the following:

1 In much of this literature the political, social, economic, cultural and institutional contexts are treated as simple contingency factors instead of seeing them as part of a complex context in which their effects are mutual and impossible to disentangle.
2 Models tend to confuse cross-national with cross-cultural differences, which risks confusing what will remain stable. The distinction between nation and culture is critical. Comparative approaches tend to directly compare HR practices between countries and subsequently provide an explanation for why they might exist, reducing political, economic or cultural dimensions to do this (Earley and Singh, 1995, 2000). 'Nation' is a rather loose term. Cross-national studies therefore tend to operate at the macro level, taking a gestalt view of an unrelated set of factors that might be at play. However, researchers also need to identify underlying organizational or individual processes through which behavior results and understand how these processes operate as part of a system. Cross-cultural studies operate at the micro level and look at the relationship between specific parts of the system and the notion of culture in its totality and theoretically linked outcomes at work (Holden, 2002; Schneider and Barsoux, 2003; Tayeb, 2003).
3 The issue of cultural relativity has tempted researchers to focus on the "hard" or "core" HR functional processes (Easterby-Smith *et al.*, 1995). Researchers invoke idealist HRM systems (such as the western view of HRM, which emphasizes what have become known as high-performance work systems (HPWS) as a basis of comparison. The field tends to ignore the subtle ways in which cultural/national differences influence the experienced reality of HRM (Earley and Singh, 2000).
4 Yet an overemphasis on comparative factors risks freezing the discourse on change in an overstatement of stable national differences. We need to understand the ways in which comparative systems and practice within MNCs change over time.

5 The wider convergence–divergence debate however tends to assume that the HRM system as a whole has to converge or remain divergent, rather than considering whether some parts of the overall HR system might be converging, in some regions or geographies, whilst other parts might be diverging.

6 Moreover, even within a single HR function there might be convergence at one level but divergence at another. An HR function operates at multiple levels that Schuler (1992) called the five Ps: philosophy, policy, program, practice and process.

Sparrow and Hiltrop (1997) argued therefore that any analysis of IHRM must consider the following three competing dynamics.

- *The range of factors that engender distinctive national and local solutions to HRM issues.* This requires insight into the institutional influences on the employment relationship, the nature of national business systems, modernization processes within these national business systems, the structure and operation of labor markets, differences in the historical role and competence of the HRM function, the way such factors are reflected in the cognitive mindsets of HR professionals from specific countries, and the role of cultural value orientations and their subsequent impact on behavioral processes within employees.

- *The strategic pressures that make these national models more receptive to change and development.* This requires insight into the ways in which the adoption of global line of business structures can override the role of country-level HR managers, the ways in which new forms of work organization create convergent HR needs, the impact that foreign direct investment (FDI) has on organizations and its associated effects on local labor markets; the role that technology has (such as shared service structures, or e-enabled HR) in reshaping national HRM systems, and the impact that best practice benchmarking and optimization has on HRM system change.

- *The firm-level processes through which such change and development in actual HRM practice will be delivered.* These are important for two reasons. First, they provide insight into the complex patterns of continuity and change that exist at this level. Second, they help reveal how firms can move beyond the constraints of the national business system within which they operate. Pucik (2003) for example uses the example of the Haier Group in China to show how important it is to understand atypical and "outlier" firms that are able to differentiate themselves and achieve above average competitive advantage, rather than just assume that national comparative HRM systems automatically apply to all organizations. How is it that some firms in the same context can deliver advantage? Analysis at this level requires insight into the role of political opportunism and the ways in which various potential integration mechanisms in the organization can be mobilized to support the introduction of new policies and practices, the nature of mergers and acquisitions and the impact that they have on the conduct of HRM, the nature of knowledge transfer and the role that global expertise networks and forum can have in facilitating this, and the role of new cadres of like-minded internationalists within the organization and the spread of such internationalism through alternative forms of international working.

In other areas of our writing we have given considerable attention to the first of these three dynamics – the range of factors that engender distinctive national and local solutions to HRM. Indeed, we devote much of the next chapter to reviewing the evidence in this area in order to contextualize the debate about the impact of globalization on the HR profession. However, in this book we focus mainly on the second and third dynamics – the strategic pressures that are leading multinational enterprises (MNCs) towards more global solutions in the delivery of their HRM and the processes within the firm through which such solutions are being delivered. These processes have until recently been relatively little understood (Napier *et al.*, 1995). The IHRM literature has given little attention to the issue of *how* the transition from multi-domestic to a more globally integrated network form of organization changes the role of the corporate HR function and yet it is clear that there are a series of "latent in nature and global in scope roles of the corporate HR function in a MNC [that] are different from its traditional organizational roles in administering HRM programmes and processes" (Novicevic and Harvey, 2001: 1253).

Research program methodology

Why is such a book necessary? Pieper (1990) questioned whether IHRM was more a theoretical construct than anything based on an applied reality. He argued that in order to advance the field we need research that helps us understand what the action of firms over time reveals about the impact that globalization is having on the role of international HR practitioners. We need to combine both quantitative and qualitative research approaches and direct such study towards reconstructing the "how" of IHRM. With the above comments in mind, the data reported in this book are drawn from our study for the British Chartered Institute of Personnel and Development on *Globalization: Tracking the Business Role of HR Professionals*. In particular, we would like to address the following questions:

1 What business models are driving the international HR agenda? What are the links between IHRM and business strategy?
2 How effective and important for business is the role of the international personnel and development manager?
3 Is there a difference between international HRM and HRM in a domestic context? Does international HRM influence the business agenda more than domestic HRM?
4 What is the impact of international HRM on organizational effectiveness?
5 What are the keys to success in international HRM?
6 What are the different HR models of organization being used?
7 What are issues involved in identifying best practice to support vertical global/international/regional businesses?
8 What diagnostic frameworks and processes can be defined to help international personnel and development managers make informed choices?

In order to address such questions, the study used multiple research methodologies and consisted of *four* interlinked approaches: The first was a web-based survey of 732 HR practitioners run in early 2001. The purpose of this survey was to examine the level of "role internationalization." Survey items covered: the HR functions that the professionals were engaged in domestically, internationally or both; the geographical boundaries to their role; the types of employees covered by their role; and a series of demographic items about the employing organization. The organizations employing these professionals themselves employed 2.4 million staff. The average organization size was 2,800 employees, with 400 employees in the UK. We draw most upon these data in Chapter 10 when we consider the impact that globalization is having on the role of HR professionals, the skills and competencies needed and the implications for professional institutions.

The second part of the methodology was a survey mailed out to the senior HR practitioner of the Times Top 200 companies. This survey was designed to examine the international strategy, structure and HR policies they pursued. As such, the data are used to explore *across-firm factors* associated with globalization. Sixty-four organizations took part in the study and most respondents were director-level and responsible for global operations. The following survey items were covered: the type of organization structure, staffing policies, pressures influencing the organizational strategy, priorities in the HR strategy, location of HR policy choice and implementation, accountability for HR service provision, critical competencies for HR and expatriation policies. Seventy percent of them employed more than 5,000 employees, 50 percent had operations in more than ten countries, 41 percent had revenues above £100 million. Seventy percent of the organizations had their headquarters located in the UK, while 16 percent were US based. A similar percentage of organizations (15 percent) had their HQs in either another EU country or Japan or Canada. The survey sample reflected a broad sectoral split, with the majority of organizations being from the manufacturing sector, followed by finance, consultancy and other private sector services. Average revenues were over £100 million pounds. Nearly three-quarters of the sample have more than 5,000 employees worldwide, with over 100 employees in their HQs. They operated in up to fifty countries worldwide. We draw most upon these data in Chapter 3, where we present a model of the main organizational drivers and enabling factors behind their HR strategy, based on various statistical analyzes. We also use the data on skills and competencies in Chapter 10.

The third part of the study methodology involved detailed and longitudinal case studies in seven international organizations. Process based comparative case study analysis was used, drawing upon the approach articulated by Pettigrew (1995). The data are used to explore *within-firm processes* associated with globalization. Data collection combined several approaches: structured and semi-structured interviews with key informants on the basis of a developed interview pro forma; documentary and archive data including minutes of relevant meetings, strategy and policy documents, memos, company newsletters and correspondence. For each case study a number of key actors were identified. These case studies involved recording 87 hours of material from seventy-three interviews with HR directors, business managers and service providers, attendance at key

HR strategy workshops within the organizations, and use of internal documentation and external press search. Fieldwork was conducted over a 2-year period from 2001 to 2003 in the UK, France, Belgium, the Netherlands and Singapore. In addition managers were interviewed with geographical responsibility for the US, Australia, Germany, Ireland, Brazil, Vietnam, Ghana, Kenya, South Asia, East Asia, North Asia and Japan. The interviews themselves were used to examine a number of issues. Case studies were selected in order to tap into a number of pressing IHRM issues and problems, high and low levels of institutional and cultural resistance and traditional and complex technical issues involved in convergence processes. The interviews focused on the following:

- technical and strategic pressures facing the IHRM practitioners;
- rationale and thought process behind their interventions;
- criteria for success;
- political, process and technical skills that had to be brought to bear to manage these interventions;
- contrasting stakeholder expectations of the intervention role; and
- link to organizational strategy and effectiveness.

The seven case studies each tended to have a specific issue-focus. For example, in Shell People Services the focus was on the web-based provision of International HR services and knowledge transfer across four global businesses through the development of communities of practice. In Rolls-Royce Plc the focus was on the experiences of a UK-centric organization going global, its pursuit of a global center of excellence strategy, and development of new areas of business through international joint venture working. In Diageo (originally United Distillers/Guinness, Burger King, Pilsbury) the focus was on the convergence around core performance capability management, rewards and talent development processes and decentralization of international HR through the use of global networks. In Stepstone.com the focus was on the internationalization of HR in an e-commerce setting and the management of a start-up venture under intense competition. In BOC Group the focus was on the alignment of Asian HR country management with global lines of business that had been established in all other regional geographies. In ActionAid the focus was on international management in a "not for profit" context and the development of values-based global HR interventions. Finally, in Pacific Direct the focus was on internationalization processes in an SME context. We provide various vignettes and episodes linked to the specific questions in hand in each chapter, usually after we have articulated some of the conceptual debate from the literature.

The fourth part of the study involved the running of a series of three design validation workshops, one research-sharpening validation workshop and three policy implication workshops. The first two of these were events held in June and September 2000 under the auspices of the Center for Research into the Management of Expatriation based at Cranfield University. These involved practitioners from several MNCs and were used to inform the design of the two surveys. The third event was run in October 2000 at the CIPD's Heads of Nations Meeting in which the senior HR professionals from various country professional HR institutions worked in groups on three issues: the main international HR agenda in their organizations; the business models and issues that were driving this agenda; and the questions that they wanted to see answered by the research program. In November 2001 an important research-sharpening workshop attended by senior HR Directors from Citibank, IBM, Ford of Europe, Rolls-Royce, Shell, Panasonic, Motorola and the BBC was run to provide ongoing validation of results and future sharpening of investigation. Its purpose was to:

- assess the validity of the findings emerging from the survey work and first stage case study interviews;
- provide a 'health check' by discussing the wider applicability of the research findings;
- help focus the interviewing in the ongoing case studies around generic cross-case study issues; and
- consider the most important models and frameworks emerging from the research.

This validation workshop was used to gain insight from firms within and outside the detailed case study process into four emerging research themes: e-enabled HR, global service provision and changes in the role of various intermediaries in the HR process; global knowledge management; rationalization of costs, pressures on the affordability of HR, and the creation of centers of excellence on a global basis; and the impacts on the HR function that result from the need to build a global presence. Finally, a series of other validation events were run under the auspices of the CIPD at a number of international HR manager professional meetings, aimed at providing ongoing briefing to senior HR professionals and seeking feedback on the implications of this feedback. These included CIPD Councils in June and October 2001 and Professional Policy Committee in December 2002. A series of detailed interviews were also held around the issues of e-enablement and centers of excellence in Ford of Europe in 2001 and 2003. We use opinion expressed in these validating workshops to provide structure and interpretation to the various topics discussed in the chapters.

The main challenges faced by global HR functions

The research shows that international HR functions face a number of challenges. In particular, they have to help their organizations manage:

- the consequences of global business process redesign, the pursuit of a global center of excellence strategy and the global redistribution and relocation of work that this often entails;
- the absorption of acquired businesses from what might previously have been competitor businesses, the merging of existing operations on a global scale, the staffing of strategic integration teams, attempts to develop and harmonise core HR processes within these merged businesses and the management of growth through the process of acquisition whereby new country operations are often built around the purchase of a series of national teams;

- the rapid start-up of international operations and the requirement to provide insights into the organization development needs of these new operations as they mature through different stages of the business life-cycle;
- the changing capabilities of international operations as many skills become obsolete very quickly and as changes in the organizational structure and design expose managers to more complex roles that require a general up-skilling of local operations;
- the need to capitalize on the potential that technology affords the delivery of HR services, whilst also ensuring that local social and cultural insights are duly considered when it is imperative to do so and especially when IT is being used to centralize and "transactionalize" HR processes, or to create shared services, on a global basis;
- the changes being wrought in the HR service supply chain as the need for several intermediary service providers is being reduced, and as web-based HR provision is leading to greater individualization of HRM across international operations that often currently have very different levels of "HR sophistication";
- the articulation of appropriate pledges about the levels of performance that can be delivered to the business by the IHR function, and the requirement to meet these pledges often under conditions of cost control across international operations, or shareholder pressure for the delivery of rapid financial returns in new international operations;
- learning about how to operate through formal or informal global HR networks, how to act as knowledge brokers across international operations and how not to automatically pursue a one-best way HR philosophy;
- offering a compelling value proposition to the employees of the organization, understanding and then marketing the brand that the organization represents across global labor markets that in practice have different values and different perceptions;
- the identity issues faced by HR professionals as they experience changes in the level of decentralization/centralization across constituent international businesses. As knowledge and ideas about best practice flow from both the center to the operations and vice versa, it is not uncommon for HR professionals at all levels of the organization to feel that their ideas are being overridden by those of other nationalities or business systems.

The analysis of the current strategies being used to cope with these challenges throughout this book leads us towards two key conclusions about the role of the HR function in international organizations:

- The added value of the HR function in an international organization lies in its ability to manage the delicate balance between overall coordinated systems and sensitivity to local needs, including cultural differences, in a way that aligns with both business needs and senior management philosophy.
- There is a distinction between international HRM and global HRM. Traditionally, international HRM has been about managing an international workforce – the expatriates, frequent commuters, cross-cultural team members and specialists involved

in international knowledge transfer. Global HRM is not simply about covering these staff around the world. It concerns managing international HRM activities through the application of global rule-sets.

Structure of this book

Our study therefore has set out to explore what is happening, at the beginning of a new century, to HRM in a global context. Can we build on existing models in order better to capture the complexity of modern approaches to the topic? In this book we draw together the disparate threads of what is known practically and academically in order to achieve the dual objectives of providing a broad, coherent overview of the field of global HRM and a detailed, practical analysis of what is needed to be successful in this crucial area of modern management.

In Chapter 2 we define what is meant by globalization and examine the debate surrounding its impact. We also look at the nature of HRM from a comparative perspective and consider whether there is convergence or divergence of national practice. In Chapter 3 we examine our survey data and articulate our model of Global HRM. We consider the internationalization of industries, firms and functions and look at the main factors that are driving the globalization of HR functions. In Chapter 4 we look at the impact that technology is having on the delivery of HR services on a global basis, concentrating in particular on the advent of shared service models, e-enablement of HR and future technical challenges facing the IHR function. In Chapter 5 we consider the challenges of global knowledge management and knowledge transfer within the HR function. We consider the role that expatriates, IJVs and mergers and acquisitions play in the transfer of knowledge on a global basis, the reasons why HR practices themselves are expected to be transferred globally, a number of models of the factors that lead to successful transfer (or not) of HR practices, the nature of HR knowledge that needs to be transferred from one International HR practitioner to another and some general lessons from the fields of organizational learning and knowledge management as to how such knowledge transfer can be facilitated. We concentrate on the role of global expertise networks and the development of centers of excellence within the HR community.

In Chapter 6 we look at a series of global themes. In practice, global HRM revolves around the ability of the organization to find a concept that has "relevance" to managers across several countries – despite the fact that they have different values embedded in different national cultures and despite the reality that these global themes may end up being operationalized with some local adaptation. These "superordinate" themes provide a degree of consistency to organization's people management worldwide as they attempt to socialize both employee behavior and action. We consider the role of global competencies or capabilities, initiatives in the area of employer branding and talent management. In Chapter 7 we address the pervasive problem of fostering heightened levels of international mobility. In this chapter we look at the strategic positioning of mobility in international organizations and the implications for individuals of various forms of mobility. We show why it is important that organizations take a wider view of mobility, including short-term and commuter assignments and frequent flying, and examine how the international HR function can manage both the organizational and the personal implications of mobility.

We have noted that international HR functions are under tight cost control and need to deliver strategically relevant HR services. The evaluation of the function has become a central concern. In Chapter 8 we examine the how, who, what and where questions usually raised when addressing the issue of measuring the contribution of the corporate HR function. We look at the link between HRM and organizational performance and approaches to evaluate the efficiency of the HR function through service-level agreements. We also consider how effectiveness is evaluated through the use of balanced scorecards and metrics used to evaluate strategic projects or international assignments. This takes us into a discussion of the most important competencies for the global HR function and the way that it needs to position itself within the business. Finally, in Chapter 9 we turn back to the international HR community and consider the challenges for their own development. We address a number of difficult questions. What are the roles that they must now fulfil? What skills and competencies are coming to the fore? What are firms doing about the need to develop the global competence of their HR community?

2 Globalization and HRM

Introduction

In this chapter we introduce the context in which our model of new developments in global HRM operates and note some of the main debates and questions in this field. The context of course is the increasingly international world economy and the thinking through which organizations attempt to understand their approaches to HRM. The debates and questions center around two features of discussions of international HRM (IHRM) which frequently irritate readers: one is the tendency to spend a substantial part of articles defining the term(s) involved in international HRM; and the other is the assumption that there is no need to define terms.

Discussions of international HRM involve a series of separate but closely connected subject areas. We noted in the last chapter that we need to build an understanding of three dynamics – the first of which was the range of factors that (currently) make HRM distinctive in countries around the world. This chapter builds that understanding by concentrating on the areas of contention in comparative HRM. HRM is almost certainly the one management practice that varies most distinctively between countries (Rosenzweig and Nohria, 1994). But to note this fact begs a series of important questions:

- Has there been an increase in globalization? And, if so, given the controversial nature of the term "globalization," how are we to understand it?
- How are we to understand the different approaches to studying IHRM?
- How are we to understand the differences that there are between the way HRM is managed in different countries?
- Is there evidence of convergence or divergence in the different trajectories of HRM developments in different countries? (In other words, are the differences in the way HRM is managed going to become less or remain a major feature of IHRM?)

These questions form the spine of this chapter. It examines a series of questions about the globalization of the world economy and the issues raised by the identification of differences in HRM in different countries. Some of the most important of these issues concern the different paradigms that are used to understand and research HRM; the different concepts that are used to explain the differences between countries; and the questions of convergence and divergence. These issues form the backdrop against which our subsequent analysis of new developments in global HRM should be judged.

Perspectives on globalization

The first question asks how are we to understand the nature of globalization? A few general observations are in order before we begin the main discussion. International HR professionals need to adopt a broad view of globalization. Their organizations experience a wide range of factors associated with it that are of an economic, political, cultural and sociological nature. However, as they deal with people they have to cope not just with the consequences of the globalization of markets and industries but the *impact* that these have on behavior, attitudes and mindsets. In relation to organizations, globalization is considered to exist within the action of those (relatively few) firms that look at the whole world as being nationless and borderless (Ohmae, 1990, 1996). Consequently, there has always been a focus on MNCs within the globalization literature. Whilst this is understandable, the opportunities to operate on a global basis are increasingly diverse. Although it would be nice to be able to substitute the word "organization" for "firm" in this chapter, we cannot. Most work has concentrated on firms, rather than other interesting global operations or organizations. Academics argue that a true understanding of global operation must also incorporate learning from international family business units, overseas networks of entrepreneurs and even illegal gangs, all of which have found ways of operating more globally (Parker, 1998).

Globalization is generally then, but not exclusively, seen as an economic process. Why is this? Political economists tend to use economic models to establish who the relevant "actors" are and calculate their relative interests. Then they put this information into models of politics in order to understand how these various actors will use their power to shape policy decisions or outcomes (Brawley, 2003). Economists have also established greater consensus as to how to measure many of the concepts associated with globalization (the next chapter looks at measures of internationalization of industries or firms and shows this is not entirely true). Economists have a direct stake in understanding globalization: "There is no activity more intrinsically globalizing than trade, no ideology less interested in nations than capitalism, no challenge to frontiers more audacious than the market" (Barber, 1996: 23).

Brawley (2003) has brought together the many strands that together form our views about globalization and presents a series of definitions that capture the diversity of the topic.

These perspectives represent a series of "pushes" and "pulls" that surround organizations or firms and influence the way they manage. They also reflect some important distinctions in the debate about globalization.

Stonehouse *et al.* (2000) note the important distinction between globalization of markets and globalization of industries. Industries are centered around the *supply of a product or*

Box 2.1 Definitions of globalization

From an economic perspective globalization can be defined as follows:

- a process whereby markets and production in different countries become increasingly interdependent due to the dynamics of trade in goods and services and flows of capital and technology;
- in addition, a change in the nature of goods being traded, with vertical transnational production being fragmented, more intermediate goods crossing borders and corporate strategies based on outsourcing to centers based on international specialization;
- the movement of factors of production from one country to another;
- the integration of financial markets (the most transferable factor of production) and more fluid flows of international capital;
- the creation of a global market based on high levels of cross-border flows of labor migration, trade, communication, transport of goods and other items.

Through a political, sociological, or cultural lens, these economic considerations are supplemented by the following perspectives:

- a political phenomenon in which decisions by vested interests reinforce policy options that support further globalizing processes;
- an intensification of worldwide social relations which link distant localities in ways that mean that local happenings are shaped by events many miles away;
- a state of mind, or way of thinking about the world, that means the individual conceives of their place in society or in politics in global terms;
- competing processes involving both the territorial diffusion of things, people and ideas and the process through which different parts of the world gradually become more interdependent.

Source: after Brawley (2003)

service whilst markets are centered around *demand* (Kay, 1993). The globalization of markets is driven by the needs of customers for products and services that are similar throughout the world. It is concerned with the increasing homogeneity of customer needs, but is generally counterbalanced by the fact that as customers become more aware of their apparently similar needs across the globe, their increasingly sophisticated and informed behavior tends to result in demand for more varied and complex products, not standardized ones. Globalization of industries is a slightly different phenomenon. This is concerned more with the ability of organizations "to configure and co-ordinate their productive or value-adding activities globally and across national boundaries" (Stonehouse *et al.*, 2000: 31).

Similarly, when globalization is portrayed as a new stage in world development (Parker, 1998), it is distinguished from the process of internationalization (Sera, 1992).

Internationalization connotes an expansion of interfaces between nations, the flow of business, goods or capital from one country to another, that is, an action in which nationality is still strong in the consciousness. A global enterprise, by contrast (Parker, 1998):

- draws resources from the world;
- views the entire world as its home;
- establishes a worldwide presence;
- adopts a global business strategy; and
- transcends internal boundaries (of people, process and structure) and external boundaries (of nation, time and space).

The growth of global enterprises leads to increased permeability in the traditional business boundaries, which in turn leads to high rates of economic change, a growing number and diversity of participants, rising complexity and uncertainty.

In short, globalization as a process is not one that is well defined. In the next chapter we look at the different ways in which people have tried to measure it – through the globalization of industries, the internationalization of the organization and internationalization of business functions. Here however we concentrate on the competing *attitudes held about globalization* and broad analyzes of the extent to which the *overall* level of globalization might have increased. Outside the economic, marketing and strategy literatures a more critical and problematic discussion about globalization takes place. These can be summarized under the following major themes (Parker, 1998; Sparrow, 2002):

- "nothing new" perspective
- IMF positive approach
- negative or neo-colonial perspective
- transformative perspective.

The nothing new or realist thesis

There are some important headlines that often suggest that a more global mentality within organizations is advancing at a rapid pace. For example, whilst only 3 percent of US Chief Executive Officers (as they are called) hold a non-US passport, in the more cosmopolitan British organizations, twenty-six of the FTSE 100 (in fact eight out of the FTSE 20) Chief Executives (as they prefer to be called) are non-UK passport holders (*The Economist*, 2003b). Should such data be taken as evidence of advanced internationalism? Well, the "nothing new" perspective – driven by the realist theoretical stance – would say no. It notes that the level of business interdependence is no greater now than in the nineteenth century. For example, trade in world goods and services as a fraction of GDP is only slightly greater now than in 1914 and US imports as a percentage of GDP only grew from 8 percent in 1880 to 11 percent in the 1990s (Farnham, 1994). The inequalities in national wealth that we see today are similar to those that were witnessed in the nineteenth century (Williamson, 1996). Furthermore, discussion of multi-country sourced brands is certainly not new. The example of Worcester sauce (an Indian sauce developed for the British) is used. It was developed in 1834, contained vinegar, molasses, sugar and Spanish anchovies, black Calcutta tamarinds, Dutch shallots, Chinese chillies, Madagascar cloves and French garlic. A similar historical perspective is taken by Moore and Lewis (1999), who demonstrated that global economic activity existed in the ancient world, and then as now most economic-exchange was *regionally* based, not globally based.

The "nothing new" perspective is supplemented by the "not really globalized" argument. Whilst it is true that the MNCs now have a major influence on world and local economies, they are still remarkably domestic in terms of employment. We expand on the measurement of how internationalized a firm is in the next chapter but at this stage note the general consensus that levels are lower than often assumed. Eighty-five percent of the world's MNCs still employ two-thirds of their workforce and produce more than two-thirds of their output in their home country (*The Economist*, 2000a). They are also remarkably fragile. One third of the 1980 Fortune 500 had lost their independence by 1990 and another 40 percent were gone by 1995. Globalization is presented as a relatively limited phenomenon. Most MNCs still do not pass Hu's (1992) five measures of statelessness, which are as follows:

1 the bulk of the assets and people are still found in the host country;
2 stock or firm ownership is still largely national or in the hands of families, or inter-linked networks of national owners;
3 board membership and subsidiary decision-making is still sourced largely by managers with the nationality of the headquarters;
4 the firm still has a legal nationality and turns to national institutions for political and diplomatic protection; and
5 tax authorities in a nation can still choose to tax corporate earnings.

Using data from 1999, the United Nations Conference on Trade and Development (UNCTAD) index of transnationality reported in the World Investment Report (which averages foreign assets to total sales, foreign sales to total sales, and foreign employment to total employment) found that only six organizations out of the top 100 firms score above 90 out of 100, the tenth most transnational firm (Philips) scores only 77.8 and firms likes Coca-Cola and McDonalds rank 31st and 42nd most transnational respectively (Brewster *et al.*, 2001).

Rugman's (2001) analysis, from an economic perspective, concludes that globalization is a myth because there is no single world market with free trade, triad-based production (competing trade blocks of the US, Europe and Japan) and distribution has been the past, current and future reality, MNCs have triad-driven regional not global strategies, and that whilst there is a see-saw of balance between governments and firms, the impact of MNCs and non-governmental organizations (NGOs) will continue to be held in regulatory check (Vernon, 1998). The global firm is still a myth in most instances because assets and workforces are highly domestic, systems of corporate governance distinctly national, senior management structures still tilted towards the home country and key processes such as research and development and innovation still governed by national business systems (see Dunning, 1997; Gray, 1998; Hirst and Thompson, 1999; Prakash and Hart, 2000; Strange, 1998 for skeptical views on the level of globalization).

The IMF/positive perspective

For many, however, looking at the products they use from all around the world and the influence of the international media and the Internet, globalization is a new phenomenon. Some see that as unfortunate; others as very positive. For many in the international business world and in politics in the developed world, globalization is an only slightly tarnished "good thing." Whilst the world may not be too globalized yet, steps need to be taken to push it further in that direction. Thus, the International Monetary Fund (IMF) and *The Economist* magazine see few negative features associated with increasing globalization and many positive features. The World Trade Organization (WTO) was established with the remit of encouraging and extending globalization throughout the world.

Reich (1994) noted the increasing "fleet-footedness" of businesses as technological developments made global integration easier. In the first wave, two decades ago, there was an exodus of jobs making shoes, electronics and toys to developing countries. In the second wave simple service work, such as processing credit cards and writing software code, began to move out from the US. For example, Jamaican office parks were processing US airline ticket reservations for 25 percent of US wage and there were typing factories in the Philippines that offered a rate of 90 cents per 10,000 characters – it could be done for 40 cents in China. In the third wave, beginning to start now, higher-skill white-collar jobs are relocating (Engardio *et al.*, 2003). For example, Dutch consumer-electronics giant Philips has shifted research and development on most televisions, cell phones and audio products to Shanghai. General Electric Co. employs some 6,000 scientists and engineers in ten foreign countries By 2015, at least 3.3 million US white-collar jobs and $136 billion in wages are estimated to shift from the US to low-cost countries. To put this in perspective, however, this represents little more than 2 percent of total US employment today (*The Economist*, 2003a) and, so far, white-collar globalization has not made a measurable dent in US salaries:

> The truth is, the rise of the global knowledge industry is so recent that most economists haven't begun to fathom the implications. For developing nations, the big beneficiaries will be those offering the speediest and cheapest telecom links, investor-friendly policies, and ample college grads. In the West, it's far less clear who will be the big winners and losers. But we'll soon find out.
>
> (Engardio *et al.*, 2003)

A new cold war?

Twelve years ago Boeing started recruiting Russian aerospace engineers at $5,400 a year. In 1999 it opened its Moscow Design Center, employing 700 engineers in 2002. The Society of Professional Engineering Employees in Aerospace (SPEEA) representing Boeing's 22,000 engineers in Seattle became concerned at the movement of jobs and threatened to walk out when their contract expired if the Russian venture was not cut back. Boeing had laid off 5,000 engineers since 2001 due to fall in orders from airline industry. Boeing has used aeronautics specialists in Russia to design luggage bins and wing parts on 777 aircraft. Next it might consider possible joint development of new commercial aircraft. The offshore salary is $650/month for an employee with a master's in maths or aeronautics. Their US counterpart costs $6,000/month. In the face of US industrial action Boeing agreed to reduce its Moscow engineers to 350. However, its strategy remains one of integrating the cheaper Russian engineers into the design process. Its Russian staff already work on everything from redesigning jet-wing parts to designing components for the International Space Station. Boeing's goal is to develop a 24-hour global workforce, made possible by a satellite link from Russia to Boeing's Seattle offices. Its competitors are moving in the same direction. Airbus opened its own Russian design center last year and plans to hire fifty engineers.

Source: after Holmes and Ostrovsky (2003)

We discuss the New International Division of Labor in the next section in the context of low-cost labor. However, a more positive slant argues that globalization is not just leading to a move of low-cost manufacturing jobs to other parts of the globe:

- Trickle down wealth has eroded wage differentials between advanced and advancing countries. For example, in South Korea real wages have risen eightfold since 1977. Wages paid by foreign firms in Turkey are 124 percent above the national average. Workforces in Turkey in foreign owned firms are expanding by 11.5 percent a year compared to 0.6 percent a year in local domestic owned firms (*The Economist*, 2000a).
- There is a significant shift in investment in higher-level skills. For example, a consortium of 57 companies from the US, Taiwan and France, including Hewlett Packard, Intel, Motorola, Acer and Alcatel, has funded the Malaysian Penang Skills Development Center, which is training 10,000 people in computing, programmable automation and other hi-tech subjects (Gordon, 2000).

The effects of globalization then have been to raise the bar and in turn to raise the standards of education in many countries. Wage costs are not the only factor and the level of education and public infrastructure is important. Employees are in competition with similarly educated employees around the world. Between 1995 and 2020 the population of the underdeveloped nations will increase by the equivalent of the total population of the developed nations. The latter's share of school students is falling. In 1970 nearly 75 percent of the world's employees educated to first-degree level came from the developed nations. By 1985 this figure had fallen to 50 percent. By the year 2000 it was only 40 percent (Gordon, 2000). One of the reasons behind the recent significant investment in Asian research and development skills concerns superior levels of educational attainment.

Countries such as the US have good news and bad news in this respect. OECD figures show that 30 percent of US citizens aged from 25 to 34 have a university degree compared to 24 percent in Japan and 14 percent in Germany (*Business Week*, 2003b). Figures such as this pass no judgment on the quality of the product. To counter this, the OECD now measures international competitiveness in part by assessing educational attainment of young school leavers. Its Programme for International Student Assessment (PISA) monitors educational outcomes against internationally agreed frameworks. The results from PISA2000 show performance at age 15 in reading, mathematical and scientific literacy through independently supervised tests in thirty-two countries of 250,000 students (out of 17 million), using structured samples across socio-economic range. The next data are due to be collected in 2003.

Table 2.1 Educational competition?

Country	Reading		Maths		Science	
Finland	*546*	*(1st)*	*536*	*(4th)*	*538*	*(3rd)*
New Zealand	*529*	*(3rd)*	*537*	*(3rd)*	*528*	*(6th)*
Ireland	*527*	*(5th)*	503	(16th)	*513*	*(11th)*
Korea	*525*	*(6th)*	*547*	*(2nd)*	*552*	*(1st)*
UK	*523*	*(7th)*	*529*	*(8th)*	*532*	*(4th)*
Japan	*522*	*(8th)*	*557*	*(1st)*	*550*	*(2nd)*
Belgium	*507*	*(11th)*	*520*	*(9th)*	496	(19th)
France	*505*	*(14th)*	*517*	*(10th)*	500	(14th)
USA	504	(15th)	493	(19th)	499	(16th)
Denmark	497	(16th)	*514*	*(12th)*	**481**	**(24th)**
Spain	**493**	**(18th)**	**476**	**(23rd)**	**491**	**(21st)**
Italy	**487**	**(20th)**	**457**	**(26th)**	**478**	**(25th)**
Germany	**484**	**(21st)**	**490**	**(20th)**	**487**	**(22nd)**
Hungary	**480**	**(23rd)**	**488**	**(21st)**	496	(17th)
Greece	**474**	**(25th)**	**447**	**(28th)**	**461**	**(27th)**
Russian Fed.	**462**	**(27th)**	**478**	**(22nd)**	**460**	**(28th)**
Mexico	**422**	**(31st)**	**387**	**(31st)**	**422**	**(31st)**
Brazil	**396**	**(32nd)**	**334**	**(32nd)**	**375**	**(32nd)**

Source: after OECD (2001)
Note: Above average and average performers: italic shows countries with significantly higher performance and bold shows significantly lower performance, upright text shows average performance.

By the time Japanese students have graduated from high school they have completed four more years of education than a comparable US student. Japan subsidizes 50 percent of wages and expenses for employee training programs that enhance production technology, and the population of 800,000 Japanese research and development employees is greater than that of Germany, the UK and France combined.

Globalization as neo-colonialism

Another school of thought – sometimes also called the "globalization from above" view (Falk, 1993) – takes a more process-orientated perspective to the issue. Whilst acknowledging that we start from regionally based economic systems, they argue that the *notion* and *strategy* implicit behind building a global firm is spreading, that we are witnessing global integration of economies, see the creation of more global management structures within organizations, and see a renewed process of convergence of management technique around notions of best practice. In relation to HRM, globalization is presented as a force that even if not yet leading to convergence in HR practice (we devote the second half of this chapter to this issue) is certainly leading to a challenge to national mindsets (Sparrow and Hiltrop, 1997).

Foreign direct investment (FDI) is seen as one important index of globalization. With the creation of the Single European Market in 1992, Europe became the center and focus of foreign direct investment for the first time (Sparrow and Hiltrop, 1994). The UK, Germany, Holland and France hosted 40 percent of worldwide FDI in the early 1990s. There were 3,500 cross-border mergers in the run up to the creation of the SEM (European firms buying other European firms). The UK was the single largest target of this investment – the value of acquired British firms was greater than that of the rest of Europe put together (Sparrow and Hiltrop, 1994). However, at the same time the UK was one of the biggest buyers. In the following 5 years there was a continuation of major capital flows. The UK attracted £1.7 billion from Korea – the largest single inflow into its economy in economic history. UK firms were investing $27 billion in the US – the largest single country-to-country movement in its history. Questions are typically asked then about the level of balance between inflows and outflows of FDI from economies. For example, in 1995 the ratio of FDI outflows to inflows was 3.8 in Germany, at about parity of 1.3 in the UK and US, but at a massive 674 times as much outflow to inflow in Japan.

Box 2.2 Where will the investment go?

The Economist Intelligence Unit reports on predicted FDI flows for sixty countries for the years 2001 to 2005 using econometric and competitiveness data. Despite the slump at the beginning of this decade, overall investment is expected to rise from $6,500

continued

billion in 2000 to $10,000 billion by 2005. The US will receive 26.6 percent of global investment in this period, followed by the UK (9.3 percent), Germany (7.8 percent), China (6.5 percent), France (4.7 percent), the Netherlands (4.1 percent), Belgium (3.4 percent), Canada (3.3 percent), Hong Kong (2.3 percent) and Brazil (2.1 percent). The latter exception proves the rule: that investment associated with globalization is not going into the poorest countries in the world, but into those that are already amongst the richest.

Source: after Trends International (2001)

Such patterns of investment have a major effect on national economies. The ten largest industrial MNCs each have annual sales larger than the Australian government's tax revenues (*The Economist*, 2000a). Certainly, the world's 1,000 largest companies produce 80 percent of the world's industrial output. FDI also plays a major role in technology transfer in that 70 percent of all international royalties on technology involve payments between parent firms and foreign affiliates. More importantly, the *physical location of economic value* creation is now difficult to ascertain:

> Multinational companies may increasingly operate as seamless global organizations, with teams of workers based all over the world, passing projects backwards and forwards via the Internet or the companies' private in-house intranets. This will make it more difficult for the tax authorities to demand that economic activity and value creation be attributed to a particular physical location.
>
> (*The Economist*, 2000b: 9)

MNCs are then presented as being economically dominant. Around 60 percent of international trade involves transactions between two related parts of MNCs (*The Economist*, 2000b). The $1.3 trillion a day that is traded on the world's currency markets dwarfs even the annual FDI flows (Harding, 2001). This new world order or neo-colonialist perspective therefore argues that we are witnessing a consolidation of power among already powerful business and government interests. Nations with clout are pooling resources and advancing their common economic interests by disseminating consumerism (Korten, 1995). Power is shifting to producers. Convergence in economic governance is restricting social programs, leading to greater inequalities and threats to the environment. There is renewed "imperialism" in which the stronger economic entities use their power to exact concessions (be they concessions from nations, suppliers or workers) (Wanniski, 1995).

Box 2.3 Low-cost labor shifts in the footwear industry

Low-cost labor is located in two main industrial sectors, textiles, clothing and footwear and electronics assembly (Henderson, 1997; ILO, 1998a, b, 1999a, b, 2000). Between 1980 and 1998, the distribution of employment in textiles and clothing and footwear shifted from Europe and the Americas to large gains in Asia (ILO, 2000): Asian Footwear employment in 1995 was four times its 1980 level, and further increased by 124 percent between 1995 and 1997. During 1980 and 1995, clothing employment in Indonesia had risen more than ten times, Thailand by more than ten times, the Philippines by 59 percent. Among the substantial gainers in clothing employment over the 1980–95 period from the United States, Hong Kong, Germany, Brazil, Poland, the United Kingdom, France and Japan were Indonesia, Bangladesh, Thailand, Turkey, Sri Lanka and Morocco, all in the category of less developed, low wage countries. In footwear, by 1995, the United States and Germany showed a 66 percent decline from 1980, while Indonesia and Thailand had become very large employers from a low base (ILO, 2000).

Low-cost labor is, however, only part of a New International Division of Labor (NIDL) that is considerably more complex. The NIDL displays *three* major trends:

1   As noted in the previous section, the global division of labor has been extended from the "low skilled" manufacturing sector to include diverse kinds of skilled labor, such as research and development, scientists, engineers and research technologists (Mytelka, 1987; Viatsos, 1989; Radice, 1995; World Bank, 1995). It has now reached the service sector. MNCs are increasingly sourcing both skilled and "unskilled" low-cost labor from a global market for financial services, banks, software and IT-enabled services and retail concerns.
2   Even the new "core" states, each have their own new "peripheries" (Applebaum and Henderson, 1982; Henderson, 1986, 1989, 1997; Mittleman, 1994).
3   Low-cost labor, mainly from "peripheral" states, still forms a substantial part of the NIDL 20 years later (Gereffi, 1994a, 1994b, 1997; Mitter, 1994; ILO, 1998b). Evidence of this is found in the number of foreign affiliates of MNCs located in developing countries and transition economies (Held *et al.*, 1999).

MNCs – or strong organizations with a dominant position in the customer-supply chain – are then presented as having immense position influence. Reich (2000) summarizes the future pressures as a steadily tightening noose around the neck of employees in terms of rising organizational expectations, increasing global competition, ever-wiser marketers and ever more pervasive communications technology. Social standards at work will have to be cut as employers try to compete with places where standards are much lower.

Globalization as a transformative social force

Parker (1998) has a category that sees globalization as a transformative social force: sometimes also called the "globalization from below" perspective (Falk, 1993). Attention here is directed towards those organizations working for a vision of a just world and for a redistribution of economic power – such as the charities and direct action groups. Two streams of criticism are seen to act as the catalyst for this perspective:

- labor criticisms (blue agenda) pointing to dangers of exploitative child labor, human rights abuse, unequal labor standards and destabilizing levels of job change (ILO, 1998a, 2000; Madani, 1999; Hepple, 2001); and
- environmental criticisms (green agenda) pointing towards unconstrained economic activity accelerating global warming and uncontrolled depletion of resources such as forests in developing economies (Spar and La Mure, 2003; Wild, 2003).

Barber (1996) made perhaps what was to be a chilling observation that the process of cultural merging enabled by globalization would either lead to the McDonaldization of the world, or to a form of counter-cultural Jihad. With some irony, to put it mildly, on the morning of September 11th 2001 UK time the *Financial Times* published the first part of its investigation on *Capitalism under Seige* with an article titled "Globalization's children strike back" and a cartoon showing planes flying round a tower being scaled by protesters (Harding, 2001). Literally a few hours later across the Atlantic the events at the Twin Towers were to be burned into the world's iconic memory. The series was cancelled out of respect.

The transformative social force perspective contains positive and less stark messages about human psychology. It argues that organizations have unleashed social forces that they themselves cannot contain. As businesses become more interdependent with other sectors they also become driven more by market forces, and if the market reflects more social concerns, as it does, then organizations themselves will adapt to the demands of their market (Greider, 1997). The nature of this uneasy balance of power is evidenced in the following quote: "it is easier to change things in Nigeria by boycotting Shell than by lobbying the Nigerian government" (*The Economist*, 2000a: 22). Several environmental campaigns have indeed demonstrated the role of consumer market power and "Activist groups are themselves a creation of the modern global economy . . . Non-governmental organizations are increasingly focussing their powers of persuasion on firms and . . . firms have become increasingly responsive" (Spar and La Mure, 2003: 94).

An empirical investigation of the 1999 Seattle World Trade Organization talks showed that whilst a portfolio of Fortune 500 firms suffered a 1.9 percent fall in equity value as a result of the failed trade talks, those firms perceived as being abusive to labor or the environment suffered a 2.7 percent loss in value (Epstein and Schnietz, 2002). They were penalized more by investors because of association with industries that were under attack from protestors. *Three* factors determine the strategic response of firms (Spar and La Mure, 2003):

1 *Transaction costs*: When costs of compliance are low and the benefits of doing so high then firms are more likely to concede. Where firms perceive higher transaction costs from complying they tend to resist.
2 *Brand image*: Where brand identity is valued, the more susceptible managers are to activist pressures. When we discuss talent management, a threat to the brand is often the precursor of more proactive attempts at employer branding.
3 *Competitive positioning*: Firms can occasionally create a differentiated competitive positioning by being the first in their sector to concede.

Wild (2003) argues that global firms have more to fear from the activities of corporate social responsibility (CSR) related pressure groups such as Greenpeace, Oxfam, Anti Slavery International, Clean Clothes, Amnesty International and Global Exchange than they do from the activities of trade unions, as these non-governmental organizations are now moving their attention to labor-related issues such as child labor, the operation of global sweatshops, workers rights and ethicality of business practices and are attacking organizations who may be partners across the whole supply chain. Organizers' guides for customer action campaigns show that they target an organization where:

- there is visibility and linkage to the issue (instead of targeting Mattel over child labor, pressure groups focused on its flagship iconic brand of Barbie);
- there are no-penalty alternatives (Burger King suffered from allegations of child labor because customers could cross the street to McDonald's);
- expectations are of "better" behavior (Adidas found that whilst a cheap football from a market stall attracts little concern about child labor its £25 product did);
- there is "previous history" (Nestlé was targeted for child labor campaigns because of previous negative press over powdered milk marketing); and
- the issue has attitudinal salience i.e it triggers several other concerns in the minds of people (Monsanto's approach to genetically modified foods triggers multiple feelings about environmental concerns, commercial control over poor farmers by rich organizations, unpredictable scientific innovations and so forth).

The new challenge then matters most only where firm and brand reputations are damaged to the extent that sales volumes are affected.

Box 2.4 Global people management concerns

There is increasing evidence to show that customers feel strongly enough about a firm's global people management for it to influence purchasing decisions. Surveys conducted by the national opinion poll organization MORI between 1999 and 2002 show that seven out of ten British people think that firms do not pay enough attention to corporate social responsibility (CSR) and nine out of ten take CSR into account when making a purchasing decision. The top three factors influencing a purchasing decision are quality (98 percent), value for money (98 percent) and customer service

continued

(97 percent) but the treatment of employees comes next (83 percent) and ahead of both convenience (82 percent) and impact on the environment (79 percent). Under the treatment of employees customers care, in order of importance, about health and safety abuses, child labor, forced labor, discrimination and sweatshop wages.

Source: after Wild (2003)

Why is this of any concern in a book about the globalization of HRM? Is this not territory best left to the marketing and corporate communications function rather than a corporate HR function? Three reasons are forwarded for its inclusion under consideration of global HRM:

1 The corporate HR function is best placed to understand the new risks associated with employment-related behavior of contractors or firms that form part of the supply chain.
2 HR have a historical strength in understanding the complexities of labor law. PR specialists often have a lack of understanding about labor laws where they relate to undesirable practices and the distinctly local and cultural context of people management. In making reputational promises that might not be capable of delivery as easily as assumed, they may make the firm a bigger target than before.
3 Activity closer to the heartland of a global HR function, such as the attraction of global talent, is increasingly dependent on reputation management.

Universalist versus contextual paradigms

The second question that we asked in this chapter is "How are we to understand the nature of the differences in HRM between countries and the different approaches to studying it?" There are differences between countries not only in the way HRM is conducted, but also in the way the subject is conceptualized and the research traditions through which it is explored. These differences result in two paradigms for research into HRM, which have been termed (Brewster, 1999a; 1999b) the

● universalist and
● contextual paradigms.

Many writers note that there is confusion about the most appropriate subject matter to cover when, for example, teaching HRM (Conrad and Pieper, 1990; Guest, 1992; Singh, 1992; Storey, 1992; Boxall, 1993; Dyer and Kochan, 1995; Goss, 1994; Martell and Caroll, 1995). To some degree this reflects differences between these two paradigms. The universalist and contextualist approaches are true paradigms in Kuhn's (1970) sense that they are in general unchallenged and are often held to be unchallengeable. This is unfortunate: just as the debate between the two paradigms can be depressingly sterile, or can lead to research which combines the worst of both. There are different strengths in each paradigm and we can learn most by drawing in the best of both traditions. The assumptions and preferred methods of both paradigms are briefly outlined.

The universalist paradigm, whilst dominant in the USA, is widely used in many other countries. As an approach to social science it uses evidence to test generalizations of an abstract and law-like character. Strategic HRM has the purpose of improving the way that human resources are managed within firms (Tichy *et al.*, 1982; Fombrun *et al.*, 1984; Ulrich, 1987; Wright and Snell, 1991; Wright and McMahan, 1992). The ultimate aim is to improve organizational performance, as judged by its impact on the organization's declared corporate strategy (Tichy *et al.*, 1992; Huselid, 1995), the customer (Ulrich, 1989), or shareholders (Huselid, 1995; Becker and Gerhart, 1996; Becker *et al.*, 1997). It is implicit that this objective will apply in all cases. The value of this paradigm lies in the simplicity of focus, the coalescing of research around this shared objective and the clear relationship with the demands of industry. The disadvantages lie in the ignoring of other potential focuses, the resultant narrowness of the research objectives, and the ignoring of other levels and other stakeholders in the outcomes of SHRM (Guest, 1990; Poole, 1990; Pieper, 1990; Bournois, 1991; Legge, 1995; Brewster, 1995c; Kochan, 1998).

This "best practice" approach is seen as coming from within a universalist approach. It is linked to parochialism, partly caused by the size of domestic US markets with their cultural and geographic barriers, and partly as a consequence that despite the different route taken by MNCs towards internationalization after World War II, the unchallenged post-war economic dominance of US MNCs for a period of several decades established a model that was therefore considered to be linked with superior performance across economic contexts (Humes, 1993). It has become hegemonic, partly because of the influence of US academic systems, publishing and consulting firms. The methodology generally used to research this form of HRM is deductive: to generate carefully designed questions which can lead to proof or disproof, the elements of which can be measured in such a way that the question itself can be subjected to the mechanism of testing and prediction. Built in to this paradigm is the assumption that research is not "rigorous" unless it is drawn from existing literature and theory, focused around a tightly designed question and contains a structure of testing that can lead on to prediction. The research base is mostly centered on a small number of private sector "leading edge" exemplars of "good practice" (potentially value-laden terms), often large MNCs, generally from the manufacturing or the high-technology sector, and usually non-union.

The strength of the approach is that good research based upon it tends to have a clear potential for theoretical development, it can lead to carefully drawn research questions, the research tends to be easily replicable, the research methodologies are sophisticated, and there is a coherence of criteria for judging the research. The weaknesses are that inappropriate techniques or dubious lines of causality can negate much of the value of this form of research, and relevance to wider theoretical and practical debates is sometimes hard to see (Gerhart, 1998).

The contextual paradigm by contrast is idiographic, searching for an overall understanding of what is contextually unique and why. It is focused on understanding what is different between and within HRM in various contexts and what are the antecedents of those differences. In this paradigm explanations matter most – any link to firm performance is secondary. It is assumed that societies, governments or regions, as well as just firms, have HRM. At the level of the organization (not firm – public sector organizations are also included), it is not assumed that the objectives (and strategy) set by senior management are necessarily "good"; either for the organization or for society. It is not assumed that the interests of everyone in the organization will be the same; nor is there any expectation that an organization will have a strategy that all people within the organization as a whole, or even within the top team, will "buy in to" (Kochan, Katz and McKersie, 1986; Barbash, 1987; Keenoy, 1990; Storey, 1992; Purcell and Ahlstrand, 1994; Turner and Morley, 1995; Koch and McGrath, 1996). This paradigm emphasizes external factors as well as the actions of the management within an organization. It explores the importance of such factors as national culture, ownership structures, labor markets, the role of the state and trade union organization as aspects of the subject rather than external influences upon it. The scope of HRM goes beyond the organization.

The contextual paradigm argues that the reality of the role of many HR and international HR departments, particularly for example in Europe, where lobbying about and adjusting to government actions, dealing with equal opportunities legislation or with trade unions and tripartite institutions is a central part of the HR role. This paradigm is widespread in the UK and Ireland, Australia and New Zealand and in many of the northern European countries, but has some adherents in North America (see, for example, Dyer, 1985; Schuler and Jackson, 1987; Dyer and Kochan, 1995). Research methodologies are inductive. Theory is drawn from a more diffuse accumulation of data. Research traditions are focused less upon testing and prediction and more upon the collection of evidence. There is an assumption that if things are important they should be studied, even if testable prediction is not possible or the resultant data are complex and unclear. The emphasis tends to be on the way things work and what "typical" rather than "best practice" organizations are doing (see, for example, the work of the Cranet network, as exemplified in Brewster and Hegewisch, 1994; Brewster et al., 2000, 2003).

Cultural versus institutional explanations

The third question that we asked at the beginning of this chapter was 'How are we to understand the differences that there are between the way HRM is managed in different countries?' Explaining differences in HRM practice is first of all a matter of levels. There is a sense in which all organizations in the world have to recruit, pay and manage people yet there are significant differences between, for example, Japan, the USA and Europe in the way that they do this. There are also differences between countries within Europe and between regions within countries. There is a somewhat sterile debate about the importance of this or that level. The image of a telescope encapsulates the reality

(Brewster, 2001): as the focus is pulled, so some things that were in sharp focus become blurred, but other differences become more noticeable. None is more or less true a view than any other – but some are more useful for some purposes than others. If there are differences between countries in the way they think about and conduct HRM, what causes them? There are two broad arguments:

- cultural and
- institutional.

The first set of explanations comes from *a cultural perspective* – a rich body of work, which includes many famous names (such as Hofstede, 1980, 1991; Laurent, 1986; Schwarz, 1990, 1992; Trompenaars, 1993; and many others). A familiar definition of culture is the one given by Hofstede (1991: 5): "the collective programming of the mind distinguishes the members of one human group from another – the interactive aggregate of common characteristics that influences a human group's response to its environment."

Value systems, and underlying beliefs, vary significantly between cultural groupings – which often, particularly in the longer established countries – overlap with nationalities. These explain why some societies may be more hierarchical; collectivist; more comfortable with uncertainty; and so on. An awareness of national cultural poses a challenge to management theory in many areas, particularly those where people are concerned, and most directly: in the HRM arena.

The most convincing work on how one national culture is consistently different from another has been that by Schwarz (1990, 1992, 1994) and Hofstede (1980, 1991, 1993). It is not necessary in this book to go deeply into the research (it is covered in detail in other books in the Routledge series). Clearly, however, variations on values which occur between nations are going to have a substantial effect on such issues as motivation, appraisal, reward systems and careers: the influence of values related to hierarchy, collectivism and achievement, for example, are bound to be strong factors here. These variations also influence selection methods and criteria, training and development and employee relations (Sparrow and Hiltrop, 1994; Brewster, 1995a).

A cultural explanation does not provide a complete explanation of the differences between HRM in different nations. *Institutional factors* can be seen as the main explanation of differences. Drawing in particular on the industrial relations and political economy traditions, differences in economics, governance, the legislative system and the trade unions, for example, shape what we see in HRM. Firms cannot be immune from the institutional context in which they are embedded (Dacin *et al.*, 1999) and the differences between countries and their political, social and legal institutions create differences in their strategies (Doremus *et al.*, 1998). For our purposes, they are more likely to show differences in their HRM. The differences in ruling parties, employment legislation, education, labor markets and trade unionism have a direct effect on HRM within employing organizations.

Recent work on different varieties of capitalism (DiMaggio and Powell, 1991; Whitley, 1992; 1999; Hollingworth and Boyer, 1997; Hall and Soskice, 2001) has revitalized the political-economy element of comparative HRM. The clusters that these authors present can tend to be very "broad-brush" and differ both in terminology and range of factors. One of the more widely used frameworks by Whitley (1999) suggests six types of business system:

- *Fragmented:* dominated by small owner-controlled firms engaged in competition, using short-term market contracts with suppliers and customers, with little coodination of economic activity, such as in Hong Kong. Employment relations are short-term and there is an efficient external labor market.
- *Coordinated industrial district:* dominated by small firms with extensive inter-firm integration and cooperation across production chains and within sectors. Relies on worker commitment and willingness to improve task performance and innovate. Limited to Italy, or even northern Italian industrial districts and similar European regional business systems.
- *Compartmentalized:* dominated by large firms that integrate activity within production chains and across sectors, but with low levels of commitment and cooperation between firms, business partners and employers and employees. Seen in the traditional US stockmarket-based system, which in Europe also encompasses Anglo-Saxon economies, such as the UK and Ireland;
- *Collaborative:* large units owned by alliances, typically focused on particular industries, which covers many continental European economies. Higher degree of employer–employee interdependence and trust of skilled workers.
- *Highly coordinated:* also dominated by alliance forms of control but with very high levels of organizational coordination of activity through intra- and inter-sectoral alliances and networks, such as Japan's post-war system.
- *State-organized:* dominated by large firms that integrate production chains across sectors, but with ownership retained by families or partners and economic development guided by the state. Examples include the *chaebol* in South Korea.

HRM practices and the nature of hierarchies are, then, influenced by the style of industrial relations and the "stratification of competitiveness at societal level" (Boyer and Hollingsworth, 1997: 190).

Box 2.5 Social systems of production

Configurations of the ways in which economic activity is organized, or the ways in which societal institutions deal with the organization of labor power and capital, create rules and conventions that serve to govern the nature of transactions between organizations. These configurations are called "social system of production" (SSP). By focusing on the nature of exchange transactions between organizations, it was clear that SSPs combined six governance mechanisms: markets; networks of obligations; hierarchies; monitoring arrangements; promotional networks; and associations.

Societies often have more than one SSP – in early US industrial history different systems existed for railroads, steel, automobiles, meat packing and so forth. They also change over time through the action of state policy, technology and changing perceptions of efficiency. However, one SSP tends to dominate a national system as important aspects of the ways that economic activity is controlled and coordinated seem to be more similar across sectors within a country than they vary between countries. Once dominant within a particular society, they are slow to change.

Source: after Boyer and Hollingsworth (1997)

The strength of these theories is the way that they consciously embed industrial relations and HR practices in the institutions and economy of the country or region and the way that they help us to understand variations in the nature and form of HRM in different countries. For example, more adversarial systems are characterized by lower levels of trust within and between firms. Conversely, more cooperative systems rely heavily on building high-trust relations with skilled labor as the source of their competitive advantage and prosperity (Whitley, 1999). Systemic trust allows for greater levels of openness between exchange partners, imparting high levels of flexibility in key areas, and reducing the need for contractual and monitoring devices (Lane, 1998). The role of HR departments in a high trust SSP would thus be characterized by a reduced emphasis on basic systems of monitoring, control and general administration; rather trust relations would be perpetuated by institutionalized mechanisms for involvement, consultation and participation.

The differences between the cultural and the institutional explanations for national differences HRM may be bridgeable. It is to a considerable extent a question of definition. Whilst many of the "cultural" writers see institutions as being key artifacts of culture reflecting deep underlying variations in values that they see between societies, many "institutional" writers include culture simply as one of the institutions they are addressing (North, 1990; DiMaggio and Powell, 1991; Scott, 1995).

The global convergence thesis

The fourth question that we asked at the beginning of this chapter was "Is there evidence of convergence or divergence in the different trajectories of HRM developments in different countries?" In other words, are the differences in the way HRM is managed going to become less or remain a major feature of IHRM? There is much discussion about whether differences are being reduced or not, that is, the question of convergence or divergence.

Convergence perspectives share a functionalist mode of thought. The practice of management is explained exclusively by reference to its contribution to technological and economic efficiency. Management is considered as a dependent variable that evolves in response to technological and economic change, rather than with reference to the socio-political context (Kerr, 1983). Global convergence arguments point to four main arguments.

Power of markets: Policies of market deregulation and state decontrol are (partly under the influence of bodies like the IMF) spreading from the US around the world. The power of markets ensures that those firms that are more productive with lower costs will be successful – others will be driven to copy them to survive. Since the USA is the technological leader, it follows that US management practices represent current best practice, which other nations will eventually seek to emulate as they seek to adopt US technology. Thus "patterns in other countries [are] viewed as derivative of, or deviations from, the US model" (Locke *et al.*, 1995: xvi).

Transaction cost economics: At any one point of time there exists a best solution to organizing labor (Williamson, 1975, 1985). Firms seek out and adopt the best solutions to organizing labor within their product markets, with long-term survival being dependent on their being able to implement them (Chandler, 1962, 1977; Chandler and Daems, 1980). The tendency is for firms to converge towards similar structures of organization and labor practices flow from the needs to accommodate these structures.

Like-minded international cadres: These are one of the more subtle ways in which the thinking of managers becomes globalized – or at least "de-nationalized." For example, France began to realize that Anglo Saxon (principally US but also UK) business schools were attracting a major proportion of the world's graduates. The syllabi being followed are shaping the thought process of a future generation of world leaders. In the run up to the creation of the European University Area by 2010, aimed at producing a more compatible and competitive higher education sector, the figures reveal the extent of the cultural deficit. In the USA, 515,000 foreign students produce revenues of $7 billion a year (Ferguson, 2001). In the 1990s the UK doubled its intake of foreign students (over 60 percent of whom come from other parts of Europe). The UK educates 220,000 foreign students a year. On average annual expenditures of €20,000 per student, continental Europe has a cultural deficit of over €4 billion to the USA and the UK. France plans to move from educating 130,000 a year to 500,000 with the creation of *EduFrance*. Hubert Vedrine, the French Foreign Minister, was quoted in 1998 as saying: "today, in all the world's governments you find people who were shaped by American universities. It is an instrument of power" (*International Herard Tribune*, 1998: 1).

Cost, quality and productivity pressures These show evidence of a worldwide convergence of quality standards. It is possible to meet western standards but at radically different cost. European productivity growth has lagged behind that in the US by about 1 percent and in Japan by 2 percent for the best part of a decade. By the mid-1990s Europe saw its share of exports and trade fall by 20 percent (Sparrow and Hiltrop, 1994). Comparative manufacturing labor costs in terms of wages for time at work and including other costs such as holiday pay and social security show that Germany and Switzerland are remarkably high cost countries, with Greece, Ireland and the UK being relatively cheap. A new context was introduced for labor competition. One hundred million workers from developing countries entered into competition with employees in western labor markets through relocation of production facilities and FDI. In the first two years of the 1990s from 10 to 15 percent of all European jobs disappeared. The scale of rationalization was marked. In the late 1990s if you went on the senior management development program at ABB (which was a project-based development program) your role was to go to another country from your own and help ABB export 1,000 jobs a month from its European operations. The proportion of employees that ABB had in Thailand was increasing by a factor of 3.5.

Regional and not global convergence?

An alternative convergence argument is based on *institutional analysis*. If institutions act as strong antecedents of difference, then owing to ongoing regional economic and political integration, for example of the European Union, countries may converge towards a distinctly regional practice – different from market convergence seen elsewhere. Thus, not only is the US model of HRM inappropriate to European organizations (Brewster, 1995a), institutional changes there may, arguably, be generating a specifically European model of convergence in HRM. In Europe organizations are constrained at a national level, by culture and legislation and at the organizational level by trade union involvement and consultative arrangements. In addition, there are continuing developments at the level of the EU or the European Economic Area which impact upon all organizations in Europe. In a historically unique experiment, EU countries have agreed to subordinate national legislative decision-making to European level legislation. These developments have indirect effects upon the way people are managed and direct effects on HRM.

Of course, the "convergers" recognize that in practice there are many variations in management approaches around the world. However, they argue that, in the long term, any variations in the adoption of management systems at the firm level are ascribable to the industrial sector in which the firm is located, its strategy, its available resources and its degree of exposure to international competition. These factors are of diminishing salience and once they have been taken account of, a clear trend toward the adoption of common management systems should be apparent.

Continued divergence or stasis?

Proponents of the divergence thesis argue, in direct contrast, that HRM systems, far from being economically or technologically derived, epitomize national contexts that do not respond readily to the imperatives of technology or the market. This may be based upon the institutionalist perspective outlined earlier, in which organizational choice is limited by institutional pressures, including the state, regulatory structures, interest groups, public opinion and norms (DiMaggio and Powell, 1983; Meyer and Rowan, 1983; Oliver, 1991; Hollingsworth and Boyer, 1997). Or they may be based on the notion that cultural differences mean that the management of organizations – and particularly of people – is, and will remain, fundamentally different from country to country.

Divergence theorists argue that national, and in some cases regional, institutional contexts are slow to change, partly because they derive from deep-seated beliefs and value systems and partly because major redistributions of power are involved. More importantly, they argue that change is path dependent. In other words, even when change does occur this can only be understood in relation to the specific social context in which it occurs (Maurice *et al.*, 1986; Poole, 1986). Performance criteria or goals are therefore, at any point in time, socially rather than economically or technologically selected. As such they first and foremost reflect the national culture and the idiosyncratic principles of local rationality.

There have been numerous attempts to identify *regional models within Europe* that make convergence even to a European model of HRM problematic. For example, Due *et al.* (1991) distinguish between, on the one hand, countries such as the UK, Ireland and the Nordic countries in which the state has a limited role in industrial relations. On the other hand there are the Roman-Germanic countries, such as France, Spain, Germany, Italy, Belgium, Greece and the Netherlands in which the state functions as an actor with a central role in industrial relations. A particular feature of Roman-Germanic countries is their comprehensive labor market legislation governing various areas, such as length of the working day and rest periods. The latitude for firm-level decision making in Roman-Germanic countries in regard to employment issues is relatively low, unlike either the Anglo-Irish or the Nordic systems. For example, Brewster and Tregaskis (2003), examining flexible (contingent) work practices found slightly different groupings in the manufacturing and service sectors. Spain tended to be a category on its own in both cases and, in manufacturing for example, Germany, the Netherlands, Norway and Switzerland were in the "high inclusive" group; France and Ireland in the moderately reactive, UK, Sweden, Denmark and Belgium in the moderately reactive group.

On a broader scale, Sparrow, Schuler and Jackson (1994) used the results of a worldwide survey by Towers Perrin (1992), to explore how different cultural groupings of countries might affect usage of a range of HRM variables. They found an Anglo-Saxon grouping composed of Australia, Canada, the United Kingdom and the United States; three cultural islands (France, Korea and Japan) and a further grouping of cultural allies comprising the South American or Latin countries of Brazil, Mexico and Argentina. These researchers found significant differences between cultural groupings on items within the culture change, organization structure and performance management variables. They stressed the impact of historical factors on the present configuration of HR policies and practices in individual nation-states.

There is, of course, a third possibility, albeit one that researchers are generally uncomfortable with: *stasis*. It may well be the case that firms are so embedded in their respective idiosyncratic national institutional settings that no common model is likely to emerge for the foreseeable future and there is no movement either converging or diverging.

Conclusion

The competing views about the level of globalization nonetheless raise some important messages for the International HR professionals. Those who happen to work for MNCs (many of course do not) live in organizations that have remarkable power yet remain surprisingly fragile. The high levels of FDI bring the planning for future mergers and acquisitions, or the challenge of integrating existing merged operations, to the forefront of their activity. It seems however that we have perhaps only seen the very beginning of this activity. There may yet be much more to come. The realist perspective on globalization demonstrates that there is a global war for talent. Many International HR professionals are intimately involved in the search for the best-educated people their organization can attract. They need to understand the different national VET systems and help design ways in which their organization and its managers can influence the skill formation process in these national systems. The globalization from above perspective also reveals the threats to the organization and its brands from poor management practice. The whole debate around corporate social responsibility also puts International HR professionals into competition with their marketing colleagues over who is best qualified to advise in this area.

From a more philosophical perspective, the arguments about universalist and contextualist research have been set up rather simply which, whilst it clarifies the debates, we acknowledge is setting up something of a straw man. Clearly, there is valuable research in all these traditions and much to be learnt from all of them. It has been argued elsewhere (Brewster, 1999a, 1999b) that the universalist and contextual paradigms are incompatible, but nevertheless have much to gain from adopting some of the elements of each from each other. Perhaps most importantly here, a lot of our discussions of HRM would be healthier if researchers understood and were clear about their own paradigms. For international HR professionals however the practical consequence of this debate is that it reveals the complexity and range of HR knowledge that they need (a topic picked up in Chapter 5). It also warns them against making simplistic assumptions about the existence of best practice and the importance of their role in educating their more single-minded colleagues who might demand that simple recipes are imported from benchmarked competitiors.

The debate about convergence vs. divergence, or stasis, is one where what is needed is more nuancing in the argument. We also need more longitudinal data – the work of the Cranet network is a pathfinder project here. However, from a comparative as opposed to international HRM perspective, there seems to be increasing evidence that country is a primary determinant of HRM practice (Brewster *et al.*, 2003). Yet, there is no reason why *some* aspects of HRM could not show signs of convergence, whilst others show signs of divergence. There may be convergence in structure whilst there is continuing divergence in process. There may be convergent trends, but trends which start from such different positions that they are unlikely to lead to a convergence in practice in any foreseeable future. An analysis using the Cranet data collected over four rounds of surveys during the 1990s to explore the issue of convergence in HRM over time across Europe (Brewster *et al.*, 2003) argues that there is more than one kind of convergence. There can be directional convergence, final convergence and majority convergence. They use the evidence to show a complex and multiply faceted development with different kinds if divergence taking place in different aspects of HRM. Overall, however, they find that "whilst there are some signs of convergence between countries in Europe in the direction of trends, there remain very substantial differences, perhaps even continuing further divergence, in terms of final convergence."

Understanding the limits of adaptation, in terms of which HR practices can be modified with positive effect, which need the introduction of some functionally equivalent mechanisms in order to make them work and which simply will not work in each cultural context becomes a core task of the international HR professional.

3

Organizational drivers
of globalization

Introduction

We noted in the last chapter that there has been considerable interest in the global
strategies of firms but the current consensus is that firms are not as global or international
as is often assumed. It is evident that there is a clear country-of-origin effect. US MNCs,
for example, tend to be more centralized and formalized than others in their management
of HRM issues, ranging from pay systems through to collective bargaining and union
recognition. They tend to innovate more and import leading edge practices from other
nation-states. Japanese MNCs on the other hand have been at the forefront of work
organization innovations through lean production, but expect their subsidiaries abroad
to fit in with this approach and even though standard worldwide policies and formal
systems are not as apparent as in US MNCs, there is stronger centralized direction and
ethnocentric attitudes. In short, "MNCs, far from being stateless organizations operating
independent of national borders in some purified realm of global economic competition,
continue to have their assets, sales, workforce ownership and control highly concentrated
in the country where their corporate headquarters are located" (Ferner and Quintanilla,
1998: 710). In our validation workshops this view was clearly supported by international
HR directors:

> In reality most multinationals have a culture which may be US-global (e.g. IBM)
> or Japanese-global (e.g. Panasonic) or European-global (e.g. Shell). So any moves towards
> centralization or decentralization operates in the context of what these respective national
> business systems/corporate governance systems need to see. In Japan, for example, they
> have to trust in your competence before they will decentralize.
>
> (Senior international HR director)

This results in there being tensions between the forces of globalization – which were
also held to be self-evident – and the characteristics of MNCs that still bear their
"nationality effects." So what exactly is meant by globalization or internationalization
in this context? Globalization of industries? Internationalization of the firm? How might
these be measured? It is important to understand this because international HR functions
only arise in, and need worry about the implications of, more global operations. The more
basic the level of internationalization of the markets the firm operates in, the simpler need

be its international HR function. However, even a small company operating in a highly globalized industry might need to demonstrate relatively sophisticated international HR thinking. What do we need to see in industries and in firms to evidence a need for a more global perspective on HRM?

In this chapter we establish the starting point from which any thinking about the role of HR professionals in corporate HR functions has to begin. We outline the main models and frameworks that have been used to think about the following:

- globalization of industries;
- relative levels of internationalization of the firm;
- progressive building of international capabilities within firms (and the pressure to build this capability more quickly);
- role of centers of excellence;
- need for partnership arrangements to capitalize on mutual and complementary capabilities; and
- globalization of functions and differing international orientations.

We then present and analyze our cross-organizational data and consider both the factors that are "driving" their organizational strategies and the reflection of these factors in their "enabling" HR strategies. Finally, we introduce a model of the processes involved in the globalization of HRM functions based on these data.

Firms within globalizing industries

The unique blend of competitive pressures in each industry results in varying levels of globalization, and in turn this is reflected in the strategies of firms in those industries (Morrison and Roth, 1992; Carr, 1993). However, relatively little attention has been paid to the measurement of the extent of industry globalization or indeed the manner in which industries globalize over time (Makhija *et al.*, 1997). Global industries are, however, ones in which:

> a firm's competitive position in one country is significantly affected by its position in other countries or vice versa . . . [a global industry] is not merely a collection of domestic industries but a series of linked domestic industries in which the rivals compete against each other on a truly worldwide basis.
>
> (Porter, 1986b: 18)

Rather than there being "big" industries that have no national boundaries or differences in economic structure, there are a series of domestic industries that are, however, linked significantly across countries. The same analogy of course applies to the organizations that compete in these industries.

More subjective measures of globalization at the level of industries include market drivers, cost drivers, governmental drivers and competitive drivers (Johansson and Yip, 1994).

Box 3.1 What makes a global industry?

Globalization is therefore conceptualized as ranging from high to low. At one end there are "multidomestic" industries in which all of the firms within it have their value-adding activity in a single country. In the middle there are industries in which there are some limited external linkages, seen mainly through the flow of useful knowledge and information from a headquarters in a home country to subsidiaries in other countries. Higher in the continuum are industries in which a few standardized value-adding activities, particularly towards its end markets or customer interface, are driven by the need for global scale. Finally, there are industries that are competitively linked to similar industries in other countries and in which firms must simultaneously achieve efficiencies through global scale, local responsiveness and worldwide learning (Bartlett and Ghoshal, 1989). There are many international linkages in the form of both inward and outflows from the firm. The dimensions that are often considered to evidence higher levels of globalization in an industry include the level of international trade, intensity of international competition, worldwide product standardization and presence of international competitors in all key international markets (Morrison and Roth, 1992).

Measuring the degree of internationalization of firms

What of the globalization of firms? We quickly review where the economists have got to in their work on measuring the degree of internationalization (as they prefer to call it) of the firm. The report card perhaps might read "some interesting observations and advances, but more work must be done." Despite considerable effort, estimating the degree of internationalization of the firm is still an arbitrary process. Both the choice of constructs to evidence it and the actual measures used are fraught with contention (see the debate between Sullivan, 1994; Ramaswamy *et al.*, 1996; Sullivan, 1996) and this lack of progress reflects an absence of definitive and reliable measures. It has always been assumed that becoming more international improves organizational performance. However, a review of seventeen studies in this area found conflicting evidence – in six cases there was a positive relationship, in five cases a negative relationship and in another six cases the evidence was indeterminate.

Box 3.2 Measuring the internationalization of firms

A range of "hard" measures have been used to capture relative levels of internationalization of the firm from an economic perspective. The most popular single measures used as proxies of internationalization are as follows:

continued

- foreign subsidiaries' sales as a percentage of total sales (FSTS) (Stopford and Dunning, 1983);
- export sales as a percentage of total sales (ESTS) (Sullivan and Bauerschmidt, 1989);
- foreign assets as a percentage of total assets, as an estimate of the material international character of an organization (FATA) (Daniels and Bracker, 1989); and
- number of foreign subsidiaries, to distinguish the degree of foreign involvement (Vernon, 1971, Stopford and Wells, 1972). This measure has been refined to Overseas Subsidiaries as a Percentage of Total Subsidiaries (OSTS), in order to standardize for differences in the scale and scope of the simple number of foreign subsidiaries.

Of these measures the first has been the most widely used.

However, the degree of internationalization also reflects attitudinal perspectives that exist within the firm. Some of the attitudinal measures that have been used include:

- Top Managers' International Experience (TMIE), a tally of the cumulative duration of top managers' international assignments as summarized in company-reported career histories, weighted by the reported total years of work experience of the top management team.
- Psychic Dispersion of International Operations (PDIO), based on the dispersion of subsidiaries across ten psychic zones in the world (unique cultural groupings). Ronen and Shenkar (1985) identified ten different geographical zones. Each zone has unique "principles of management" and managers within each zone are considered to have unique "cognitive maps" (Adler et al., 1986; Hofstede, 1993: 84).

By combining a range of these measures into a composite scale, economists hope to get a better picture of the critical antecedents and consequences of global expansion. However, there is still debate over whether these different measures in fact show that the degree of internationalization exists across several independent dimensions – with organizations being high or low in different combinations across these measures (Ramaswamy, 1992; Ramaswamy et al., 1996).

The notion of organizational capability

At the level of the organization, then, coping with or taking control of globalization is all about building the "capability" of the organization. The term organizational capability was in fact first used by Igor Ansoff and was subsequently developed by both Ulrich (1987) in the HR field and Prahalad and Doz (1987) in the strategy field. As a concept it combines ideas from the fields of management of change, organizational design and leadership. Ulrich and Lake (1990) brought these perspectives together and developed the following theory. They argued that organizational capability was about competing "from the inside out." Organizational capability therefore focuses on the ability of a firm's internal processes, systems and management practices to meet customer needs and to direct both the skills and efforts of employees towards achieving the goals of the organization. This collection of capabilities reflects things such as a firm's "key success factors," "culture," "brand," "shared-mindset" or "processes" (Ulrich and Lake, 1990; Lawler, 1997).

The idea also has its root in theoretical work that was done in the strategic management field in the early 1990s. This became known as the *resource-based view of the firm*. It argued that in an environment characterized by the globalization of markets, changing customer demands and increasing competition, it is the people and the way that they are managed that takes on more significance because other sources of competitive advantage are stable and therefore less powerful (Wright *et al.*, 1994, Lado and Wilson, 1994). These newer models of strategy argue that competitive advantage is derived from both internal knowledge resources and the strategic resources or capabilities of the firm. It is "bundles of resources" – generally considered to be complex, intangible and dynamic – rather than any particular product-market strategy – that provides an organization with the capability to compete. Capabilities, then, capture a firm's abilities to integrate, build and reconfigure its internal assets and competencies so that it can perform distinctive activities (Teece *et al.*, 1997). Hence, organizational capability is defined formally as "a firm's capacity to deploy resources, usually in combination, applying organizational processes to effect a desired end" (De Saá-Pérez and García-Falcón, 2002: 124). These resource-based theories of strategic management "emphasized the importance not of the organization's position in relation to its industry, but rather the way in which it manages its resource inputs in developing core competences and distinctive capabilities" (Stonehouse *et al.*, 2000: 15).

Box 3.3 Globalization and resource-based theories of the firm

Early authors of competence-based theories of strategy considered that core competencies represented the collective learning within the organization about how best to coordinate diverse production and integrate multiple technologies and then exploit this in a wide variety of markets. Organizations have to develop core competences – such as distinctive and superior skills, technology relationships, knowledge and reputation of the firm – by *employing its tangible and visible assets* (be they human, financial, physical, technological, legal or informational) *in the activities of the organization*. By deploying these resources and progressively integrating them into the most value-adding activities, then the organization can build a series of capabilities (such as industry-specific skills, relationships and

continued

organizational knowledge). These capabilities tend to be more intangible. Building new capabilities to account for changes in the business environment and leveraging capabilities to establish an advantage in a new market is considered to be key to the success of organizations.

Source: after Prahalad and Hamel (1990)

The whole concept of building international capability is rooted in this resource-based view of strategy. Building rapid capability, in the context of the internationalization of a business, might actually mean developing new competencies necessary to compete, or leveraging (applying) existing competencies to develop existing strengths, for example, by:

- exploiting a core competence globally in a large number of countries and markets;
- identifying new resources found in untapped markets or countries and using them to strengthen an existing core competence; and
- reconfiguring value-adding activities across a wider geography and range of operations in order to enhance an existing competence (Stonehouse *et al.*, 2000).

There is then growing consensus about the attributes that represent organizational capability. Many current models of MNCs have been described as having a "*capability-recognizing*" perspective. This means that firms possess some unique knowledge-based resources. However, these resources are typically treated as being home-country based or somehow belonging to the corporate function and top team. Tallman and Fladmoe-Lindquist (2002) argue that we need a "*capability-driven*" perspective: an understandable theory of MNC strategy based on *how* they attempt to build, protect and exploit a set of unique capabilities and resources. This is also known as the "*dynamic capability*" perspective. In order to understand how organizations develop, manage and deploy capabilities to support their business strategy (Montealegre, 2002) we generally have to conduct longitudinal studies. Only a handful of strategists have considered specifically how MNCs develop organizational capability (see, for example, Collis, 1991; Fladmoe-Linquist and Tallman, 1994; Hedlund and Ridderstråe, 1997; and Kogut, 1997). Our study, as reported in this book, is an example of the dynamic capability perspective as applied to the field of international HRM.

An important task, then, for international HR managers is to grasp which overall business-level and corporate-level capabilities are relevant to the particular international strategy of their organization. Tallman and Fladmoe-Linquist (2002) have outlined what they consider these capabilities to be against three contingencies:

- type of strategy for international expansion or global integration;
- requirement to continue generating competitive advantage *or* to innovate through global learning; and
- skills and activities operating at the business level or corporate-level routines that integrate these skills across operations.

Building rapid global presence and capability

How do organizations build these specific capabilities? Organizational capability is created out of the international networking that surrounds building research and development or production centers, logistic networks or indeed HR systems and processes on a global scale, and the conduct of these activities in global contexts: "the world becomes an important source for new knowledge as well as new markets" (Tallman and Fladmore-Lindquist, 2002: 116).

However, the international management literature has always adopted a fairly traditional stance to the building of capability within organizations. The vast majority of models of organizational design and internationalization, for example, suggest a clear sequence of evolutionary stages through which the organization has to evolve. In reconstructing the sequence of events and relationships associated with internationalization, early studies of British, Swedish, French and American firms all supported a gradual pattern of internationalization (Cavusgil and Godiwalla, 1982). A sequence of stages of organization design – variously called international, multinational, global and transnational/network/heterarchy – have been outlined (Bartlett and Ghoshal, 1989). There is then a pattern to be found in the way in which the internationalization process has to be managed. In general, the organization structure has to respond to a series of strains that are faced, such as the challenges of growth, increased geographical spread, and the need for improved control and coordination across business units. Organizations have to build capability in each stage sequentially in order to maintain integrated standards for some business lines but remain locally responsive in others (Hamel and Prahalad, 1985; Yip, 1992; Ashkenas et al., 1995). Some firms might develop through the various phases rapidly, and might be able to accelerate the process through acquisitions, but any attempt to leapfrog over intermediate steps is generally considered to result in dysfunctions.

However, the questions asked today by organizations are as follows:

- can we accelerate the pace at which we progress through various phases; or
- indeed must we really work through each one?

These are questions about the building of capability at a more rapid pace. As we noted in Chapter 2, an often-overlooked type of organization in research on global HR is the rapid start-up operation. The challenge for such organizations is that they have to be global almost from day 1 of their operation, or must build capability in international markets at a rapid pace (Oviatt and McDougall, 1995).

Box 3.4 Global start-ups as an exception to the rule?

Is it possible to by-pass these stages of development? Global start-ups, in which entrepreneurs act on a world stage, have become a more popular form of international

continued

business venture. Logitech (a manufacturer of computer mice) is seen as a prototypical start-up. Founded by one Swiss and two Italian entrepreneurs in 1982, it was headquartered in California and Switzerland from the start, and soon expanded into operations in Taiwan and Ireland. By 1989 it had gained a 30 percent market share and revenues of $140 million. In their study of twelve global start-ups, Oviatt and McDougall (1995) noted seven common principles:

- A global vision exists from inception
- Managers are internationally experienced
- Their entrepreneurs have strong international business networks
- They exploit pre-emptive technologies or marketing strategies
- They have clearly unique intangible assets in the form of tacit knowledge
- Product or service extensions are closely linked to the original business concept
- The organization is closely coordinated worldwide.

Source: after Oviatt and McDougall (1995)

Amongst our case studies Stepstone provided insight into the challenges for the HR function created by this rapid internationalization. We provide a fairly detailed case example as the story presents in graphic detail the pace, complexity and fragility of organizational life – and international HR existence – involved in this kind of environment. It also provides a different perspective in comparison to the usual picture of slow, planned internationalization that follows a set of predefined stages. While many companies are faced with similar challenges, the e-business environment and the immense time pressures Stepstone was exposed to meant that they had to manage all these challenges at the same time which exposed the company, and its international HR function, to an unusual amount of complexity, uncertainty and dynamism. The picture accords with work done by Wright and Dyer (2001) as part of their state-of-the-art study into HR issues in e-commerce. This work showed that organizational capability has to be developed in an environment driven by:

- high levels of uncertainty and anxiety, where there is no institutional memory and so no models or learning comparators;
- a sense of entrepreneurialism, innovation, creativity, experimentation all of which come with a limited financial tolerance for failure;
- a sense of speed and real-time feedback;
- a reliance on a knowledge-base that becomes a strategic necessity; but is imitable;
- a lack of stable structures; and
- short duration project based work and inefficient problem solving due to a lack of mature, cross-country, coordination systems.

The race to build rapid capability at Stepstone: from dot com start-up to pan-European player

The viability of online firms depends on their economic ability to be able to survive as a profitable operation, but also on their organizational capability – seen in terms of their methods of operation, processes, customer relationship management skills, and human resource systems. In order to be able to capitalize on the benefits of its business model, Stepstone had to internationalize *its own* operations at a very rapid pace whilst also managing the evolution of the e-commerce business model. The latter task was in itself risky. After its 1996 foundation, Stepstone gradually opened operations in five European countries. By 1999 it employed 200 people and had made £7m in revenue and a loss of £15m. Its goal was to become Europe's leading recruitment and career portal. It embarked on a massive expansion throughout Europe in 2000–2001 that almost led to its collapse. In order to fund this expansion Stepstone floated the company at the Oslo and London stock exchange at the height of the Internet boom in March 2000 when it was valued at £530m. The floatation was twenty times oversubscribed and initial enthusiasm doubled the share price, valuing the company at more than £1 billion. Stepstone already had a strong position in the UK market and beyond that in Europe but in order to become *the* leading recruitment and career portal in Europe it had to grow rapidly.

Stepstone's business model was based on using technology to make the recruitment process more efficient and to provide pan-European organizations with a consistent platform for their recruiting. A lot of business needed to come from big corporations to provide Stepstone some economies of scale. Competition was rising fast. Its competitive advantage was built around technology that was both innovative but easily imitable. Staying ahead of the technology curve and competition in order to provide customers with leading edge information and tools to manage their portfolios *and* expanding throughout Europe became a constant struggle. Expansion incurred immense costs and as a pure-play dot com (i.e., e-business being the only route to market that it operated) the company started each of these operations with no brand, no jobs, no infrastructure. High costs were incurred through the founding of new offices and take-overs of competitors, the recruiting and training of sales forces in new countries, together with brand building and marketing activities. While internationalizing, Stepstone was faced with simultaneous pressures:

- maintaining a technological lead ahead of competition;
- integrating various acquired and organically-developed businesses to provide "one face" to the pan-European customer;
- managing the internationalization process in the fastest possible time;
- managing the changing skill requirements of a maturing business "on the fly"; and
- operating in an "untapped" business environment.

By October 2000 Stepstone had extended its service into sixteen European countries including: the UK, Belgium, Luxembourg, Germany, Austria, Switzerland, France, Holland, Spain, Portugal, Norway, Denmark, Sweden, Finland, Ireland and Italy. Furthermore, the company had also launched an Indian operation in July 2000. This move was based on the recognition of the demand for quality IT professionals from many of its European customers.

continued

From just 200 employees in 1999 the company had increased its headcount to 1,385 staff in the year 2000. It still had a formidable cash position as a result of its floatation, but the losses were accumulating. The options were to build capability rapidly, be acquired, or go out of business. In 2001 losses ballooned to £89m as expansion was still being funded, though costs were expected to plateau once the roll-out was complete.

The fast build up of individual European sites meant that people were hired at high speed and did not therefore have the range of skills or development potential to be productive in all phases of Stepstone's evolution. Responsibility for finding people was spread. As a reaction to the massive expansion and the necessary integration work that this entailed Stepstone professionalized its management team by attracting a number of seasoned managers, including the post of Group Human Resources Director. The rapid and ongoing pace of new country operation start-ups dominated the everyday activity of the firm, as well as the role of the international HR function:

"I started in June 2000, so there had already been a lot of opening in countries anyway. I signed my contract in April and there were 400 people. I joined in June and there were 600–700 people. Now (February 2001) there are 1400 people . . . Basically the process is to get your country manager in place, and you work with them to recruit their own team. Then you work to make sure they have the resources below them" HR Director Europe.

Managing a process of rapid internationalization brought a wide range of complex HR problems to bear. The HR agenda in the race to build rapid organizational capability was quite clear. It set about:

- establishing processes to manage the quality of recruitment and to handle inherited problems of skills obsolescence, imbalances and equalization across operations
- facilitating senior board appointments to import people who had business models from other sectors that could be used to bring some learning into an e-business environment in which there were no models;
- introducing a sense of "managed speed", by helping to realign staff numbers in some of the early start-up misjudgments (a *plan sociale* process was needed to readjust numbers in France, UK Web design and IT support operations were outsourced to India) so that resources could be used in other start-ups;
- creating some zones of stability, reincentivizing the top team through stock options to ensure continuity of leadership;
- mobilizing internal communications to get managers to move from an action culture to thinking "beyond tomorrow" about a post break-even world;
- introducing a regional HR structure to help coordinate organization development and training initiatives across highly independent country operations; and
- introducing a series of supporting HR processes, such as changes in the performance management process, incentivization approach, and customer relationship management process.

All this was done within the space of one year. However, would the City allow Stepstone to survive long enough to complete this task?

Source: Braun *et al.* (2003b) and secondary sources[1]

As the Stepstone case shows, the challenges facing the HR professionals as they tried to help shepherd the organization through its early start-up phase were significant. International HR roles such as this are themselves complex. In more mature organizations, some work has been done to try and understand exactly what capabilities are needed by the HR professionals themselves to work in these roles. This was seen, for example, in Diageo. For them, building organizational capability entailed the alignment of strategic planning, investment decisions, management development and executive rewards to the single governing objective of building global brands. The development of strong management teams with world-class brand management and international management skills was an important way in which this capability was to be realized. It was possible to tease out the capabilities needed by the HR function. These are detailed below.

Organizational capability and HR capability at Diageo

Case Example

In 2001 Diageo specified a series of HR capabilities that were needed to help it deliver the organizational strategy. These set out what it took to be a "master" of global HR. Capabilities were established around five themes: strategic HR; organizational capability and change; talent recruitment, development and retention; performance and reward; and developing an employee value proposition. Business strategy involvement required a highly developed understanding of Diageo's consumers, business, and competitor strategy and how it created value. HR professionals had to deliver performance and value by explicitly seeking to leverage the contribution of the individual and the organization to driving business performance. They had to take a lead on the use of technology (including e-HR) to enhance the performance of the individual and the organization. They had to vigorously ensure that the people strategies throughout Diageo directly supported the business strategy. They had to orchestrate the HR function and set out to gain commitment to a clear vision, build and motivate strong teams, focus on business partnering and lead the function to maximizing its economic profit contribution. They had to lead in the identification of organizational capabilities designed to drive business strategy at the global level and articulate the implications of potential gaps to the business. They needed to develop organization design methodologies and coach managers in deploying these to deliver solutions that increased business performance. They had to develop change methodologies and be recognized as a "champion of change." This involved ensuring that the organizational culture was "change ready."

They had to drive the development of global capability to meet business needs through the creation of global resourcing strategies, benchmark against other organizations to seek new opportunities and approaches to source top talent for Diageo, deliver value through the retention of key talent and actively drive initiatives to embed a coaching model of talent management within Diageo. A focus on performance and reward required a deep ability to diagnose the root causes of organizational performance issues and the facilitation of senior management in thinking through how it could improve organizational performance. It involved clearly and convincingly articulating the implications of using different reward

continued

tools/techniques and their impact on individuals and the business. Finally, developing a value proposition for employees brought with it the need to deliver an effective communication strategy on a global perspective, managing complex conflict situations through to resolution, acting as an advocate of employees on a global scale, and creating strategies that engaged senior employees and encouraged commitment to the business.

Source: Braun *et al.* (2003a)

Partnership arrangements

The resource-based view of strategy also emphasizes the potential advantages of more collaboration between organizations, especially if they have mutually complementary competencies (Sanchez and Heene, 1997). When organizations build capabilities, these tend to be generated internally, but they may also be shared or created across organizational boundaries, between an organization and one or more of its suppliers, distributors or customers (Stonehouse *et al.*, 2000).

In our case study work, the not-for-profit charity, ActionAid, had as a central part of its strategy the importance of decentralizing its activities to local operations and local staff. This involved working closely with other aid groups to ensure the delivery of the necessary support. Similarly, Rolls-Royce was keen to develop its partnerships with plane builders and airlines.

Partnership arrangements at ActionAid

In the late 1990s, ActionAid undertook a strategic review of its work, aware that the external environment was changing rapidly and that the organization was in need of a new direction. The outcome of the exercise was a new strategy document, *Fighting poverty together*, which set out ActionAid's understanding of the causes of poverty and strategic priorities for action for 1999–2005. The strategy has four main goals, one of which involves working in partnership with others to achieve greater impact. ActionAid works with over 2000 organizations that have a deep knowledge of local conditions, customs and politics in poor communities, from local support groups for HIV-positive people in Africa to national workers' movements in Latin America. Local people and partners in twenty-four countries help review the effectiveness of the work, enabling ActionAid to hold itself accountable to them and to their donors. These alliances help it to work more effectively with poor people as well as strengthening the global anti-poverty movement. However, the accent on partnership, taken to its logical conclusion, also meant a loss of jobs for some staff in the HQ and a rebalancing of employment between the HQ and the regions as part of an associated drive towards decentralization.

Source: Hegewisch *et al.* (2003)

Case Example

Building centers of excellence within organizations

Strategists, then, have shown that technological and business skills can be developed by international diversification into multiple markets, collaborating with organizations that have mutually complementary competencies, emphasizing strategic leadership roles for national subsidiaries and gaining access to foreign-based clusters of excellence (Tallman and Fladmoe-Linquist, 2002). In recent years the latter two approaches have become increasingly important. As MNCs change their organization design in response to the need to build more international capability, then as part of their natural development they often establish centers of excellence (Ohmae, 1990, 1996). Centers of excellence have been considered in the context of national or regional clusters of skills and capability – such as the location of IS work in India or in Ireland. More recently center-of-excellence thinking has also been applied to the location of HR work. We introduce the broad concept here but shall develop some of the deeper HR implications in Chapter 5.

MNCs have relied on specialized and often network-based structures to coordinate their activities for a while, but today they have increasingly dispersed activities. The response of the corporate headquarters to this dispersion has typically been to adjust its level of coordination and control to reflect the role of the subsidiary and the strategic importance of the mandate that it has (Bartlett and Ghoshal, 1989). Although a variety of missions can be assigned to subsidiaries one particular type of subsidiary has recently gained prominence – the center of excellence. Centers of excellence tend to be established as a general consequence of a long and slow internationalization process within the organization or as a deliberate part of organization design where HQ managers decide to grant autonomy to units that have also been given a specific strategic mandate. However, they have some important characteristics:

1 They take on a strategic role in the global organization that reaches beyond their local undertakings.
2 They have to be tightly integrated with their surrounding technical or professional communities.
3 They must have both high competence and high use of its competence throughout surrounding units.

Increasingly, small teams or units within subsidiaries are taking a lead center of excellence role in one area, with other units taking the lead in different areas of capability. Indeed, whilst the leadership of a center of excellence might still be vested in a physical location, the actual center itself may be quite virtual, spread across networks of teams in many different geographies. In many cases, experts argue that these centers actually need to be quite loosely tied into the organization and coordinated with other units if they are to help search for new knowledge and augment the capability of the MNC (Hansen, 1999; Kuemmerle, 1999). Control typically varies between being direct or indirect and through personal or impersonal mechanisms – what Harzing (1999) calls centralized personal control, formal bureaucratic control, output control or control through socialization and networks. Recent research suggests that controlling these centers of excellence through socialization proves dysfunctional (Ambos and Reitsperger, 2002). Therefore understanding and building these more globally distributed centers of excellence into viable operations has become a significant challenge.

In the longer term, global HR functions that themselves establish their own centers of excellence will begin to learn from research that has already been conducted into research and development and other technical centers of excellence. This research has provided insight into how such centers should be fostered and nurtured. They must be more than just specialized in their knowledge (Holm and Pedersen, 2000). They have to be able to maintain one or several critical fields of knowledge that have a long-term impact on the development of activity in the other subsidiaries and units of the MNC.

Technical centers of excellence at Rolls-Royce

Case Example

At Rolls-Royce the relocation of businesses was not just on an international basis. As part of a centers of excellence strategy they also relocated businesses within the UK. For example, within the Naval Marine business they moved the center to Bristol away from Derby (the nuclear marine facility remained in Derby). It was considered that their work on propulsion systems for Navies across the world was better run out of Bristol, in part because of Rolls-Royce's need to operate from a reducing number of sites, but also because of their concentration on building technical centers of excellence. Similarly in the Airlines business the intention was to set up Rolls-Royce Deutschland as the center of excellence for two shaft engines (the smaller engines in its range), whilst Derby would become the center of excellence for the three shaft engines (engines used in transatlantic jets) and Indianapolis the center of excellence for all the business/corporate jet engines.

What are the roles for international HR professionals in this development of centers of excellence? We would argue that there are three particular ways in which the IHR function is being driven by the development of these centers of excellence:

1 Managing the international relocation of staff as organizations:
  (a) move these centers of excellence nearer to the global center of gravity of their core customers;
  (b) reconfigure their core competencies on a global scale moving manufacturing, research and development or logistics operations closer to the best national infrastructures in terms of education or transport facilities; or
  (c) set up new centers as part of international ventures or as a result of mergers.

2 Advising on the best HR strategies to coordinate and control such activities.

3 Understanding the centers of excellence that can be created within their own activities, and building networks of HR experts within these areas of competence on a global basis.

In Chapter 5 we pick up the last of these roles and examine the ways in which global centers of excellence have been used to facilitate the transfer of best practice and HR knowledge within organizations.

Functional realignment surrounding global HRM

As a final section of theory, we consider the functional impact of globalization. Many researchers argue that globalization within organizations is driven by what happens within business functions as they seek to coordinate (develop linkages between geographically dispersed units of a function) and control (regulate functional activities to align them with the expectations set in targets) their activities across borders (Kim *et al.*, 2003). In addition to understanding what happens at the level of the firm in its totality, which has been the traditional focus of many researchers (see for example Doz and Prahalad, 1981; Ghoshal and Nohria, 1989; Gupta and Govindarajan, 1991), we need to understand how organizations enhance the ability of specific functions to perform globally. "Globalization occurs at the level of the function, rather than the firm" (Malbright, 1995: 119). Clearly, then, attention needs to be devoted to understanding the ways in which the HR function itself contributes to the process of globalization. However, as was evident from Chapter 2, the HR function is not one that can be considered currently as being highly globalized. Yip (1992) argues that some of the most global functions in outlook include manufacturing (inventory control, fabrication, assembly, quality control, testing, machining and equipment maintenance), research and development (experiments, design, prototype development and testing and technical support for new products and processes), marketing (advertising, promotion, branding, market research, packaging, pricing and channel selection). More recently, information systems and knowledge management functions have been highlighted too as leading the process of global functional integration (Hansen *et al.*, 1999). This is because information is the only integrating mode that seems to be beneficial across manufacturing, research and development and marketing: "Information-based integration will be a more important and effective form of integrating various business functions and operations in the coming years. Despite its importance, previous research on global integration has given limited attention to this mode" (Kim *et al.*, 2003: 340).

Together, these functional activities are being better connected across geographical borders through flows of information that are intended to enhance levels of innovation and learning. In practice, MNCs utilize several integrating mechanisms simultaneously and with different levels of intensity in order to improve global coordination and control. Each form of integration is more or less suited to facilitate global coordination of control of the different functions.

Aligning international assignments with organizational strategy has historically been thought of in respect to the dominant *orientation* of the international organization. One of the most helpful typologies is derived from the work of Perlmutter (1969) and later Heenan and Perlmutter (1979). These orientations are seen in aspects of organizational design such as decision-making, evaluation and control, information flows and complexity. They also describe how MNCs approach the staffing and management of their subsidiaries, thereby perpetuating their underlying orientation.

Box 3.5 The main integration modes used to coordinate and control global functions

There are four integration modes in the repertoire of most organizations:

People-based integration: Transfer of managers, meetings, teams, training, committees and integrators (for example expatriates). Brings with it varying degrees of personal control, and socialization or cultural control. Built around a process of sharing visions, values, norms and building of trust. We cover this form of integration in Chapter 5 in particular.

Information-based integration: Use of international flows of information and development of systems such as databases, e-mail, Internet, intranet and electronic data exchanges. Control exerted through information systems or through data management. Used to communicate knowledge or bring together individuals with common interests and issues.

Formalization-based integration (also called standardization or bureaucratic control): Formalization of the ways in which functional activity is performed through the use of standardized work procedures, rules, policies and manuals. Used to integrate highly codified activities.

Centralization-based integration: Centralized decision-making authority at higher levels (usually a head office but not necessarily located there) in a chain of command. Used to locate decision-making in areas where a more complete understanding of widely dispersed activity exists in order to capitalize on the benefits of global scale, scope or learning.

Source: after Kim *et al.* (2003)

Typology of MNC international orientations

- *Ethnocentric:* Few foreign subsidiaries have any autonomy; strategic decisions are made at headquarters. Key positions at the domestic and foreign operations are held by headquarters' management personnel. In other words, subsidiaries are managed by expatriates from the home country (PCNs). This form of structure and type of control system most closely relates to the *hierarchy* approaches described above.

Case Example

- *Polycentric:* The MNC treats each subsidiary as a distinct national entity with some decision-making autonomy. Subsidiaries are usually managed by local nationals (HCNs) who are seldom promoted to positions at headquarters. Likewise, PCNs are rarely transferred to foreign subsidiary operations. This typology relates to the *multinational* type of organization.

- *Regiocentric:* Reflects the geographic strategy and structure of the multinational. Personnel may move outside their countries but only within a particular geographic region. Regional managers may not be promoted to headquarter positions but enjoy a degree of regional autonomy in decision-making.

- *Geocentric:* The MNC takes a worldwide approach to its operations, recognizing that each part makes a unique contribution with its unique competence. It is accompanied by a worldwide-integrated business, and nationality is ignored in favor of ability. PCNs, HCNs and TCNs can be found in key positions anywhere, including those at the senior management level at headquarters and on the board of directors. This final form of structure and control system relates to the *network/heterarchy* approaches.

These differing underlying orientations are still alive and kicking today. As noted in Chapter 1, the Benchmarking Survey of Global Human Resource Management formed part of the Chartered Institute of Personnel and Development's (CIPD, 2001; Brewster *et al.*, 2002) flagship research into the impact of the globalization of business on the role of the international HR professionals. The aim of the survey was to provide sixty-four organizations with a unique insight into how they compared with similar companies on the most pressing strategic issues for the international HR function. The survey questions reflected much of the literature that we have summarized in this and preceding chapters.

The results from the survey showed that organizations are still adopting a number of orientations to globalization. These range from exerting strong central control from the HQ (this ethnocentric orientation was identified by 12 percent of the sample) to allowing international subsidiaries almost complete autonomy (this polycentric orientation was identified in 16 percent of the sample). A regional orientation to management strategy was only noted in 5 percent of responses. The hallmark of a truly global company, however, is the desire to create an organization where there is a balance between central coordinating processes and flexibility at the local level, with a strong global culture that fosters integration. Over 67 percent agreed with the statement "Top management strives to create an integrated organization" as a description of their organization's management strategy. These organizations were striving to create a geocentric organization.

It is important to note that no one orientation is necessarily the best. The skill of the IHR professional is to determine the approach that best fits the organizational strategy. Whilst many people would regard an ethnocentric approach as outdated, Mayrhofer and Brewster (1996) point out that this orientation is effective when strong control and coordination of subsidiaries is required. In addition, sending expatriates out from head

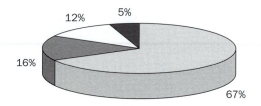

□ Top management strives to create an integrated organization

▨ Top management emphasizes environmental/cultural differences and makes deliberate choices to make foreign operations as local as possible

□ Top management attempts to implement values, policies and sentiments of parent company regardless of environmental or cultural differences

■ Top management emphasizes environmental/cultural regional differences and makes deliberate choices to make foreign operations as regional as possible

Figure 3.1 Management strategy

office is a major vehicle for diffusing central values, norms and beliefs throughout the organization.

A global orientation in management strategy (i.e., a balance between loose and tight control of HR policies) was also reflected in answers to questions concerning the standardization of HR policies, responsibility for policy determination and scope of policy implementation. On a seven point scale, with total localization of HR policies scored as 1 and total standardization scored as 7, nearly 60 percent of respondents plot their organizations between 3 and 5. This is further evidence of a desire to balance global coordination with local determination. This global orientation was reflected in the location of responsibility for global HR policy and practice, where certain key areas were determined by worldwide *corporate HQ* HR managers. The CIPD survey of global human resource management practice (CIPD, 2001; Brewster *et al.*, 2002) found that the most centrally determined areas of HR were as follows:

- expatriate management
- management development
- succession planning
- performance management
- equal opportunity/diversity
- health and safety
- HR planning
- compensation.

However, in line with the need to be sensitive to local environments, *regional* HR managers were most responsible for the following:

- non-managerial level recruitment and selection (with business unit HR managers)
- training and education

- communication processes
- employment contracts/employment law
- employee involvement/work councils
- industrial relations (with business unit HR manager).

Of course, there are usually powerful political debates about which particular aspects of HR should be managed globally or regionally. Looking at Figure 3.2, which shows the percentage of organizations that determine policy through worldwide corporate or regional HR managers, it is clear that some HR activities lie at the cusp, with organizations being relatively evenly split between adopting a more centralized or regionalized control over the activity. We would argue that it is over these activities (i.e., compensation, benefits, job evaluation and cost reduction) that most contention within the profession will be found.

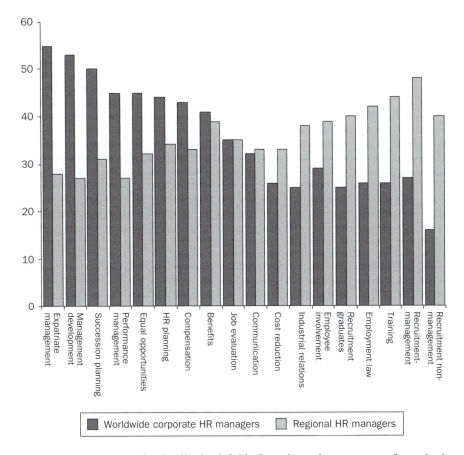

Figure 3.2 Corporate–regional policy battlefields. Data shows the percentage of organizations that manage the international HR activity either through worldwide corporate HR managers or regional HR managers

Factors driving organizational and international HR strategy

Organizations were asked about a series of key drivers of their organization and HR strategies. The IHRM directors, who were the respondents, were asked to rate the extent to which twelve features were an integral element of the organizational and international HR strategy, a peripheral part, or were not applicable (see Table 3.1).

The organizational strategy to which the international HR function has to respond is one driven primarily by the need to maximize shareholder value and control costs. In some cases maximizing shareholder value was an implicit business objective. In others it was more plainly stated. Thus, Diageo, when it was established, made clear commitments to its shareholders as to where the new conglomerate would be within a stated time period. The Internet job market provider, Stepstone, was having problems surviving in a highly competitive field and needed to keep its shareholders with it.

Internationalization also requires the building of a global presence, in increasingly short periods of time. Building a global presence was important in all of our case studies. For example, Rolls-Royce identified the fact that the market for aero engines was increasingly global, with much of the business in North America. It was important for them to have a presence there. Stepstone, as an Internet-based company was inevitably international, but needed to make its operations match its reach. Pacific Direct had operations in China, the Czech Republic and the USA almost as soon as its number of employees reached double figures. Again, it needed to be visible where its markets were.

Internationalization is also driven by the need to create strategic partnerships, as we saw in ActionAid and Rolls-Royce. Finally, it requires the management of knowledge on a

Table 3.1 Percentage of organizations rating element as a key part of the strategy

Feature	Key part of organizational strategy (%)	Key part of international HR strategy (%)
Maximizing shareholder value	70.5	42.4
Creating core business or HR processes	59.0	51.9
Building a global presence	54.8	45.5
Rationalization of costs	46.6	38.9
Forging strategic partnerships	45.0	18.9
Knowledge management initiatives	39.0	44.6
E-enabling business or HR processes	37.1	30.2
Creating centers of excellence on a global basis	33.3	24.5
Industry-wide convergence	9.3	4.3
Decentralization	9.1	13.5
Outsourcing business or HR processes	8.8	12.0
Centralization	1.8	10.2

global basis and the creation of centers of excellence. The most important factors for the HR function to be effective at the global level (and implicitly position the function as a strategic business partner) are shown in Table 3.2 in order of importance.

Internationalization also often requires the creation of, and e-enablement of core business processes. IHRM responds to the development of core business processes and the movement away from country-based operations towards business line driven organizations. However, it does more than just respond. It is often a key part of the re-orientation of strategy.

Table 3.2 The most important factors for the HR function to be effective at the global level

Factor	Percentage
Ensure flexibility in all HR programs and processes	51.6
Have ability to express the relative worth of HR programs in terms of their bottom-line contribution to the organization	37.5
Have ability to express the relative worth of HR programs in terms of their bottom-line contribution to the organization	37.5
Have ability to market HR globally as a source of strategic advantage	35.9
Develop global leadership through developmental cross-cultural assignments	29.7
Foster the global mindset in all employees through training and development	29.7
Design and implement an international HR information system	29.7
Develop relationships with international HR counterparts to encourage information exchange	23.4

These findings are discussed in relation to Stroh and Caligiuri's (1998) study, from which several of the items were drawn, in Chapter 8 and in the context of the changing role of IHR professionals in Chapter 9.

Towards a model of factors involved in the globalization of HRM

In order to begin to model the factors involved in the globalization of HRM we needed to see how these responses patterned across the sixty-four organizations. First, the series of features of the organizational strategy and HR response were factor analyzed to identify the central components of the proposed model.[2]

Our model of the processes globalizing HRM is shown in Figure 3.3. The various organizational drivers can be explained by five factors, interpreted as follows, based upon significant item loadings. As a consequence of the statistical analysis, not all of the drivers shown in Table 3.1 necessarily end up being involved in these factors:

1 *Efficiency orientation*: this included the two organizational drivers centralization and outsourcing of business processes.

2 *Core business process*: this was based on the single organizational driver of creating core processes.
3 *Building rapid global presence*: this included the two organizational drivers: building a global presence and e-enabling management.
4 *Information exchange, organizational learning and partnership*: this included two organizational drivers of forging strategic partnerships and knowledge management initiatives.
5 *Localization of decision-making*: this was based on the single organizational driver of decentralization.

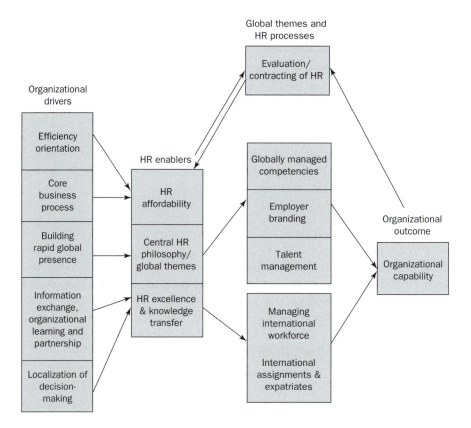

Figure 3.3 Model of processes globalizing HRM

We believe that the items central to the HR strategy are best considered as enablers of the organizational strategy. In order to identify the HR enabling factors, the twelve issues affecting the HR strategy (shown in Table 3.1) were similarly factor analyzed using the same approach adopted to examine the organizational driver factors. Based on the responses of the IHRM directors to the questions about the factors shaping their HR strategy, there were *three* significant HR enabling factors, which are introduced here in detail, but which form the focus of the next few chapters in the book:

- HR affordability
- global themes/central HR philosophy
- HR excellence and knowledge transfer.

HR affordability: As a factor across the sixty-four organizations this included the creation of core HR processes, maximizing shareholder value and rationalization of costs. Organizations are devoting much attention to ensuring that they are putting their people where they can be most cost-effective and that central overheads are as low as possible. Behind most global HR functions' recent restructuring efforts has been the need to deliver global business strategies in the most cost-efficient manner possible. This is not to be confused with "cheapest possible" – although it sometimes feels that way – because many of the companies we saw are making substantial investments in getting things right. But they are assessing their activities to cut out duplication and waste, to ensure added value and to move from purely *transactional* work, which can often be delivered directly by new technology towards those activities that deal with *capability* and *business development*. There is an increased interest in an organization's ability to measure the output of the HR function, reflecting the need to be able to deliver cost reductions and ensure HR affordability. We devote Chapter 4 to examining the impact of technology on the delivery of global HRM, focusing in particular on the shift towards shared service structures, much of which is predicated on the need to deliver HR services at a much more affordable cost and against higher expectations of customer service.

Global themes/central HR philosophy: The second factor across the sixty-four organizations included centralization of decision-making, industry-wide convergence of HR practice, and forging strategic partnerships. This is where organizations are applying generic themes to their HRM that are relevant to all organizations or partners and require a degree of central coordination or establishment of rules. We devote Chapter 6 to this topic and the initiatives typically involved.

HR excellence and knowledge transfer: As a factor across the sixty-four organizations it included building a global HR presence, creating HR centers of excellence on a global basis, capitalizing on e-enablement of HR and the pursuit of knowledge management initiatives. We devote Chapter 5 primarily to this topic. There has been an increased focus on knowledge management in organizations. International HR departments are taking on responsibility for the conscious development of operating networks, both as practitioners within the HR community and as facilitators elsewhere in the organization. The impact of new information and communication technology on global HRM could be immense. Many of those we spoke to had started down this path: none felt they were anywhere other than at the beginning of it; but most realized that it would dramatically change what HRM could do. The ability to get HRM information to and from, and support onto, line managers desks without a formal HRM intervention opens up new and exciting possibilities allowing HR to focus on its capability and business development roles and this e-enablement of HR is being engineered on a global basis. Part of the response to this, in HR as elsewhere, is the move towards developing centers of excellence. In many instances, the HR function itself is also being viewed as a series of centers of excellence best organized on a global basis.

In Figure 3.3 we suggest some possible links between the organizational drivers and the HR enabling strategies. These links are untested, but it would seem likely that an HR strategy concerned with HR affordability is likely to be more important when the organizational strategy is driven by an efficiency orientation and a focus on the creation of core processes in all parts of the business. An HR strategy focused on knowledge transfer is likely to be more important when the organizational strategy itself is driven by attention to information exchange/organizational learning, and a more decentralized strategy. Finally, an HR strategy based around attention to global themes and a central HR philosophy is likely to be more important when the organization needs to build a global presence in fairly short order.

In Chapters 6, 7 and 8 we give attention to a series of important HR processes that play a central role in the globalization of HRM. In Chapter 6 we highlight three global themes that are being used to coordinate initiatives across country operations. These are the use of management competencies or capabilities applied across the organization on a global basis, the pursuit of employment branding, and need for attention to talent management. In Chapter 7 we focus on the development of higher levels of international mobility, the management of an international workforce and the more traditional concern with expatriates. In Chapter 8 we give attention to the process of evaluation. In an environment of efficiency, cost control and concerns about HR affordability, clearly evaluation of the international HR function is important. There is likely to be a virtuous circle in which more positive evaluation and performance is likely to reduce future concerns over HR affordability. The sum product of the different HR enabling strategies and attention to core HR processes, we would hope, is the development of a sense of superior organizational capability.

Conclusion

One of the central findings of our research – and a theme that cuts across much of the material in this book – is that the future of the global HR function is both heavily dependent upon and will be shaped by the globalizing activity of two contiguous functions. These are information systems and marketing or corporate communications. We discussed organizational capability earlier in the chapter. In addition to the management of people – it is considered to include the means through which the organization implements policies and procedures. These means are centered around – and require international HR professionals to understand – economic and financial capability, strategic/marketing capability and technological capability (Ulrich, 2000). As the HR profession becomes more involved in developing organizational capability, then it has chosen to build alliances with – or depending on your viewpoint has been forced to work with – the dictates of the last two of these capabilities. In some organizations this may be seen as a "push" towards globalization of the HR function, as the consequences are not always seen as desirable by isnternational HR professionals. In other organizations the alignment of the HR function with the global integration activity of these other functions is welcomed. Much of this depends of course on how central manufacturing, marketing, research and development and information systems are to the core business of the organization.

From our own data, Table 3.1 has showed the importance of both creating core and e-enabled HR processes to the international HR strategy, whilst Table 3.2 has showed the relative importance both of marketing the HR function but also HR IT systems to the effectiveness of the function.

Figure 3.4 summarizes some of the functional realignments taking place. Strategic or marketing capability thinking is based around offering uniqueness to customers. This marketing perspective has in fact been a significant driver behind approaches to talent management. The second alliance, based around technological capability, involves building uniqueness and customer focus in the delivery of products and services. We shall see in Chapter 4 that the development of shared service models and the e-enablement of HR systems are but two ways of delivering this type of organizational capability. Perceived customer value is considered to result from responsiveness (meeting needs more quickly than competitors), the formation of endearing and enduring relationships, and the pursuit of service quality through guarantees.

The message is that as organizations continue to globalize and design themselves around processes that can be managed on a global scale, then the interdependencies between previously discrete business functions continue to grow and become embedded in every

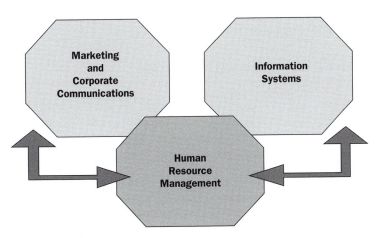

- Global talent wars and employment branding
- Employee value propositions
- Corporate social responsibility
- Insights into employee segmentation
- Engagement and psychological contract
- Building/protecting an HR brand

- E-enabled HR systems and removal of intermediaries in service delivery
- Service centers and global business process integration
- From manpower planning to enterprise modeling and enterprise resource planning

Figure 3.4 The positioning of the global HR function and key power threats/alliances

© Paul Sparrow, Chris Brewster and Hilary Harris

facet of their operations. The main interdependencies are shown in Figure 3.3 and we shall develop each of these dependencies throughout the book. Information-based integration is covered mainly in Chapter 4 and people-based integration is covered mainly in Chapter 5 on knowledge management and Chapter 7 on international mobility. These two modes appear to be the most fruitful routes in the global integration of the HR function, supported by some more limited formalization-based integration in the form of a series of global themes. This form of integration is covered mainly in Chapter 6 – with its discussion of global themes being driven across the HRM-marketing interface, such as talent management and employment branding. It is also picked up in Chapter 8 under the topic of evaluation.

Notes

1　Draws upon secondary sourcing including: Dickson, B., Morgan, M. and Skorecki, A. (2001) "World stock market report: Alcatel falls, but Lucent deal may be close," *Financial Times*, 25 May; Morgan, M. (2001) "World stock market report: Techs fall further on rate move," *Financial Times*, 22 March; Reuters News Service (2001a) "Stepstone ASA moves to cash positive trading in Germany," *RNS*, 21 May; Reuters News Service (2001b) "Stepstone ASA Grants Options," RNS, 23 May; Snoddy, J. (2001) "e-Finance: Stepstone expected to write off 4m," *The Guardian*, 21 March; Svenska Dagbladet (2001) "Amerikanska Monster slukar svenska Jobline," *Svenska Dagbladet*, 26 May.

2　For the statisticians amongst our readers, this was done as follows. The twelve features driving organizational strategy were factor analyzed using PCA with varimax rotation to reveal five factors accounting for 63 percent of the variance that characterized the organizational strategy. We term these organizational drivers. (See Table 3.3.)

Table 3.3 Factor analysis of organizational strategy drivers

Factor	*Eigenvalue*	*Percentage of variance*	*Cumulative variance*
Efficiency	1.82	15.2	15.2
Global provision	1.68	14.0	29.2
Information exchange	1.60	13.4	42.6
Core business process	1.37	11.4	54.0
Localization of decision-making	1.21	10.0	64.0

A similar procedure was followed for the analysis of the HR strategy factors. There were four types of firm shown by the cluster analysis across these factors.

The impact of technology
on global HRM

4

Introduction

A series of generic international management issues involved in globalization inevitably create a search for optimal HR practice that it is hoped will, if managed appropriately, increase the importance of the international HRM function. In other words, globalization of itself brings the HR function closer to the strategic core of the business and also leads to considerable changes in the content of HRM (Pucik, 1992). The effective management of human resources internationally is a major determinant of success or failure in international business (Stroh and Caligiuri, 1998). Therefore those organizations that underestimate the nature and complexity of the HRM problems involved in managing increasingly international operations face avoidable implementation problems (Dowling *et al.*, 1999).

In their search for the changing role of the corporate human resource function in international firms Scullion and Starkey (2000) consider that the answer has to do with unique competencies. The bottom-line question faced by all corporate centers is: "What is it that the corporate HQ can do that cannot be done by financial markets or the business units, acting as independent market contractors?" (Foss, 1997: 314). For Ghoshal and Gratton (2002) the answer has to do with four important integration activities that the corporate HR center can make a unique contribution to. These are noted below, along with some reference to analogies found in our research:

1   *Operational integration through standardized technology*. We look at the impact of technology throughout this chapter when we consider the e-enablement of HR on a global scale. Portals can provide a common front to employees and help integrate the HR function around common processes. This is a form of information-based integration within the HR function (see Chapter 3 for an outline of the different forms of functional integration). However, we also consider operational integration in Chapter 6 when we look at the challenges of globalizing talent management processes, particularly those to do with recruitment, selection and assessment.
2   *Intellectual integration through the creation of a shared knowledge base*. By focusing on creating, sharing and exchanging knowledge both within and beyond the HR community, corporate HR functions can ensure that the intellectual capital of the

function is rapidly codified and shared across constituent HR functions. In Chapter 5 we shall discuss knowledge management, the delivery of HRM through networks and the process of intellectual integration around concepts of optimal HR.

3 *Social integration through the creation of collective bonds of performance.* This is where the function develops a clear sense of what it wants to achieve and how it wants to achieve this goal. The shift within global HR towards working through global networks is an example of new patterns of social integration.

4 *Emotional integration through a sense of shared identity and meaning.* This concerns the mobilization of hearts and minds behind change processes. In this chapter we shall examine the need for international HR professionals to act as guardians of national culture as they negotiate a new balance between the application of global rulesets to HR processes and the need for local responsiveness to cultural imperatives. In Chapter 6 we provide another example of emotional integration when we look at efforts to develop a sense of identity around employer branding and values-based HRM in global organizations.

In this chapter we examine the latest technical developments that have the most powerful impact on the ability of the international HR function to offer the above sorts of integration. These four developments are as follows:

1 the advent of shared service thinking;
2 the e-enablement of HR service delivery and move towards self-service models;
3 the removal of various intermediaries in the delivery of HR services; and
4 the continued adoption of enterprise resource planning systems and advent of enterprise modeling techniques.

Shared service models

Considerable attention has been paid to the development of shared services. As Ulrich (1995: 13) noted in the earliest days of the trend: "the impetus for shared services is the intersection of five management concerns: productivity, re-engineering, globalization, service and technology. Productivity demands have required that managers do more with less through improved efficiency and reduced costs."

He argued that global alliances, acquisitions, joint ventures and competitors have led to a more complex organizational arrangement in which companies may be simultaneously customers, vendors, competitors or distributors. The global HR function now must respond faster and with more specialized knowledge of both its own field of HR and of its application to the business.

Shared service thinking forces a distinction between transaction-based services (dealing with processes and activities related to meeting the administrative requirements of employees) and transformation-based services (non-routine and non-administrative HR activities that transform a firm by helping to implement strategy, create a new culture, or accomplish business goals). Transactional work can be put into a service center – typically created when the organization chooses to concentrate its administrative personnel activities into a centralized "back office" function. Administrative processing is therefore carried out separately from the main HR group. Transformational work can be put into a service center, but may also be combined into a center of excellence. We discussed the nature of centers of excellence as strategic subsidiaries or indeed as networks of experts in Chapter 3. In the context of HR services, however: "Centers of excellence combine distributed talent throughout a corporation into a shared service, then invite businesses to use these resources to solve business problems" (Ulrich, 1995: 15).

Although shared services tend to denote centralized provision, a better word to use is common provision. Ulrich (1995) argues that whilst shared services might look like centralization, they could imply the opposite. The corporate center does not need to control the resources or dictate the policies, programs or procedures. Central structures are balanced by the presence of more HR managers close to the customer, bringing in elements of decentralized service. Central organization of HR resources comes hand in hand with local (or in an international sense more likely regional) tailored advice, policy, or practice designed around business needs. Administrative functions may be centralized but decision-making remains decentralized. Moreover, a wide range of services can be considered in terms of this need for common provision to recipients – not just administrative work.

The relevance of this development to international HRM is considerable. Shared service thinking – and the associated technologies being used to enhance delivery – represent a force for a fundamental realignment of the HR function. It carries implications for the level of centralization–decentralization and devolvement evidenced across countries, regions and corporate headquarters. Moreover, it changes the economics of HR service provision and introduces competing dynamics for both the standardization of HR processes but also the potential for mass customization. We argue that few international HR functions will be able to ignore this development.

Practice however rarely matches theory. Central organization can also imply that a small subset of HR experts hold sway over HR system design and if they are not internationally minded then their perceptions of (country-level) customer need may themselves be stereotyped. Lentz (1996) noted that successful organizations walk the tightrope between integrating competitive features of customer focus and flexibility on the one hand and creating economies of scale on the other. Therefore the activities and responsibilities that end up being devolved both to the local line managers and to local HR staff vary considerably (Reilly, 2000). Shared service models might in effect offer a "take it or leave it" option to local management – seen, for example, in Eisenstat's (1996) reporting of a quip made by a manager at Apple that "my HR representative is not a person, its a floppy disk." On the other hand, the models can also be ones in which HR acts as an "intelligent agent" guiding staff and managers through a maze of complex policy. Reilly points out that opinions as to the eventual impact of this development still diverge. Although in 1999 it was still considered that shared service models were a side issue and possibly another technical fad (Arkin, 1999), events moved on rapidly. By 2003 a number of professional conferences and networks had been established to help practitioners understand the implications of this development (for example the Shared Services Network on http://www.sharedservicenetwork.com). Several large firms have recently developed shared service models for their HRM and some multinationals believe that shared services represent a fundamental change in HRM: "Separation of strategy from service delivery and the creation of shared services is in that league of change with the switch from welfare to personnel in the 1930s and from personnel to human resources in the 1980s" (Alf Turner, Director of HR Services, BOC; cited in Reilly (2000: 2).

By separating out those elements of the HR role concerned with business strategy from those elements concerned with service delivery, it is argued, there are deep implications for the skills and competencies of HR professionals. The radical perspective links the development of shared service structures to parallel changes in technology that have enabled greater outsourcing of HR activity. Whilst technology (notably organizational intranets, web-based portals, interactive voice responses and document and information management systems) has been an important part of the equation in the move towards more global models of HRM it is a facilitator rather than a driver of such change (Reilly, 2000; DeFidelto and Slater, 2001). Technical innovation has simply enabled organizations to consider a much wider range of HR services on a common basis around the globe, though the reasons for introducing shared services have been more to do with cost, quality and the general nature of organizational change, as we saw from our survey data reported in Chapter 3.

Box 4.1 Impact of shared service models on HR functions

Shared services help to reduce costs by cutting the number of HR staff needed, reducing accommodation charges and by introducing greater efficiency into choices both about what services are provided and how they are delivered. Cost savings in particular come from the following:

- falls in HR headcount of between 20 and 40 percent;
- moving operations from high locations to low cost locations in terms of either office space or employee costs;
- centralization of focal points used to buy external services (for example the centralization of recruitment services in 1999 saved ICL £2 million a year); and
- development of high volume partnership arrangements with a restricted set of suppliers.

An indirect impact is that the introduction of shared services makes the cost of HR administration far more transparent to the business.

Source: Reilly (2000)

As well as shared services there has been a desire to improve the quality of HR delivery and to enhance levels of customer satisfaction. Improved quality of service is evidenced in a number of ways:

- greater professionalization of technical skills within the HR function;
- more consistency and accuracy in HR transactions and less rework;
- more awareness of and conformance to both internal and external best practice; and
- higher specifications of service levels for the internal organization – and the development of greater trust and transparency – through service level agreements or through activity-based pricing.

For international HR professionals there are some immediate consequences. Issues that invoke cross-national working and interpretation are more likely to be escalated upwards to international specialists or centers of HR excellence. Shared services, then, can change the way in which international HR professionals are sourced with their work and can also bring with it new control systems to govern and monitor their response.

Another implication of the move to shared services is that the structures of HR at country-level changes. By the end of the 1980s most multinational organizations had decided that splitting up the HR function on a country-by-country basis when the rest of the organization was increasingly aligned behind global lines of business was not helping the function to achieve its objectives. However, concerns about diversity in employment law and the continuance of strong national influences on the employment relationship meant that total alignment of the HR function with other business processes remained problematic. As a compromise, many organizations installed global HR directors as an extra layer in the reporting structure in order to create a position that acted as a strategic business partner. However, the result was often confusing as HR functions attempted to interweave their day-to-day administration work with the more strategic activities open to them. The advent of shared service thinking in the late 1990s provided the opportunity to transform HR.

Global e-enablement of HR processes

We have noted that to date there does not appear to be a common path to the internationalization of shared service models. Many organizations have chosen to create regional centers as part of a single international organization structure. In contrast to IBM, Hewlett Packard changed their country-based systems to regional centers but allowed the managers to stay in their original offices. They sent the work to the people, not the people to the work (Reilly, 2000). Another arrangement has been to use service centers to support global business streams rather than organize them at a regional level on a geographical basis.

Future developments in the shared service models described above are likely to come about through technological change. The impact of new information and communication technology on global HRM is potentially immense. Most organizations have only just started down this path but already realize that technology will dramatically change what HRM can do. The ability to get HRM information to and from, and support onto, line managers' desks without a formal HRM intervention opens up new possibilities that allow the HR function to focus on roles that are more to do with capability and business development. There is clear evidence that the e-enablement of HR is being engineered on a global basis (Harris *et al.*, 2003). This technical evolution is intimately connected with the development of service center models outlined above. Consequently, more and more service center activities can now be put online in order to develop the ethos of employee self-service or self-reliance. Operations behind the scenes to handle this service may be managed in-house or may be outsourced to firms that have the technological expertise to offer such services at low cost, but the ability to answer employee questions on behalf of the employing organization (Ulrich, 2000).

In practice a simple evolution has occurred through which web-based systems allow employees from anywhere in the world increasingly to manage their own requirements. Initially simple HR administrative transactions such as payroll processing, benefits administration, stock purchase plans and regulatory compliance were made available on intranets. The move to more sophisticated forms of employee self-service has become more practicable.

The adoption of technical routines can be used to introduce disciplines into management or employee behavior, whether such disciplines are considered culturally desirable or not. As these technologies develop, then the following developments are expected to be seen on a sporadic basis:

- e-enablement of more transformational HR work and more sophisticated HR practices such as parts of the recruitment and selection process, or the appraisal and performance process;
- current online access rights and limited update rights used as a stepping stone to managers authorizing pay changes and performance management data and to employees providing not only factual data about their preferences but also more dynamic and interactive information around skills and personal aspirations;
- computing power being directed at developing what are called "proactive pull technologies" (modeling systems that allow individuals to see the consequence of their decisions, or decision-support mechanisms to assist managers in areas of discipline, training and selection); and
- mass customization of terms and conditions as variations and combinations can be recorded and monitored.

Practice of course lags behind the rhetoric, and the web-enablement of training programs, learning communities, compensation system administration, employee relations surveys, communications, grievance procedures is as yet still a rarity. Even protagonists of e-enablement, let alone doubters, sensibly observe that the "speed of progress will probably not be determined by technological capability but by culture" (Reilly, 2000: 37).

Implications for global HR

Nonetheless, these developments are having a significant impact on existing international HR functions. They are moving the focus of the IHR away from its traditional focus on being able to manage a global set of managers, towards becoming a function that can operate a series of value-adding HR processes within the business internationally (Sparrow, 2001). Historically, considerable energy has been spent translating central initiatives into what works within different countries. Countries therefore had much freedom in the operation of several HR processes and there was only a light "touch of hand" from the center. Now, however, there is a much stronger focus on cross-country and cross-business border implementation issues. HR is moving towards a world where it has to satisfy line of business – and not just country – needs and this is shifting the way that HR professionals think about problems (Harris *et al.*, 2003). The main change is that they now consider whether their organization has good information systems in place, and whether this gives them the capability to deliver people-related services without them having to pass through the hands of the HR function.

In practice, most organizations are pursuing regional but not yet global e-enablement strategies. Scale is an important consideration. Many international organizations do not have sufficient numbers of HR professionals in particular geographies and so the policy is hard to justify. There are not enough intermediaries to cut out from the process to justify the investment. Moreover, not all countries are supportive of the service center concept. In part this is because there is still a lot to learn about the operation of global service centers as evidenced by the professional networks that have been set up. Rather than confront countries around the world with an over-standardized solution – which is fraught with political and cultural problems – MNCs are persuading various businesses and country operations to support the concept of global service centers and then managing a step-by-step migration towards them. The strategy has tended to be to establish the principle of e-HR first, and then to reorganize the supporting infrastructure that is needed to enable this, such as the service centers.

Box 4.2 The Gulf Stream effect

As with many HR innovations, service centers appear to have followed the "Gulf Stream," "drifting in from the US and hitting the UK first, then crossing the Benelux countries and Germany and France and proceeding finally to southern Europe." Towers Perrin consulting reports suggested that by 2001 within Europe the UK was host to 66 percent of HR Shared Service centers, France and Germany 8 percent apiece, Ireland 4 percent and a further 14 percent in other European countries. When looking at country coverage, the overwhelming majority of HR Shared Service Centers (70 percent) were national, i.e., covered a single country. Thirteen

continued

percent operated on a pan-European basis and only 7 percent operated on a global basis (many of these were in fact single regional centers operated as part of a global network).

Source: DeFidelto and Slater (2001: 281)

IBM's European HR Service Center demonstrates the challenges created by greater pan-national coverage. We provide some detail on this because the early adoption by IBM of this approach and relative success has led to them being consulted by other HR organizations on how best to handle this type of model. This process of implicit knowledge transfer from one organization to another through best practice consultation is important. Within our validation workshop process it was clear that as IBM began to understand the escalation process through experience, they learned to make some important distinctions between call centers, service centers and competency centers. Enquiries can rapidly raise the level of handling an issue to that which requires detailed insight. IBM realized that call centers were different from central service centers. The latter needed to bring together some of the leading expertise, for example, in the HR compensation area. The competency centers created new sets of careers for international HR professionals, for people who had sophisticated and detailed insight into technical issues (this is discussed in the next chapter in the context of centers of excellence within the HR community at Shell People Services).

What is the understanding that IBM might pass on in this instance? Its European HR Service Center is based at their UK headquarters in Portsmouth. It was established in 1998 and now provides support to over 100,000 employees in more than twenty countries. These twenty countries are serviced by ninety people representing fifteen different nationalities (Industrial Relations Services, 1999). The majority of these people are young and speak several languages. In 2001 the center received 252,000 telephone calls, 71,000 e-mails and over 2 million Web hits (Stevens, 2002). Delivering a quality service requires enhanced internal control and issue escalation procedures to ensure people know their area of expertise and do not go beyond their capability. At IBM's Ask HR, the average routine telephone call is dealt with in two minutes. The target set is for 80 percent of calls to result with the customer being satisfied. These are level 1 issues that can be handled by generalist staff in the service center. A further 19 percent of issues require more sophisticated responses. These enquiries involve a degree of program interpretation, issue resolution, training and trouble-shooting. They are answered by specialists within the European Service Center with a target response time of two days. The remaining 1 percent of enquiries have to be referred to a small number of HR process experts who reside within the general HR function.

One of the striking points of the above data – which seems to be fairly typical across many organizations – is the amount of activity that is really just of a transactional nature. In one of our case studies when an activity analysis was carried out 75 percent of HR activity fell into this category. Care should be taken in assuming that just because activity is transactional it is of lower value of course. Line managers in any geography expect these transactions to be carried out efficiently and to the highest quality standard, and if they are not then the reputation of the HR function can be imperilled for several years to come. Dave Ulrich has said at many conferences that HR managers may get promoted for good strategic work, but they get fired for mistakes at the transactional level. Indeed, any event that leads to an interruption of service – for example loss of IT service – can have very damaging effects given the volume of work carried out this way. Nonetheless, a figure of 75 percent demonstrates the potential for automation that exists within HR work.

Ford of Europe's Customer Operations Delivery Model was originally based around the re-engineering and centralization of transactional and administrative HR processes in order to enable more consultative HR roles (Brewster *et al.*, 2001). The delivery of standardized HR processes, across countries where feasible, was intended to achieve high customer satisfaction levels whilst also delivering efficiencies within the function. Service centers were designed to ensure that managers, employees, HR colleagues, pensioners and external customers can have their policy queries dealt with in a consistent, efficient and effective way. Ford reorganized into regional business units, linked through global centers of excellence in 2000. In response to this, the HR function, which traditionally focused on delivering services at a national level, changed its emphasis in 2001 in order to become a pan-European organization. The aim was to serve its customers more effectively and to strengthen its role as a strategic business partner. To support the new regional focus, Ford of Europe re-engineered the function to help reduce the level of transactional work that HR was involved in.

Constraints limiting the impact of technology on global HRM

It is important to note that there is a clear danger that the sorts of technical developments outlined above can lead to a fragmentation of the international HR function. Gratton (2003, p. 18) has expressed the nature of this danger. It concerns the fragmentation and ultimate perceived irrelevance of remaining work within the function:

> during the past decade we have fragmented the roles and responsibilities of the function. We have outsourced the lower value, operational work, and we are beginning to develop the staff profiling work that will enable us to act as "employee champions." We are also putting the "change agent" roles back into the streams of business to work closely with their line manager partners. Meanwhile the "business partners" are either going into the businesses or clustered around "best practice" centers, which may be located in different places . . . this fragmentation of the HR function is causing all sorts of unintended problems. Senior managers look at the fragments and are not clear how the function as a whole adds value.

An example of planning for the changes in the role and structure of HR can be seen in one of our case companies. After making a series of divestments Diageo's strategy centered around creating global consistency, organic growth and long-term sustainability. Diageo also believed that it had the potential to be an employer of choice in most of its markets. In its desire to be an "authentic and iconic" company senior management realized that it needed to nurture and manage corporate reputation as a critical asset, but also that this could be damaged very quickly. Consistency of service delivery was important.

A new HR model at Diageo

Case Example

In December 2002 Diageo began work on a new HR model designed to ensure ownership for shared processes and policy, clear accountabilities and consistent deployment of the core HR strategy. Although the people resources were distributed over a wide geography, the function had to be better connected at a global level. Project Perfect Serve involves the design and implementation of a new operating and organizational model by mid-2006. The project involves investment in common technology, process and data platforms to support the HR function and the business to improve decision-making, especially in the area of talent management. The challenge is to accelerate the deployment of the HR strategy and make sure that the new structure and operating model will be delivered at lower cost with less duplication, with common processes, systems and ways of working and with improved levels of service. This project, like those in other functions, is based on a set of common Diageo operating principles that have been developed and communicated as part of the strategic drive towards an organization that facilitates sustainable organic growth.

Applying these operating principles the HR Leadership Team confirmed a set of organization design principles for Project Perfect Serve. The model will connect the function globally, but Diageo's people resources are likely to be distributed geographically. Diageo is not building a decentralized model where policy and practice decisions are invariably made locally, nor a centralized organization model where decisions are made from a narrow geographic mindset, with policy makers sitting in one location. The HR organization model will ensure coordination of key policy and practices in a country. It will be built around *three* activity and process categories:

- *Global*, where the desired outcomes necessitate that policy practice and data are developed and deployed for the whole organization
- *Business support*, where the local HR resource will contribute to and execute global policy and practice, or develop and execute local policy and practice needs
- *Service delivery*, where policy, process and transactional support are pooled to service multiple markets and business entities.

The bias is to place as much activity into service delivery as possible, beyond the traditional remit of "service centers." A number of HR activities currently taking place within business units will be pooled, eliminating costly duplication and improving consistency, quality and effectiveness. The operating principles are based on a clear underlying philosophy:

- *Customer-orientated HR service delivery*, "strategic partnering with" rather than "policing" the business

- Promote *accuracy, self-service and self-reliance* in employees and line managers people management requirements
- Act as a *global community* with *consistent execution* of the global HR strategy
- Provide *integrated HR services and data*
- Where beneficial to Diageo, the provision of HR *services will be based on standardized processes, common data and standard applications*
- Provide actionable management information at all levels of the business (local, regional, global) for use in the *execution of the Corporate Strategy.*

The global HR service delivery model foresees HR delivery specialists in areas such as recruitment, deployment, development, reward, performance and reward providing value-added services in response to requests from the business unit managers in addition to administration and transaction services provided out of service centers. This will be tracked and measured by service-level agreements. Diageo's new e-enabled global service delivery model will go way beyond just the transactional side and will incorporate more sophisticated HR processes.

Some of the threats noted by Gratton – as well as a series of practical constraints – became clear both through our validation workshops and also through developments over time in our case studies. There are clear risks and constraints inherent for international HR functions in pursuing an e-enablement strategy:

- *The long cycle of investment*: with the risk of sophisticated but unattractive or culturally unacceptable systems.
- *The scale of IT investments*: HR functions have to ride on the back of investments by IT function, yet its service delivery is dependent upon the ability of IT to deliver uninterrupted resources.
- *Risk management*: if a global organization experiences technical problems and the server goes down there is a need to have local expertise in place to sort out the problems.
- *Fractured delivery*: the creation of several web sites leads to global inconsistency, not consistency, in messages portrayed.
- *The need for pan-regional policies and processes first*: conflicting policy interpretation often exists across regions.
- *Data protection concerns*: the main constraint to complete global integration of e-enablement strategies.

Sharing information worldwide

Developing the last issue, the constraints tend to be around those HR services that are affected by employment law, employee relations, works councils, procedures governing dismissal and setting up an employment contract – all more country-focused activities (Industrial Relations Services, 1999). One of the biggest cultural differences affecting shared service models and the e-enablement of HRM concerns data protection. As one example, the holding and processing of personal data in EU countries invokes requirements to gain consent from employees and is associated with different restrictions in different countries (data listing religion and ethnic origin is forbidden for German and Italian companies, for example).

There is as yet an absence of coherent worldwide legislation on data privacy. Until this exists the onus is on multinationals to develop their own organization's internal compliance structures and codes of practice for what they deem to be legally safe use of data.

Box 4.3 Data protection legislation: a brake on global service centers

In 1998 the European Union passed a directive laying down strict rules about how data can be used. This banned transfer of data to other countries deemed to have inadequate protection. Transfers can only take place within the European Economic Area. Individual data controllers have some freedom to make their own decisions as to whether adequate levels of protection for specific transfers of data. At the time of introduction the US did not have a general data protection law and so was excluded. A "safe harbour" system is being worked on whereby individual US companies that sign up to restrictions and regulations of the directive and "adequate" designation by the EU is sought for countries such as Australia, Canada, Hong Kong, Switzerland and Hungary. However, the holding and processing of personal data in EU countries invokes requirements to gain consent from employees, is associated with different restrictions (data listing religion and ethnic origin is forbidden for German and Italian companies).

Source: DeFidelto and Slater (2001)

The European directive on data protection covers the processing of personal information. "Processing" includes obtaining, holding, disclosing, organizing, deleting and transmitting across national borders whilst "personal information" can be facts and opinions about individuals and information on an organization's intentions towards them.

Processing of personal HR data is legitimized by employment contracts, collective agreements, national laws or consent of the data subject – the rights and freedoms of individuals. The risk is one of employee claims on breach of privacy. National legislation is also important. The UK's Data Protection Act 1998 requires that employees give their specific and informed consent to data transfers outside approved areas. Privacy laws are complied with by blanking certain fields in employee data files and obtaining employee consent to data being put on the system.

It has been pointed out that "although the software to help manage a global workforce is available, shipping data around the world remains a legal minefield." (Evans, 2003: 32). For example, Daimler-Chrysler used Peoplesoft to create integrated e-HR systems on a regional basis, first for the US, Canada and Mexico and then for sixteen locations in Germany and Spain. The system had to cope with different tax laws between states, separate workforce bargaining structures and local laws governing the privacy of employee records. Once both systems are live the potential exists to move to a global e-HR system. The management development and share option systems are already managed globally, but further integration will be slowed because of international differences in HR structures.

Changes in the role of intermediaries in the HR supply chain brought about by e-enablement of HR

Implicitly, one of the benefits to customers of the new business model afforded by the e-enablement of HR processes such as online recruitment is the opportunity for what IT and marketing professionals call "disintermediation." The noun is based on *intermediate*. The adjective and participle is *disintermediated*. It describes the concept of removing links from a trading chain as part of a trend towards direct interaction between consumers and producers, which reduces or eliminates the need for intermediaries such as wholesalers, retailers, brokers and agents. These intermediaries tend to either facilitate a transaction (transaction brokering) or provide a "hands on" service themselves. The term is used by the computer technology and Internet marketing community[1] as a popular buzzword to describe many Internet-based businesses that use the World Wide Web to sell products directly to customers rather than going through traditional retail channels. Examples include Amazon.com's success in online book retailing, General Motors Corporation bypassing dealerships to sell cars directly to consumers, and insurance companies skirting their own agents to sell products and services. Providers of services therefore are using electronic communications and the Internet to bypass intermediaries, lessen the trading distance between themselves and their customers and capture a larger segment of a particular business market.

In short, it is a market force considered to be as important as globalization because of its power to transform certain business sectors – with the delivery of HR services being one such sector. By eliminating middlemen, companies can design HR processes that are more customer-responsive and efficient. Intermediaries survive by adding value. If changes in the marketplace render an intermediary's role less valuable, then the intermediary must adapt or otherwise be replaced either by a new, more valuable intermediary or by one of the other agents in the supply chain moving up or down the chain.

An example of this process and global changes in the delivery of HR services was seen in our research at Stepstone. Job-hunting services and associated recruitment and selection activities have proved to be one of the most successful areas of dis-intermediation. Much of the activity is information-intense and therefore the Internet can be used to automate activity and reduce both search time and costs. As an online recruiter it defined itself as a "new media entity operating as the interface between the job opportunity and the potential employee." Online recruiters began operating in an environment where other agents (intermediaries) – such as search, recruitment and selection consultancies and advertising agencies – took a slice of the value-chain through their control of media including magazines, newspapers and exhibitions. However, database interrogation tool expertise resides within online recruiters and so their development of online products and services was designed to take a slice out of the value chain by transforming them – and not the other intermediaries – into becoming the primary "shop window" for job hunters. Having gained control of the main recruitment shop window, then their technological expertise, and economies of scale were expected to help persuade client organizations to re-engineer their own internal processes in ways that would draw more upon the services of external providers such as online recruitment agencies. Or so the plan went. The example below shows that there are often unforeseen complexities when attempting to capitalize on this technical development in a more global context.

Disintermediation within the HR service chain: global complexities faced by Stepstone

Case Example

Stepstone is an independent career and recruitment portal. The company was founded in Oslo, Norway in 1996 and today still has operations in twelve European countries including: Austria, Belgium, Denmark, Finland, France, Germany, Italy, Luxembourg, Netherlands, Norway, Sweden and Switzerland. It is an integrated e-business. Internet technology is not only used as an added distribution channel for job adverts but also to manage and integrate Stepstone into its customers' and suppliers' value chains. Business-to-customer, business-to-employee, and business-to-business interfaces are integrated through such things as: job seekers searching job databases online; targeted alert service via e-mail to job seekers; candidates presenting CVs to future employers online and database management services; career and educational/training course advice; the running of corporate recruitment web sites; the provision of automated data transfer for volume advertisers; and proprietary online sifting software.

In 2001 Stepstone aspired to cater for organizations of various size, for both single positions and global recruitment projects by building its capability to provide pan-European market reach. State-of-the-art technological development meant that it could provide customers with a consistent pan-European recruitment platform. To do this it had to integrate its own systems within its customer's value chain – a form of reverse integration process – and in order to be invited to do this on a significant scale it had to be able to treat its customers consistently across the national markets that it was in. It needed to provide customers with a relatively standardized experience so they knew what to expect and could therefore understand how to build their own HR processes around this offering.

However, one of the problems soon faced by Stepstone was that the intermediary relationships in the recruitment market were in reality very different from one country to another. This was to slow down its ability to build its capability of offering a common pan-European recruitment solution thereby taking out other intermediaries. This constraint almost led to the collapse of the business. In the UK recruitment consultancies were far more dominant than in Germany or Scandinavia. Intermediaries handled 25–30 percent of the recruitment market in Germany. In the UK IT and public sector this figure was 50–55 percent. For example, in France the recruitment market was dominated by newspaper/web site alliances. In the UK partnerships with other intermediaries seemed the best route to gain market share (i.e., rather than attempt to attract more direct clientele): in other countries direct competition with newspaper media made more sense. An indication of the differences between individual European countries in terms of recruitment can be seen in the fact that recruitment agents are generally unknown in Germany but commonplace in the UK. This of course had an impact on the kind of customer relationships Stepstone had in each market. It also made transfer of the business model from one start up to another more difficult. Therefore it was always going to be the case that local strategies would emerge to deal with brand constraints and the different values and actions necessary to maintain market share in notably different labor markets.

Source: Braun *et al.* (2003b)

Is there a consequence for international HR professionals? In our validation workshops it was considered that at a simple level, the e-enablement of HR and delivery through service centers can potentially take out the intermediary intervention of several layers of country-management in a high volume of transactions. From 80 to 90 percent of first-call transactions can be handled on a self-service basis, clearly replacing the need for mediation by HR professionals through a set of automated protocols. However, it was pointed out that such dis-intermediation is often more an aspiration and plant-HR or country-level professionals still have to deliver a wide range of HR processes.

Enterprise modeling techniques

As much of this chapter has attempted to explain, the ability to understand and optimize business processes is considered to be a cornerstone of organizational success (Mabert *et al.*, 2003). In this final section we consider the fourth technical development that is impacting the provision of services in International HR functions. The adoption of enterprise resource planning systems and their combined use with enterprise modeling systems represents another example of the way in which the HR function is having to come to grips with – and absorb some technical knowledge from – developments emanating from the IS function (see Figure 3.3).

The HR function perhaps first began its strategic role by developing expertise in manpower planning – how to resource the business with appropriate numbers and categories of employees. In a couple of our case studies the HR function is now being asked some searching questions by the business. Central to this is the question: "How do we resource *the business*?"

There is an important difference between resource planning and *human* resource planning. The former concern requires the ability to model the enterprise and the complex interworking between human, organizational and technological systems. It centers around the ability to model the business and its strategic purpose in order that appropriate decisions can be made to help integrate a series of "strategic actors," rebalance their relationships or indeed end or outsource the relationship.

If the global HR function cannot rise to the challenge of advising on such fundamental organization design and scale questions, then who can? Quite possibly computer scientists, systems analysts and IS departments. As we have seen, HR Service delivery is being designed around ever-closer technical integration with information systems. IT has provided a new class of planning and resource management software that enables optimum management of resources across global distribution channels, numerous international plant sites and supply chains. These systems are now spreading into supply chain management and customer relationship management systems. It is this last link – customer management – that has brought these IT-based planning techniques ever closer to the heart of the HR function. In the context of the earlier discussion of shared services, outsourcing and global redistribution of work that is taking place consider (whether for right or for wrong) the language associated with the following techniques sounds appealing to senior managers? Ask yourself who owns the technology and expertise? Consider who can apply such expertise wisely?

Enterprise Resource Planning (ERP) systems have so far served to integrate accounting, finance, sales, distribution, materials management, human resources and other business functions to a common architecture that links the firm to its customers and suppliers. Around 30,000 firms worldwide are in the process of implementing such systems. *Enterprise modeling* is a natural extension of this process thinking combined with knowledge management interests. It is defined as the process of building models of the whole or part of an enterprise from knowledge about the enterprise (Vernadat, 1996). These techniques represent knowledge about the organization and its business processes, and provide business analysts with tools to move from high-level enterprise objectives through to detailed specifications of business processes and dependencies used to realize these objectives. They model (Yu and Mylopoulos, 1997):

- strategic opportunities to take advantage of or make use of a units' capabilities and the vulnerability of the unit if the dependency fails;
- intentional desires, expectations and commitments among organizational players;
- mutual dependencies and relationships in terms of tasks, resources, or soft goals shared across roles, positions, agents/actors or processes;
- consequences surrounding the dependency in terms of the degrees of freedom and control (open and uncommitted, committed and critical);

- enforceability (sense of mutual dependence);
- assurances (other dependencies with the unit that reinforce a sense of trust that the dependency in question will be delivered); and
- insurances (the back-ups or second sources in case of error or failure).

Fortunately for the global HR function, its own knowledge at least is not so easily codified. We hopefully make a convincing case for this in the next chapter. Nonetheless, as a function it is being brought into dialogue with other global business functions such as IT and has to be able to present a role and contribution to the organization that is considered to be of equal value.

Conclusion: optimization or standardization: HR as gatekeepers of national culture

What should be concluded from this chapter? Organizational and customer needs are already altering – and in future will alter more radically – in response to the globalization of business and the internationalization of resources within organizations. Nationally based service provision is slowly being replaced by cross-national operations. For example, the advent of the Euro led to a drive to harmonize reward structures on a pan-European basis and this work was considered to be best supported by common shared service centers by many multinational organizations. The environment will be one in which global firms will:

- extend the shared service concept to other parts of their business operations, subsidiaries or satellite companies;
- use it as a force for integration across recently merged or acquired businesses or joint venture operations; and
- seek common platforms for the HR, finance and logistics shared services.

However, the impact of shared service models on the international HR function has been to create a number of pressures:

- Consider the cost efficiencies of delivering HR services across different geographical areas.
- Identify the new HR coordination needs as organizations continue to move away from line of country reporting arrangements towards global lines of business.
- Provide the systems necessary to support strategy on a global basis.
- Understand which HR processes really needed to be different, and which ones are core to all countries.
- Manage a process of migration towards regional and then global HR Service Centers.
- Cope with problems of information deficiency where country-based systems do not provide the information needed to support a global line of business.
- Manage deficiencies in its own staffing, where headcount savings mean that there is not a good match between HR professionals in each area and the functional data that is needed.

Organizations have to re-engineer their HR processes before they e-enable them. Most attempt some form of "optimization" at the same time that they make the move to service centers and e-enabled delivery of HR. Given that many service centers are national, even within MNCs, pan-national optimization is still a relatively rare activity. How do organizations ensure that appropriate decisions are made as to which aspects of the local (country) process may be simplified and which should be deleted only at the organization's peril?

Box 4.4 Optimization of HR processes

As organizations design optimized HR processes they have to ensure that decisions made about which HR protocols they should keep or discard are based on sound judgments. They also have to find ways of capturing the learning that results from these judgment processes so that it may be used to inform and educate other HR professionals or the broader community, especially when decisions are made on a pan-national basis. In one organization that was converting its resourcing activity (in the broadest sense) to a service center model, over sixty different scenarios were generated representing different service requests, problems possibly faced and different types of client perspective. For each scenario a series of "swimlines" were established that represented flows of activity handled by different roles throughout the process. The team then designed an optimal way of handling each swimline, seeking input from internal and external professionals and other experienced organizations in the area.

A distinction has to be made between the simplification of transactional work and the removal of it. When organizations become truly e-enabled this does not mean the removal of all transactional work, but generally implies the simplification of many transactions. In the international arena however, many transactions will still require specialist and high level-input – such as advice on corporate taxation or employment law.

Galaxy project at Shell

The Galaxy project at Shell in 2001 focused on transactional HR practices and the need to develop web-based global HR services provision to enhance the availability and range of employee and manager self services. Shell People Service's vision with regard to the Galaxy project was that the system should provide direct support to employees and enable them to manage their basic HR needs on a self-service basis. The project re-engineered HR

Case Example

processes. It was expected to change the perception of the HR department at a country level and drastically change the roles of country-level HR managers. The system architecture was designed to generate significant cost savings achieved through the standardization of transactional and administrative processes, the lowering of processing costs, less system maintenance, lower upgrading costs, less hardware and licensing costs, fewer HR staff and less staff training needed. Pursuing this agenda on a global basis was necessary in order to achieve a desirable level of cost savings. Galaxy enabled access to globally consistent management information, which was expected to generate a lot of new activity and new ideas. Galaxy allowed truly global management of people resources and would lead to the facilitation of Internal benchmarking and more consistent talent management across the Shell Group. The Galaxy project clearly was a flagship activity. The Galaxy project was expected to transfer work from the businesses to central services. A major challenge was how best to map a set of generic HR processes into the established – and often quite unique – country roles for HR? In considering the options, it was clear that no matter how this was done, the organization would have to go back to each HR process and revamp the country roles in relation to it. By late 2001 Shell developed the first major "delivery project," which covered countries such as Malaysia, Taiwan and the Philippines. Managers in this region had to finalize how the system would work in these countries. Internal businesses globalize at different paces – for example in Shell the chemicals business had recently moved towards a single performance management process on a global basis. Such initiatives acted as a supporting argument that global processes could work.

The introduction of e-enabled HR, with the associated generic HR processes supported by IT systems that it entails, brings a significant change in the focus of the international HR role. The shift is to move away from being able to manage a global set of managers, to being able to help organizations operate internationally. Rather than a pure country focus, the emphasis shifts to cross-country and cross-business border issues and on satisfying the various lines of business as opposed to just country needs. Country-level HR employees will have to think in terms of global line of business processes while being able to become the "care-takers of national culture." Rather than being part of an independent country-level organization, international HR specialists will need to become "brokers" between host country localization demands and global line of business consistency requirements. This new brokering role will be key in ensuring quality assurance of the e-enabled processes.

Being able to locate the right balance between global processes and local specificities – "knowing where the line in the sand is" – will become a key HR competence. HR managers need to be able to see where communality of HR practices are a necessity under conditions of market competitiveness and the need to develop authentic and consistent employee value propositions (we explain this development in Chapter 6), and where the conditions of the local market cannot be overridden. However, traditional country-level HR jobs, as well as jobs dealing with basic transactions will likely disappear in the future.

For those HR professionals who can make the transition, opportunities will be enormous. The new level of information will mean that HR people can get involved in strategy formulation. There is huge opportunity to increase the visibility of the HR function. Having the accumulated information on the HR transactions will get HR people into the offices of business managers. It opens up the door for an internal consulting side of HR. This opportunity, however, can only be grasped, if HR is able to convert the new strategic HR information into messages of value to the business, whilst also being able to convey unique insight into how best to interpret the data, including the ability to assess the business risks associated with both the information, or its misinterpretation.

In our validation workshops it was made clear that there is a danger that despite attempts to put in place optimization forum and decision-making bodies, e-enablement results in standardization "by the back door." The following quote highlights the dangers of this back-door standardization:

> A key challenge is finding the people who have got the skill to translate the need to evaluate the true benefits or risks of e-enablement into practice. Currently there are "pockets of HR information" that are being e-enabled, but there is no knowledge management strategy behind this piecemeal approach.

This critical issue in the current process of globalization is considered in the next chapter.

Note

1   See, for example, sites at: http://www.computerworld.com/managementtopics/ebusiness/story/
    0,10801,37824,00.html

    http://www.webopedia.com/TERM/D/disintermediation.html

    http://www.marketingterms.com/dictionary/disintermediation/

Knowledge management and global expertise networks

5

Introduction

In the last chapter we noted the current opportunity afforded to the international HRM function in helping to build organizational capability. Perhaps the most critical component in terms of international HR positioning lies in its role as knowledge management champion. Thirty-nine percent of the sixty-four organizations in the CIPD study saw knowledge management as a key driver of their organization's strategy (Brewster *et al.*, 2002). It was also a central element of the international HR strategy – what we would call a key delivery mechanism – for 45 percent of the sample. This was the one issue that received more attention in international HR strategies than in the organizational strategy. Moreover, 25 percent of the sample saw the creation of centers of excellence on a global basis as a central part of their international HR strategy. As we shall see in the opening sections in which we present the main theories, frameworks and ideas in the field, these data are in line with current strategic thinking. We outline the latest ideas in *five* areas, and then go on to examine actual practice. The five areas are as follows:

1 the role that expatriates, IJVs and mergers and acquisitions play in the transfer of knowledge on a global basis;
2 the reasons why HR practices themselves are expected to be transferred globally;
3 models of the factors that lead to successful transfer (or not) of HR practices;
4 the nature of HR knowledge that needs to be transferred from one international HR practitioner to another; and
5 some general lessons from the fields of organizational learning and knowledge management as to how such knowledge transfer can be facilitated.

We shall see that the creation of shared knowledge bases represents an important integration activity to which international HR functions can contribute. Gratton (2003) calls this intellectual integration. However, despite the attention paid to knowledge management, "to date there is yet to be a significant undertaking that looks at issues in managing knowledge across borders" (Desouza and Evaristo, 2003: 62). We respond to this challenge by looking at the role that knowledge transfer plays in the work of international HR managers. Having outlined the main frameworks, theories and models, this chapter shows how the way that the process of globalization taking place within international HR functions helps exploit the knowledge stock within the organization. This will demonstrate, however, just how intrinsic or tacit is the nature of HR knowledge (Brewster *et al.*, 2002). Transferring HR knowledge and HR practices on a global basis therefore presents both a significant challenge but also a remarkable opportunity for organizations.

Transferring best practice globally

How do the strategists view the transfer of HR best practice on a global basis? In a competitive marketplace the act of integrating disparate sources of knowledge within the bounds of the organization becomes a source of advantage (Grant, 1996). Indeed, one of the basic premises of internationalization research is that in order to succeed internationally a firm has to possess some highly advantageous, but intangible, knowledge-based asset. International expansion is only possible when firms can transfer their distinctive knowledge-assets abroad into new international markets (Dunning, 1993; Caves, 1996). If one chooses to follow this logic, if there is any strategic advantage to be found in a firm's HRM capability (its philosophy, policies and practices) then this HR capability itself must also be transferred into different geographies around the world. Writers such as Ghoshal, Bartlett and Nohria (Bartlett and Ghoshal, 1997; Ghoshal and Bartlett, 1988; Nohria and Ghoshal, 1997) argue that it is the utilization of organizational capabilities worldwide that provides MNCs with an important source of competitive advantage. The role of the corporate center in MNCs is generally assumed to be one of shaping the strategic direction of the organization and designing the strategic change programs pursued in the subsidiaries. Considerable tacit knowledge is considered to reside within the whole HRM system (Lado and Wilson, 1994; Huselid, 1995). Consequently, the capability to effect internal cross-border transfers of HRM practice (along with the knowledge needed to link this practice into local organizational effectiveness) becomes a core competence (Flood *et al.*, 2003).

One of the ways in which this core competence is evidenced is through the process of "design influence" over local HR practice exerted from the center – exerted either as the direct source of innovation or by tacitly structuring the agenda in terms of what might be deemed acceptable in subsidiaries (Martin and Beaumont, 2001). However, *early* perspectives on "knowledge diffusion" tended to assume a unidirectional flow of knowledge from the MNC's home base to its subsidiaries and alliances. Martin and Beaumont (2001) note sadly that most attempts to transfer best practice have still been predicated on centrally designed change programs intended to:

- modify the culture of subsidiaries through vision and values programs (Buller and McEvoy, 1999); and
- assign a central role to new and reformed HRM policies, usually based on concepts of best practice (Martin and Beaumont, 1998).

This central design influence exists despite the view that has emerged from both early theoretical work on MNCs (Hedlund, 1986) that noted that MNCs may also be designed around more horizontal, relational networks of influence, as well as more recent models of MNC center–subsidiary relationships based on the "knowledge leveraging" perspective of Grant *et al.*, (2000). This more recent perspective appreciates that knowledge is created in many sites and functions and is accessed in many locations. It argues that: "the movement of knowledge between different geographical locations is central [to the process of adding value in knowledge development]" (Grant *et al.*, 2000: 115–116). Knowledge flows are now understood to be multidirectional, unplanned and emergent (Iles and Yolles, 2002). Influence is not considered just to be a one-way and hierarchical process. Patterns of "reverse diffusion" have been shown to exist through case study analysis (Birkinshaw and Hood, 1997; Edwards, 1998; Edwards and Ferner, 2003 forthcoming). Indeed, our discussion of centers of excellence in Chapter 3 exemplifies one of the types of organizational unit that can exert upwards influence.

Knowledge transfer within globalizing organizations: the role of expatriates, joint ventures and acquisitions

The role of knowledge transfer in international management has mainly been confined to discussion of *three* topics: expatriation; international joint ventures; and mergers and acquisitions (Hodgkinson and Sparrow, 2002).

Bartlett and Ghoshal (1995) noted that expatriates are an important vehicle for knowledge transfer in transnational organizations. There has been little empirical study of or theorizing about this phenomenon, excepting work on the following:

- the spread of tacit knowledge within top management teams through "advice networks" (Athanassiou and Nigh, 2000);
- the "social capital" that accrues to international managers as a consequence of their boundary spanning roles (Kostova and Roth, 2003); and
- the application of knowledge transfer theory to the topic of expatriation (Bonache and Brewster, 2001).

Cerdin (2003) has modeled how expatriates help diffuse HRM practices across international borders (see Figure 5.1). Indeed, we found examples of this in our research. For example, in Chapter 6 we note a global set of competencies used by BOC. These competencies were, however, only adopted in their attempts to integrate their Asian operations into a global line-of-business structure because the expatriate HR manager in charge of the project had had prior experience of working on the development of these competencies in another region. He judged that the process would be beneficial to changes taking place in Asia and drew upon his connections in the headquarters to import much of the work that had already been done.

Organizational learning has also been considered to be central to the success of international joint ventures (Barkema *et al.* 1996; Glaister and Buckley, 1996; Inkpen, 1996; Pilkington, 1996; Schuler, 2001). Iles and Yolles (2002) focused on the HRM practices involved in the migration of knowledge, knowledge appreciation and practice

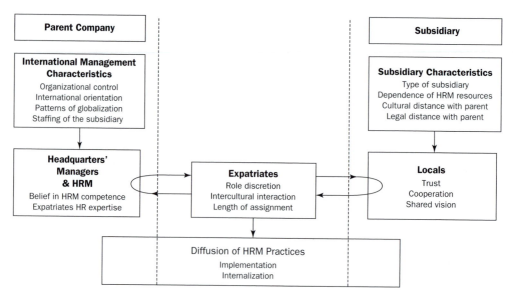

Figure 5.1 Model of the role of expatriates in the international diffusion of HR practices
Source: Cerdin (2003)

of "knowledgeable action" in IJVs. This perspective features much in the opening volume of this series by Schuler *et al.* (2003: 30) who, in discussing motivations to enter into IJVs, note that "the reasons that appear to be gaining substantial momentum are learning and knowledge sharing and transfer." They argue that a main source of both instability and potential gain in competitive IJVs is the relatively greater learning capacity of one or other partner.

Considerable research has demonstrated the limited performance gains associated with international acquisition strategies (Hitt *et al.*, 1996). Serious problems with senior management behavior have been highlighted (Schuler and Jackson, 2001), including tendencies to: pursue personal goals that do not necessarily coincide with the interests of shareholders; imitate others that have made acquisitions; and to overvalue their ability to manage acquired businesses. Acquisitions then present a series of managerial challenges, including differences in organizational culture and managerial style, the need to absorb new product lines and varying dominant logics (Vermeulen and Barkema, 2001). However, acquisitions as viewed through the lens of organizational learning and knowledge management can be seen in a more positive light. They can act as a counter-force to the problem of "progressing organizational simplicity." This is the natural situation in which repeated use of a knowledge base leads to the tendency of organizations to become rigid, narrow and simple, relying only on routines that have made them successful in the past (Miller, 1993). Acquisitions can revitalize organizations, through exposure to manageable levels of shock, and can therefore lead to superior long-term survival; that is, organizational learning gains might outstrip the short-term downsides to acquisitions. Differences between managerial teams can create the opportunity for synergies and learning and added value might be created through processes of corporate renewal (Haspeslagh and Jemison, 1991; Krishnan, *et al.* 1997). Empirical examination suggests that acquisitions – whether in related markets or not – do indeed tend to bring powerful forces of cognitive change (Vermuelen and Barkema, 2001). The conflicts that they engender serve to unfreeze the "cognitive maps" of senior managers, structures and processes, preserve healthy levels of doubt, diversity and debate, create new knowledge from the combination of existing forms of knowledge, infuse unique knowledge and inculcate practices that lead to the creation of new knowledge. The international HR function, then, through the assistance it gives the organization in the management of expatriation, design of IJVs and absorption of mergers and acquisitions, can help engender the transfer of knowledge and assist the long-term competitive advantage of the organization. But what of its own knowledge and practice? Need this be transferred?

Why bother transferring practices across borders?

In order to transfer its knowledge effectively a firm needs a range of technological and organizational skills. When strategists look at the process of internationalization they argue that some organizations have built a superior "knowledge transfer capacity" (Martin and Salomon, 2003). This involves two mutually reinforcing capabilities:

1   the ability of a firm (or business unit within the firm) to articulate the uses of its own knowledge, assess the needs and capabilities of the main recipients for the knowledge, and transmit knowledge so it can be used in another location ("source transfer capacity"); and
2   the ability of the transferee to assimilate and retain information from a willing source, that is, evaluate external knowledge, take in all its detail and modify or create organizational procedures to accommodate the new knowledge ("recipient transfer capacity").

Clearly, one role of the international HR function in facilitating the process of globalization is to help develop the above two capabilities. However, is this transfer so easy to engineer, so automatic, and can it actually be managed? Two models, each coming from a different theoretical perspective, have served to shape thinking about the global transfer of HR practice (see Fenton-O'Creevy, 2003 for a review of a range of theoretical stances that inform the field).

The first model (see Figure 5.2) developed by Taylor *et al.* (1996) adopts a resource-based view of the firm. It asks "why should firms want to export their HRM system in the first place?" Specifically, the model considers the circumstances under which strategic HR capabilities are considered to be generalizable and therefore capable of transmission or diffusion from the parent organization to affiliates. Two factors shape an organization's "strategic international HRM system orientation": whether the parent company actually has a global (as opposed to multi-domestic) strategy or not; and whether top management believe that the HRM capability of the organization is a source of strategic advantage. The resulting orientation is of one of three types, the first of which results from a multi-domestic strategy and the second and third of which result from a global strategy as the organization develops:

1 *Adaptive*: seek to adapt affiliate HRM system to local conditions;
2 *Exportive*: seek to transfer HR policies that are seen as successful in the parent organization to the affiliates;
3 *Integrative*: focus on the transfer of best practice from wherever it might be found among affiliates in the organization.

At the subsidiary level four factors influence the similarity between parent and subsidiary HRM systems:

1 *Subsidiary's strategic role*: this affects the power balance between the two and the parent's ability to impose HR practices;
2 *Method of subsidiary establishment*: HR practices are easier to impose on a greenfield investment than in an acquisition;
3 *Parent–subsidiary cultural distance*: greater distance restricts the potential for HR practice transfer;
4 *Parent–subsidiary legal distance*: greater distance restricts the potential for HR practice transfer

Finally, consideration has to be given to the transfer of HRM practices not across subsidiaries, but at the level of strategically important employee groups. A particular employee group – for example, design engineers in Rolls-Royce, corporate sales representatives in Stepstone or brand teams in Diageo – might require common training across the world given their centrality to the delivery of a strategic imperative such as customer service, innovation or quality.

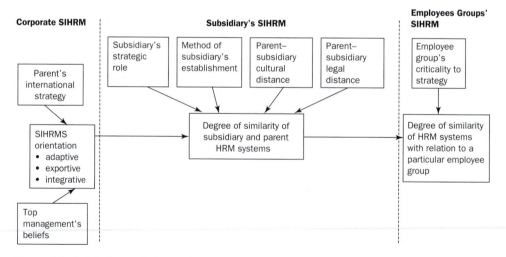

Figure 5.2 Model of strategic international human resource management

Source: Taylor *et al.* (1996)

However, global strategies are characterized by particularly intense levels of uncertainty (Weick and Van Orden, 1990). Moreover, efforts at globalization within organizations are hampered by problems of information overload, managerial complexity in the form of numerous conflicts and paradoxes (what has been called "domestic myopia" or only seeing things from within the mindset of the headquarters), and problems created by differences in national culture (called "expanded socio-cognitive diversity") (Sanders and Carpenter, 1998).

It has long been understood that foreign subsidiary managers frequently become frustrated with requests to implement "yet another program" from headquarters and may – whether by intention or not – end up implementing one thing whilst reporting another (Kostova, 1999; Martin and Beaumont, 2001). So what does it take to ensure the implementation of acceptable corporate-wide strategic change whilst allowing for differential development across subsidiaries?

The complexity of transferring cross-border ideas across multiple layers of management

The second model of factors that contribute to the success of transnational transfer of organizational practices that we outline here was developed by Kostova (1999: 311) who defines the successful transfer of practice as "the degree of institutionalization of the practice at the recipient unit." Convergence of practice ranges on a scale from at the very least actual implementation, to at the most, evidence of internalization. How might an outsider make a judgment that an HRM practice has successfully transferred or not? By measuring two things:

1 *Implementation* – requires the following of rules implied by the practice and the reflection of these rules in objective behaviors and actions. It requires the diffusion of sets of rules to subsidiary employees and can be seen in – and measured – by the actions of employees.
2 *Internalization of these rules by subsidiary employees* – requires the ability to make sense of and attribute meaning to these rules in the same way as that achieved in the host country or headquarters employees, and the ability to infuse the practice with value. How is this measured? The ways in which employees at the recipient unit attach meaning to the practice is reflected in three psychological states: a sense of *practice commitment* (the relative strength of an employee's identification and involvement with the practice); *practice satisfaction* (a positive attitude towards the practice); and *psychological ownership* (the extent to which the employee claims that it is their practice).

We shall consider some global themes that invoke such rulesets in the next chapter when we look at the use of capabilities, employment branding and talent management. However, in the context of this chapter it is useful to note that Kostova (1999) argues that ideas will only transfer successfully internationally if they can be embedded into *three* contexts or variables:

- *Social context:* three factors – regulatory systems, the mindset (cognitions) of managers and norms of behavior – together make up the institutional profile of the home and host country. An "institutional distance" exists between home and host countries based on these factors (we expand on the issue of differential cognitions of managers a little later when we discuss the problem of "surface level agreement")
- *Organizational context:* the organizational culture of host country subsidiaries is important – in particular the extent to which this culture favors learning and change and is compatible with the values underlying the proposed changes in practice.
- *Relational context:* four factors reflect the nature of the relationship between host country and subsidiaries and the successful transfer or not of practice: commitment of the subsidiary to the parent; sense of shared identity with the parent; trust in the parent; and the dependence on the parent for resources.

Kostova and Roth (2002) found support for this model when they examined the transfer of quality practices within an MNC to 104 locations in ten countries through questionnaires given to 534 managerial informants and 3,238 employees. They made a distinction between *ceremonial* or purely formal adoption and more *substantive* adoption of practices. Fenton-O'Creevy (2003: 46) provides an example of ceremonial adoption: a Chinese manager in the Chinese subsidiary of a US MNC noted that his fellow managers "formally comply with an appraisal based annual bonus scheme but construct the appraisal profiles retrospectively to fit decisions about bonuses made on different criteria, such as the status of the employee in relation to important company and external networks."

Martin and Beaumont (2001) consider that Kostova and Roth's model of factors that determine the transfer of best practice is consistent with two important theoretical perspectives. First, it fits the strategic process perspective on the management of change (evidenced in the work of Pettigrew (1995) and touched upon in Chapter 1) in that it points out that international HR professionals have to make the three contexts outlined above more receptive to change. We would argue that international HR functions can influence the second and third of these contexts, if not the first. Second, it fits the business system and comparative literature (evidenced in the work of Whitley, 1992) in that it demonstrates the need for international HR professionals to understand how local practice is embedded in a complex set of relationships between national market structures, ways of organizing firms and authority systems. They also note that this model "has usefully identified measures for evaluating the extent of institutionalization [but] . . . is relatively silent on the process by which such states might be achieved" (Martin and Beaumont, 2001: 1238). We examine some of these processes in this chapter.

The nature of HRM knowledge to be transferred

In Chapter 7 we touch upon the different skills, competencies and mindset between expatriate managers and global managers and outline the importance of four different "cognitive orientations" (Perlmutter, 1969). Indeed, from the earliest debates on international management strategy it has been noted that strategic capability is dependent on the "cognitive processes" of international managers and the ability of the organization to create a "matrix in the minds of managers" or a transnational mentality (Bartlett and Ghoshal, 1989: 195). This international orientation or "attitudinal attribute" is assumed to correlate with the extent of a manager's international experience, although this relationship is complex and highly dependent on the quality of international experience (Kobrin, 1994), not just the length of it as suggested by the measures of firm internationalization outlined in Chapter 3. Some researchers have even developed measures that correspond to the core dimensions of managers' thinking about international strategy and organization and have shown how this mindset changes over time – as for example a study of cognitive change over a three-year period towards a more global mindset in 410 managers within a single MNC (Murtha *et al.*, 1998). It was possible to identify a core value-set or logic that was associated with global operations.

Here, however, we consider the challenges specifically of creating a more global mindset amongst HR professionals. Is such a thing possible? What exactly is the nature of knowledge that has to be transferred between these professionals? In a global environment, physical and cultural distance present powerful barriers to successful knowledge transfer amongst HR professionals. We noted in Chapter 3 that one of the measures used to reflect the degree of internationalization of a firm was called Psychic Dispersion of International Operations (PDIO) – based on the dispersion of subsidiaries across a series of unique cultural groupings (Ronen and Shenkar, 1985). Each of these zones was considered to have unique "principles of management" and managers within each zone therefore to have unique "cognitive maps" (Adler *et al.*, 1986; Hofstede, 1993: 84). Agreeing the content of the knowledge to be shared and creating knowledge networks that can engage HR professionals from across these different cultural groupings is a significant challenge in HR globalization efforts.

What then is the nature of HRM knowledge that has to be transferred? What is the nature of knowledge within the minds of the individual international HR professionals that has to be shared? In Chapter 2 we examined the debates around universalist and contextualist paradigms in HRM in some detail. In Chapter 1 we also outlined three areas of insight that HR professionals needed concerning the following: the range of factors that engender distinctive national and local solutions to HRM issues: the strategic pressures that make these national models more receptive to change and development; and the firm-level processes through which such change and development in actual HRM practice will be delivered. This framework provides an outline of some of the most important content items of the knowledge needed. Knowledge about the nature of distinctive contextual factors – the institutional context, labor market properties, HR career paths and values-linked behavior – is broadly about the role of "cultural pathways" in HRM. This requires insight into the ways whereby different values might be engaged to produce common outcomes

If such knowledge is complex enough, then the challenge of knowledge transfer is made all the more difficult by the fact that apparent agreement between International HR professionals often only exists at surface level.

Box 5.1 Surface-level agreement

When an international HR director gets his or her HR managers from around the world together at some global forum and presents the HR strategy and constituent practices that will come to the fore, just because the country HR managers nod at the mention of certain practices means little in relation to the way in which they will (or will not) support the business logic behind the strategy, or indeed the outcomes that they intend to create by the pursuit of a particular practice. Two empirically supported findings show the nature of the challenge:

- *Logic recipes:* Research has shown that when asked about the perceived relevance of specific HR practices to the competitive advantage of their organizations, there is a clear imprint of nationality. HR professionals packaged HR practices into a series of recipes concerning for example the range of practices that created a sense of empowerment through changes to organization structure, the range of practices that accelerated the pace at which human resources could be developed within the organization, the practices to develop an employee welfare orientation, an efficiency orientation or a long term perspective. Practitioners agree on the practices and the implicit logic represented by these underlying recipes, but they will rate their importance to the creation of competitive advantage in fundamentally different ways from one country to another (Sparrow and Budwhar, 1997).
- *Cognitive maps of the resultant cause-and-effect processes:* Even when there is agreement around the assumed importance given to a best practice, there are marked differences in the perceived reasons why such a practice might be of importance and the assumed outcomes or effects that it will have. For example Budwhar and Sparrow (2003) examined the logics of British and Indian HR professionals around the issues of integration of HR with the business strategy and devolvement of HR to line managers. Although in surveys both sets of professionals rated these policies as being extremely important, when cognitive mapping techniques were used to reveal why they were important and what the assumed cause-and-effect outcomes would be, the professionals were working to fundamentally different logics.

Knowledge is information embedded within a context. HR knowledge is no different in this. Davenport and Prusak (1998) define knowledge as information combined with experience, context, interpretation and reflection. Sackmann (1991, 1992) identified four kinds of cultural knowledge:

- *procedural in nature*, concerning definitions and classifications of objects (called "dictionary knowledge");
- information on *how things are done*, that is, descriptive in nature (called "directory knowledge");

- information on how things *should preferably be done*, that is, prescriptive in nature (called "recipe knowledge"); and
- *fundamental beliefs* or final causes that cannot be reduced any further (called "axiomatic knowledge").

So how can organizations transfer such insights and effect change in HRM across their subsidiaries? Martin and Beaumont (2001) incorporated work on the ways in which managers create a "strategic discourse" (Barry and Elmes, 1997; Ford and Ford, 1995) and the work on institutionalization described above (Kostova, 1999; Tolbert and Zucker, 1996) into their model of HR change in MNCs (see Figure 5.3). International HR practitioners have to "habitualize" other parts of the organization to the new strategy, make the messages for change more objective as they are shared among employees and ensure that the messages become "sedimented" into the organization. This strategic influence role has been examined by Napier *et al.* (1995). It includes being "the change agent of corporate culture; the top management team's symbolic 'communicator' to other levels of the organization; the senior manager's mediator in development/career planning opportunities; and the corporate top management team's and particularly the CEO's reliable internal informal advisor" (Novicevic and Harvey, 2001: 1252).

The tensions between corporate HR and the more globally-minded HR professionals, and the country-based HR managers become evident from this work. In their efforts to "habitualize" and "sediment new ideas" into the minds of the country HR managers, did the corporate HR professionals listen to both sides of the story?

Lessons from the field of knowledge management

Clearly, then, organizations have a major challenge on their hands if they wish to create a more shared and global perspective within the minds of global HR professionals. As the above perspectives highlight, in the field of HR a much more open and unprescriptive discourse between professionals is needed if HR practices are to be transferred in a successful way, or allowed to operate to different purposes in different geographical operations. This accords with recent work on the nature of knowledge management in general within organizations. We briefly review some of the latest thinking on how best to manage the transfer of knowledge within organizations.

It has been argued that managers now add more value to the business process through their brokering of information, their access to a distinct set of suppliers of information who gather, select, edit, codify and publish knowledge; and via their active participation in this "information market" (Hansen and Haas, 2001). This is equally true of International HR practitioners. The knowledge management and organizational learning fields make two sets of important distinctions:

1 *Explicit versus tacit knowledge and learning:* as well as explicit knowledge, the need to enquire into *implicit intelligence* – or forms of knowledge, thinking and learning that lie outside the more overt and rational model of managing is emphasized (Spender, 1998).

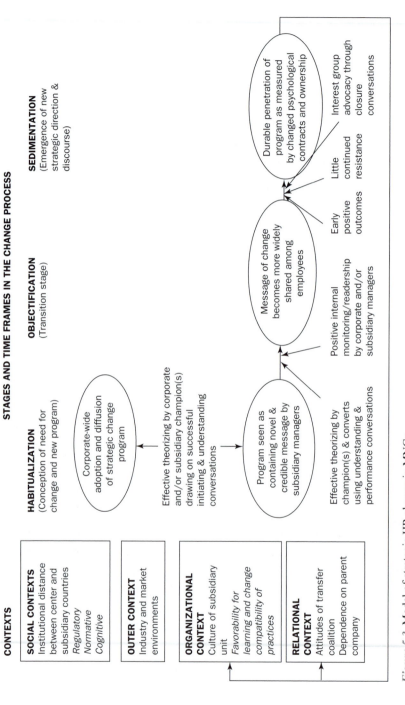

Figure 5.3 Model of strategic HR change in MNCs

Source: Martin and Beaumont (2001)

2   *Knowledge and learning that resides within the individual versus that which resides within collectives:* some strategic management theorists view knowledge creation as a process that primarily resides within individuals, whilst for others knowledge creation is primarily a process that is considered to occur within institutions or professions (we expand on this when we discuss the nature of HRM as a profession in Chapter 10).

In order to integrate knowledge, the organization must be designed and administered in ways that first create, capture and protect it (Liebeskind, 1996). The rapid transfer of knowledge across units (be these business units or HR country operations for example) can only be achieved through the pursuit of broadened networks – called "communities of practice," "communities of interest," or "global expertise networks" (Brown and Duguid, 1991; Orr, 1990). A community of practice (COP) is defined as "a group of people who have common tasks, interact, and share knowledge with each other, either formally or informally" (Desouza, 2003: 29). They have been used widely for example in Shell. Networks have to operate in ways that allow "communities" to create themselves and understand their own trajectories (where did we come from, where are we now, where do we want to go next and how do we get there?). These communities learn through the development of their own identities, professions and skills (Elkjaer, 1999). This in turn means that organizations have to have cultures, structures and systems that enable the acquisition of learning through: team processes of learning, reflection and appreciative enquiry; co-enquiry, as opposed to a simple expert–student relationship (headquarters–country operations); joint planning forums; long time-span projects; and discussions across communities.

Communities of practice at Shell

Case Example

Shell uses the COP method for knowledge exchange in isolated environments, that is, to link globally distributed projects and provide them with a forum for exchanging experiences. The technical communities span more than fifteen subsidiaries and are supported by technology. Each community has a leader whose role is to coordinate events and facilitate connections between members. The various local leaders form a global expertise network, holding the entire network together. For example, the Wells Global Network is one of eleven global knowledge communities set up by Shell International Exploration and Production (SIEP) since 1998, covering technical functions and support functions like HR, IT and procurement. A "New Ways of Working" group was set up to bring together people in three networks. New communities are set up with "seed groups" of around twenty-five people from anywhere in Shell's global operations. This group initiates initial traffic. Successive layers of potentially interested people are invited to join. In the engineering areas communities were easier to set up because the culture was based on knowledge sharing and factual information. Communities are regulated by a moderator or coordinator, who is responsible for encouraging contributions, controlling the content of discussion, ensuring answers to traffic flow or searching for an expert who can answer. In the operating

continued

companies each network has a regional ambassador called a hub-coordinator. They build the community locally. As material in the network amasses it is archived and the list of experts grows. This requires accreditation of the role by senior managers. They are allowed to make themselves available for up to 15 days a year, which in an organization that operates jointly owned operations requires the development of financial and legal arrangements. Expertise at team level is acknowledged through centers of excellence. In 2002 there were thirteen such technical centers in SIEP. Shell estimated that it had saved $200 million from the knowledge sharing initiatives within these global networks.

Source: Carrington (2002); Desouza (2003)

The role of global teams

As we have seen from the review of the literature, expatriates are seen as important carriers of the implicit knowledge needed to capitalize on any HR practices that are transferred. In this role, expatriates represent one form of people-based integration within the HR function (see the discussion of functional integration mechanisms in Chapter 3). However, our research highlighted the importance of two other important people-based integration mechanisms: the creation of global expertise networks; and the formalization of individual expertise within HR centers of excellence.

What is the difference between global teams and networks? Global teams – defined as semi-permanent groups that are assembled to facilitate cooperation and communications between headquarters and subsidiaries – have become a central aspect of global organization operation (Harvey and Novicevic, 2002). They have been studied for a while. They take on an especial importance when subsidiaries are considered to be rich in knowledge, or when it is appreciated that there are continuous changes in the state of knowledge within the organization (Ireland and Hitt, 1997) and help renew the organization during times of heightened need for inter-unit learning, trust, commitment and coordination (Ghoshal and Bartlett, 1995). Global teams perform three key roles (Mohrman *et al.*, 1995):

1 collaborative global project initiation
2 headquarters–subsidiary conflict mediation
3 mobilizing support in the headquarters for cooperation with a subsidiary.

Global networks however are a much more loosely connected group of people or units that interact on a regular but more informal basis. They are potentially a far more powerful vehicle for organizational learning, yet we still know little about how they can be managed and coordinated effectively:

> [The IHRM literature has generally not explained] . . . how the transition from the
> multi-domestic MNC to a global integrated/co-ordinated network can affect the change in

roles of the corporate HR function . . . these new latent in nature and global in scope roles of the corporate HR function . . . are different from its traditional organizational roles.

(Novicevic and Harvey, 2001: 1253)

Global networking represents a powerful process through which the international HR function can help build organizational capability across international operations. It has always been important within international HR. However, it is now considered to be critical because of the structural and technical changes within HR functions outlined in Chapter 4. As a consequence of these structural changes: "the focal point of the corporate human resource function in global organizations appears to be moving toward the need to design a supporting infrastructure for managers to manage competently the complex and competing demands for network co-ordination" (Novicevic and Harvey, 2001: 1251).

We begin with an examination of global networking and then move on to consider more formal approaches.

Historically, global information, insight into local conditions and best practice tended to be shared through the process of international HR professionals just talking to each other – getting groups of people together within the organization to facilitate some transfer of learning. Indeed, international HR professionals have to set up informal networks all the time – it is one of their key objectives. Networks suit a more decentralized model of international HR. They are not put in place just for the purpose of knowledge transfer. They are also used to cut through bureaucracy and to act as important decision-making groups. They serve several important purposes:

- providing a forum to encourage innovation and growth throughout the business and a vehicle to get the right people onto the right teams in order to make this happen;
- encouraging HR professionals and line managers to think beyond their "own patch";
- creating a situation whereby membership of the network provides better quality implementation to both the line managers and the HR professionals;
- getting stakeholders (the senior HR community, presidents in businesses) to buy into business changes; and
- forcing the business agenda in forums outside the networks in subtle ways based on shared insight within the network.

However, in flat and constantly changing organizations, networks tend to break down. Many global organizations are therefore developing more formal processes to transfer knowledge that capitalize on technology (Brewster et al., 2002). International HR departments are taking on responsibility for the conscious development of operating networks, to handle both the transfer of knowledge within their own community as HR practitioners, but also to handle their role as facilitators of change elsewhere in the organization.

> ## Box 5.2 The role of global HR networks
>
> - Provide and enable value-added cost-effective global, regional and local solutions in a series of core HR processes.
> - Identify customer driven pan-national issues.
> - Design solutions to meet specific customer needs and support the corporate people management strategy.
> - Demonstrate to customers that global connectivity adds value by sharing knowledge and expertise.
> - Ensure that knowledge and intellectual property that resided within HR silos were made freely available to all of the organization.
>
> Source: Brewster *et al.* (2002)

Global knowledge transfer through HR networks

International organizations are experimenting with global expertise networks that serve a knowledge management role, making use of "team rooms" established on the intranet to provide access to common implementation materials or live record updates to transfer and share insights into cross-cultural implementation issues (Harris *et al.*, 2003). A technological infrastructure to support the formation and initiation of global HR networks is important, but not always necessary. For example, global leadership networks that were not strongly reliant on technical support formed an important part of operations at Diageo, ActionAid and Stepstone. Diageo initially constituted a series of global teams but, through their way of working, these teams began to develop into much looser networks of influential people. Diageo believed it was important that these teams did not just become debating clubs, dumps for technical data, or another layer of bureaucracy. They had to be decision-making bodies in their own right with the right level of authority. Therefore a common global team process was established through which teams:

- worked out development priorities;
- developed world-class and internal benchmarks against which the results of the initiative would have to be compared;, and
- formed their own network of expertise and decision-implementors.

Work carried out in 2001 on the HR networks proved an important foundation for the new global operating model introduced two years later (outlined in Chapter 4). Networks were of central importance. They drove consistency and communality into geographically dispersed operations, but through a process of finding out what was happening, what could be learned to create a new global system and what good things were going on in the business that could be capitalized on. It was the "softer" "processual" information that facilitated most learning within the networks.

Case Example

Global HR networks at Diageo

In 2001 Diageo decided the global HR agenda had to be orchestrated on a network basis. HR Directors in the various markets had part of their time and responsibilities geared towards the global agenda. Ownership and accountability lay in a lead "market" or one of the global functional HR positions. HR directors from either would take an initiative and develop networks that drew people in from around the organization to work on the issue. Global HR networks focused on recruitment, performance and reward, organization development and international assignments. For example, the need for a global employee value proposition was orchestrated and managed by Diageo's HR Director in the USA. A global network on international assignments was headed by the HR Director for Key Markets. An initiative on Building Diageo Talent Workshops (a form of assessment center to make people understand how a capability agenda supported their strategy) was driven out of a major market rather than the central HR function.

Source: Braun *et al.* (2003a)

Networks were important at ActionAid, where a "joint learning" director was appointed to help coordinate HR people and operations spread across the world in developing countries, often with limited access to the information technology infrastructure. The purpose of networks in Stepstone was motivated by the need to drive the learning associated with the process of internationalization into a set of highly independent country activities. It became clear that the success of Stepstone's strategy of a gradual integration of a complex set of merged and organically developed country operations depended mostly on the development of informal networks, and the relationships developed between the individual corporate functions and country managers. A bundling of corporate functions in one location was considered undesirable. While there was a bias towards London, Stepstone made the decision very soon after start-up to put different corporate functions in different locations, for example, HR in France, marketing in the UK, the CEO in Germany. This was a deliberate attempt to create a "European" company. It reinforced a decentralized culture. However, Stepstone also had to cope with a very rapidly maturing skill-set implicit in its business model. It was managing a series of rapid country start-ups but already the skills in these international markets were maturing. New systems and processes in line with a business model based on the development of a strategic partnership with clients and the offering of pan-European recruitment systems to increasingly global customers had to be exported across its European operations.

The role of global networks, then, is often to develop the level of capability within all of an organization's local or line manager or HR communities. Global HR network leaders may need to get an organization's country or local HR operations to a position where if network were to no longer provide the ideas exchange forum or service for them, then the solution would still be implemented effectively. From our case studies it was evident that global HR networks are used to:

Learning from country initiatives at Stepstone

Stepstone chose a strategy of gradual integration through the use of pilot countries and gradual export of best practices across the European operations in order to develop greater operational consistency. Integration was pursued by using countries as pilots and then based on the experience of these countries, exporting certain processes across Europe. An example of a country level development that served as a basis for possible export was the "Stepstone Academy" established in Germany. Stepstone's Country Manager for Germany – the most successful of the European start-up operations – detected that the longer life-cycle of customer accounts created a need to change the attitude of the salesforce from "hunter" to "farmer." In order to develop a long-term partnership with customers, employees needed to both deepen their knowledge of Internet recruitment, and also develop their insight into the workings of the human resource management function [in the client organizations]. Stepstone Academy provided new models of team leadership training and training focused on dedicated sales techniques to equip staff with key factors for their success. The export of such models and knowledge that was being developed within independent countries initially relied on two things: the appointment of a corporate training role within HR, the holder of which trouble-shooted across countries and acted as a conduit between country managers, and the establishment of a new forum for managers. This operation began as an informal network and problem solving mechanism that became known as Country Managers' Meetings. These informal meetings set up on their own initiative were organized around small workshops in which three or four country managers worked together on a particular project. These small teams were responsible for working out a proposal for the whole company. Similar workshops were also created at the functional level in Marketing and Sales.

Source: Braun *et al.* (2003b)

- capture learning across the HR community and serve as a source of leadership for this broader HR community;
- demonstrate to customers that global connectivity adds value by sharing knowledge and expertise about core HR processes;
- identify customer driven pan-national issues and both provide and enable value-added cost-effective global, regional, and local solutions; and
- ensure that knowledge and intellectual property that reside within "HR silos" are made freely available to all of the organization.

Global knowledge management strategies

We have said that technology need not be central to global networks. It has however generally played a significant role. Desouza and Evaristo (2003) examined the issue of managing knowledge within organizations that span multiple countries through interviews with twenty-nine senior managers from eleven firms in the telecommunications, insurance, pharmaceutical, manufacturing, software and consulting sectors. They considered how these organizations integrated disparate sources of knowledge across different geographical contexts, noting that: "the literature addressing management of knowledge in a global context is best described as sparse. To date there is yet to be a significant undertaking that looks at issues in managing knowledge across borders" (Desouza and Evaristo, 2003: 62).

The study of thirty-one knowledge management projects in twenty-four global companies by Davenport *et al.* (1998) showed that the success of the projects depended on the creation of an effective culture and process, a common purpose and the creation of common language to help identify knowledge. When Chiesa and Manzini (1996) looked at the transfer of knowledge within twelve multinational firms, the main instruments and mechanisms for knowledge flows were found to be electronic communication systems, forums, temporary assignments, international teams, internal markets, cross-border assignments, boundary spanning roles and personnel flows.

Drawing on the work of Desouza and Evaristo (2003), Table 5.1 presents the different competitive, IT system and knowledge management strategies that are generally found within organizations. These are examples of information-based integration as discussed in Chapter 3. There is some, but not total, overlap between each of the different classifications.

It is interesting to note that the regional HR Shared Service infrastructure discussed in Chapter 4 most closely associates with the regionally commissioned and locally executed knowledge management system shown in Table 5.1.

The range of approaches to global knowledge management systems used by organizations tends to fall into one of two strategies: codification or personalization (Hansen *et al.*, 1999).

1 *Codification strategies:* individual knowledge is amalgamated, put into a cohesive context and made available to members through central databases and data warehouses. Document-to-person approach, assuming that knowledge can be extracted and codified. Prominent for creation of global knowledge repositories driven by need for efficiency, lower costs, standard scheme and representations and ease of access. The enterprise modeling techniques introduced in the last chapter fit into this category.
2 *Personalization strategy:* no distinction imposed between the knowledge and the knowledge provider. Tacit knowledge recognized as being important with transfer best achieved through person-to-person contact. IT serves to facilitate communication only. Used to manage knowledge within global projects using e-mail, intranets and discussion boards and to catalyze a subsequent period of socialization with peers.

Given the comments made earlier in the chapter about the role of expatriates in diffusing the meaning behind practices (Bonache and Brewster, 2001; Cerdin, 2003) and the complex social processes involved in the internalization of best practices as they transfer across international boundaries (Kostova, 1999), it is clear that personalization strategies will be more effective than codification strategies in the realm of HR knowledge transfer. As Cerdin (2003: 49) observes:

Table 5.1 Global knowledge management classifications

Bartlett and Ghoshal's (1989) competitive strategies	Ives and Jarvenpaa's (1991) global IT strategies	Desouza and Evaristo's (2003) global knowledge management strategies
Multinational: Foreign subsidiaries run with high autonomy and as a loose federation. This enables subsidiaries to respond quickly to changes in local markets	*Independent global IT operations*: Subsidiaries develop own systems. Collaborative system development is rare	Not present
Global: Actions of subsidiaries heavily regulated and controlled by HQ to achieve global efficiency through economies of scale	*Headquarters-driven global IT*: Corporate and worldwide IT systems imposed in the parent organization	*Headquarter commissioned and executed*: HQ provides technology solutions, support, training, policies and procedures. Standardization of interfaces and uniform approach to best practice
International: Knowledge of parent organization is exploited, diffused worldwide and adapted. Principle of rapid deployment of innovation	*International*: Cooperation and mutual assistance creating strong links between parent and subsidiary IT systems	Not present
Transnational: Dynamic interdependence between the parent and subsidiaries through coordination of efforts, local flexibility, but exploitation of the benefits of global integration and efficiency	Not present	*Headquarter commissioned and regionally executed*: HQ sets out broad guidelines and policies, chooses tools initiatives KM dialogue. Execution commanded by regions. Regional hubs ensure common themes and mission, customizes technology, language, interfaces and type of knowledge base. Own scheme and interactions
	Not present	*Regionally commissioned and locally executed*: Vision and initiative for KM efforts come from regions. Recognition of need for local offices to exchange expertise on frequent basis. Locale-specific KM efforts with actors, networks and inter-relations managed at regional level. Tools and initiatives to capture and exchange knowledge required significant effort across regions

Box 5.3 *Managerial issues with cross-border knowledge management systems*

A number of common issues are generally experienced in the management of knowledge across borders:

- The mindset of employees has to be changed from sharing on a "need to know basis" to one of "continuous sharing of new insights."
- The rate of contribution to central repositories for knowledge-hosting and knowledge-distribution tends to be below expectations.
- Contributing insights to knowledge repositories serves to identify relevant knowledge in a domain.
- Knowledge sharing and usage varies across cultures, making global standards and protocols on how to initiate knowledge difficult to implement.
- Strong informal ties, however, can only be generated once participation is initiated and this requires modification of reward structures to encourage knowledge sharing.

Source: Desouza and Evaristo (2003)

information technology can relay HRM knowledge to subsidiaries, such as HRM guidelines available on an intranet network, but it cannot transfer know-how. It is often left up to expatriates to put into full and efficient practice the knowledge acquired at headquarters and demonstrate and transfer know-how . . . [to be] a carrier of HRM practices.

Formalizing global HR centers of excellence

In flat and constantly changing organizations, networks tend to break down. Many global organizations are therefore also developing more formal processes to transfer knowledge that capitalize on technology. From our validation workshops it was clear that much of the transfer of credibility within organizations comes down to the level of "network brokerage" that can be achieved by individuals or units. The expertise might lie in an internal center of excellence tied strongly into complex and numerous interactions within the organization, but it might also be a relatively small source of activity – for example the possession of knowledge about international benefits – that at a local level would be seen as a target for outsourcing because of the relatively few information requests initiated. For a short time an organization therefore might have a group of people who act as a loose network around the world, whose expertise can be called upon as and when needed. There are a number of different roles played by international HR professionals in these networks:

Box 5.4 Three different contributions IHR professionals can make to global networks

- *Network coordinator* – their role is to liase with the "owner" of or "expert" in a core HR process and then ensure that this expert responds to global customers.

- *Knowledge manager* – their role is to control the HR skills pool, keep people connected, minimize any reinventing of the wheel and maximize the sharing of good ideas and "best practices" where appropriate.

- *HR practice leader* – their role is to take responsibility and accountability for managing a set of resources within a geographical region or on a global basis, so that the HR function meets customer and business objectives and delivers on key targets and revenues.

As described earlier in the chapter, Shell has taken a longer-term approach to global expertise networks. Whilst its approach to knowledge transfer is technical, it has also combined this with the ideas discussed earlier in the chapter surrounding "communities of practice." Shell makes a distinction between a network and a center of excellence. It considers that global knowledge is first *brokered* within informal communities or networks but then needs to be more formally *supported by a strong infrastructure* provided through centers of excellence.

Global expertise networks in Shell People Services

Shell People Services (SPS) experimented with global expertise networks that also serve a knowledge management role. The purpose of SPS is to provide common HR services to group companies and to participate in the setting of the group's HR direction and policies. A critical success factor in being able to meet these goals is to maintain a repository of HR knowledge and expertise. International HR staff are split over three continents and increasingly need to share information and work in virtual teams. Shell has developed several successful global communities that enable practitioners in a particular field to "meet" other practitioners and exchange ideas, problems and best practice. In order that all HR staff, regardless of geographical location should be able to access an information store of best practice, agreed procedures and expertise and to deploy this knowledge when working in collaborative and distributed teams, SPS pursued a strategy based on selecting pilot international HR teams with a proven need for collaborative working and team sharing. The objective of the knowledge sharing strategies across the regional structure of SPS was the creation of communities of practice in each of seven HR expertise areas: compensation, benefits, expatriation, diversity, organization development, learning and talent pipeline.

Case Example

Center of Excellence Coordinators (CECs) in specific HR expertise areas were put in place. People in this role needed to be empowered in order to execute their knowledge management roles and fund the process. A series of community of practice workshops was started in December 2000 and ran through the year 2001. Each of the seven HR expertise areas ran their own workshop resulting in a final workshop where all CECs shared their own learning. By the end of 2001 the internal "communities of practice" were working as a general function. The role of the CECs was to provide information and advice to central HR process leaders and regional HR managers, act as a resource negotiator, facilitate the networks and ensure it met the needs of the HR community, guide the expansion of the HR networks across Shell and ensure appropriate movement of knowledge, learning and ideas across Shell, and finally through their expert understanding of their respective fields and overview of the network, develop the link between HR and the business strategy.

There is an implicit logic behind the development of centers of excellence within global HR work. This is the assumption that organizations can pull things out from the HR process or knowledge base that is not country-specific. If a unit proves to be good at this activity then it can take the lead within the organization, and the knowledge can then be leveraged across other parts of the organization. For an organization to be able to go through this structural transition successfully it has to be able to transfer credibility, and there are often a lot of internal forces within an organization that can act against this kind of transfer.

The HR function at Shell learned much from its global expertise networks and centers of excellence experiment. In building networks of experts, it did not consider that it was building data libraries. The value provided by the CECs was through their connections with each other, not the documents that they put onto the intranets. The notion of "best practice" depended on a variety of things and often what was successful in one area might be seen as such without regard to transferability. Globalization was not about doing the same thing everywhere, especially in HR. The network, however, was about conveying the different HR choices that might be made. These choices were values-based and these values were dependent on cultures. Similarly, a key conclusion from our validating workshop process was that within the field of HR it is virtually impossible to lift an idea – a practice, policy or philosophy – and then transplant it into another country. In the context of global knowledge transfer, HR knowledge management systems are about providing mutual insight into the context for change, HR networks are about managing the strategic change process and HR centers of excellence are about adapting knowledge and then learning from this process of adaptation.

Conclusion

We noted in Chapter 4 that the practice of global HRM through networks represents two forms of Ghoshal and Gratton's (2002) integration: intellectual and social. Intellectual integration can be developed through the rapid codification of knowledge, creation of a shared knowledge base and emphasis on sharing and exchanging knowledge both within and beyond the HR community. We saw this in the example above of global expertise networks within Shell People Services. Similarly, we saw an example of the creation of social integration – the development of collective bonds of performance through which the HR function builds a clear sense of what it wants to achieve and how it wants to achieve this goal, in the development of global networks at Diageo. The potential advantages of global HR networks are self-evident. A number of important lessons can be drawn about them.

Box 5.5 Learning about global expertise networks

- *Implementation speed and quality:* Key individuals must demonstrate commitment and "buy into" initiatives at an early stage. Projects can move more quickly, with higher quality joint work time, more business focus and a higher chance of success.

- *Incentives to participate:* International HR functions have to do something to make it worthwhile for an HR professional from one particular country or business to share the knowledge that they have in a proactive way.

- *Development potential:* Through network initiatives, talented HR professionals can be given temporary global exposure by working on projects that are bigger than those experienced in their countries. Networks also develop HR expertise and attract HR professionals into new careers.

- *Social capital:* In order to build on the reputation that resides within global expertise networks, HR professionals have to build strong relationships and this still requires considerable face to face contact.

- *Technology as an enabler:* HR communities have to work on real business issues with people working together to solve business needs – technology enables, but does not cause, the required connections and sharing.

- *Communities of practice:* The mechanics of how international HR insights get "written up," how they get preserved and how they are shared are important. Networks have to operate using principles from the fields of knowledge management and organizational learning.

- *One size does not fit all:* Global HR networks vary in nature depending on the size of the HR community, character of the HR disciplines comprising the network, customer needs and relative levels of regional vs. global focus.

HR networks are however not without risk, especially if they remain too informally based. Within our validation workshops it was clear that for some international HR professionals the concept of HR centers of excellence built around informal networks can be troubling. This "troubled" line of thought runs as follows. On the technical side the attractions of having global centers of expertise seems clear. However, when applied to HR work, the concept actually goes through a number of transitions. One of these transitions depends on the size of the network required to deliver the expertise. The smaller the network size, the more that there is gravitation to core areas of HR that might reflect political issues. The example was given of a chief executive who likes stock options. An opportunistic person in HR is capable of spreading this expertise even though more considered data might show the cultural problems inherent in such a strategy. In short, considerable social capital can be captured and owned by an individual, a small team, network or organizational unit as a result of the granting of center of excellence status. If the interests of this social capital are not aligned with the reality of organizational behavior that results from the application of its ideas, then dysfunctional arguments around policy and the relative interests of different stakeholder groups can arise. Not surprisingly, then, it becomes critical that the activity of HR networks and the sharing of knowledge across the organization is guided by some higher-level themes that bring a degree of structure and consistency to global activity. It is to this topic that we turn in the next chapter.

Developing global themes: capabilities, employer branding and talent management

6

Global themes and superordinate themes

Janssens and Brett (1994) have noted that there have been three traditional and distinct approaches to managing and integrating global firms:

- *Centralization:* where decision-making is left in the hands of a core group of executives
- *Formalization/standardization:* where decision-making is structured around a set of rules and procedures
- *Socialization:* where decision-making follows a set of norms and values established in the firm.

We have already outlined Kostova's (1999) model of factors involved in the successful transfer of cross-national ideas when we examined the role of networks and knowledge management systems in shaping this transfer. We noted that this involves the articulation of rules across operations, the attribution of a common meaning to these rules and finally their subsequent "internalization" into the minds and activity of employees. Effective global implementation requires the diffusion of sets of rules to subsidiary employees (an example of Ghoshal and Gratton's (2002) operational integration), the following of these rules is implied by the presence of the practice and the reflection of these rules in objective behaviors and actions.

However, we argue that when one takes a more process-based approach to understanding the nature of global HR knowledge or HR practice transfer, any distinction between centralization, formal rulesets and socialization through norms and values, whilst conceptually neat, does not actually fit the data. We argue that, in practice, global HRM seems to revolve around the ability of the organization to find a concept that has "relevance" to managers across several countries – despite the fact that they have different values embedded in different national cultures and despite the reality that these global themes may end up being operationalized with some local adaptation.

Organizations use these *superordinate themes* to provide a degree of consistency to their people management worldwide and as an attempt to socialize both employee behavior and action. However, in doing this they are attacking the issues of centralization, formalization and socialization *in parallel*. They are attempting to re-negotiate a new position across these three dimensions – rather than seeing these as alternative "either–or" forms of control. As a Chief Information Officer from one of our case studies noted:

> Today, most people believe that there is a set of global processes. However, in [this company], when people use the word "global" they mean different things. Is it a common set of rules that can be applied to HR, or is it about the management of a group of people who work globally? . . . Global means that there is a common set of rules that can be applied to all countries . . . However, are the rules the most important thing? No. Where culture comes into it is in terms of how the people behave around those processes.

In short, in applying global themes, organizations also must seek through their global HRM strategies, to engage the hearts and minds of a diverse workforce (Ghoshal and Gratton, 2002). Our research found that the most common superordinate themes that were articulated in the process of globalizing HR were as follows:

1 The corporate strategy. This is usually expressed through performance management systems applied globally that measure and manage a balanced series of outcomes that must be achieved (Kaplan and Norton, 1996).
2 Core strategic competencies that are considered to differentiate the firm and lead to its competitive advantage. These are usually reflected in a series of organizational capabilities or competencies that once specified are integrated into career development or performance management systems (Sparrow, 1997).
3 The pursuit of talent management initiatives.
4 Corporate and global brands, whereby organizations think about their external brand image and corporate reputation, and the ways in which their employees identify with and actively support the brand (Harris and de Chernatony, 2001; Hatch and Schultz, 2001; Davies *et al.*, 2003; Martin and Beaumont, 2003).

The themes of linkage to the business strategy and the role of processes such as balanced scorecards we have left for Chapter 8 where we discuss evaluation of the international HR function. We focus our attention now on the use of organizational capabilities, employer branding and talent management.

Integration around core strategic competencies or capabilities

We introduced the concept of "core competencies" in Chapter 3 in the context of having to build capability rapidly. We pointed out that core competencies describe the resources and capabilities of the organization that are linked with business performance and are generally identified through market analysis methods and the strategic planning process. We have also noted, in Chapter 5, that the HRM system itself can facilitate the development of strategic capabilities that provide competitive advantage (Lado and Wilson, 1994).

Grant (1991) examined what lies beneath core competencies (such as the ability to innovate and the development of a learning organization). Organization competencies and capabilities represent a meshing together of organization resources (such as the skills of individual people), leadership and more tangible assets such as capital resources, brand reputation and patents held. Klein *et al.* (1991) argued that as product life-cycles shorten and skill development life-cycles lengthen the skill base of an organization must be actively managed as the mainstay of its competitive strategy. They view "corporate skills" as strategic combinations of individual (human) competencies, hard organizational factors (such as equipment and facilities) and soft organizational factors (such as culture and organization design). Core competencies therefore indicate what makes an organization more successful than others, representing fixed sources of competitive advantage (Hamel and Prahalad, 1994). The performance criteria used to assess this are superior records of innovation, learning, quality or other long-term business criteria. They are applied to marketing and product strategies and the design of business processes. In terms of ownership, this competence is shared by the organization and the individuals. The assessment onus is to articulate the unique key success factors and proprietary know-how.

It is argued that there should be a connection between the following three issues:

1 the capabilities and skills of the organization's human resources;
2 the distinctive areas of high performance and technical know-how of the organization; and
3 the dominant logic or mental models of the top management teams.

The richer that connection is, the more effective both strategy analysis and execution will be (Reed and DeFillippi, 1990; Sparrow, 1997). Strategists therefore view management skills – evidenced by the organization's behavior and the skills of the total pool of human resources – as being based on the possession of core corporate-level skills, coherence across these skills and unique know-how in the context of strategic key success factors. Organizations need to actively manage their competency portfolio, analyzing emerging and future needs for competence in line with the strategy development process (Whipp, 1991).

Organizations first began to develop domestic HR strategies based around competencies in the early 1990s, but with the exception of BP's Project 1990 (Sparrow, 1995) there were relatively few attempts to develop global HR systems around them. In our study, BOC used a global set of competencies. It realized that the move towards a global line-of-business structure had to be backed up by a global managerial mindset and a unifying global corporate culture. In 1998 it defined a set of values or pillars on which the new organization would be built – known as the ACTS model:

● accountability – "We know what we are accountable for and are empowered to deliver";

- collaboration – "We maximise our achievements by working together";
- transparency – "We can solve problems that are visible and make better decisions if we're informed"; and
- stretch – "We always push the boundaries of performance."

Initially specified as a set of values, they were revised into behavioral competencies called the ABCs (ACTS behavioral competencies) and deployed globally.

A more sophisticated form of integration of HR around a global theme to do with capabilities was seen in Diageo. In order to get the best from their people, in 2000 Diageo developed "The Diageo Way of Building Talent." This was a framework of three key processes intended to help build capability and also specified the behaviors that committed Diageo to "winning through people." Under this banner, new initiatives were brought together on external resourcing, talent benchmarking, deployment decision forums, high potential review processes, a focus on reward and recognition in order to link individual performance, development and reward more closely with organizational performance, and development partnering or coaching.

A capability-based performance management system in UDV North America, Diageo

Case Example

One of the most visible initiatives to support the creation of such common systems and processes was the establishment of a consistent People Performance Management process across the four merged businesses. It was an obvious starting point for any cultural change to facilitate integration and development of the business. The core People Performance Management system started with a set of six organizational and five leadership capabilities – defined for the organization as a whole. There were four Organizational capabilities, core to all four businesses: Consumer Insight, Business System Transformation, People Recruitment, Development and Retention and Rapid Capability Building.

Two of the organizational capabilities were allowed to be different for each business. For example, in UDV North America, they were Managing for Value and On-Premise Leadership. The adoption of two localized Organizational capabilities reflected the particular strategies of each business. However, apart from the necessary professional and functional skills, Diageo put a strong focus on the leadership capabilities and competencies that influenced the way in which people at Diageo worked and interacted. The five leadership capabilities were also generic to all businesses. These leadership capabilities were:

- People performance: The ability to inspire and support people to realize their full potential.
- Emotional energy: An ability to actively communicate and to demonstrate this drive to create positive energy in others.
- Edge: The ability to live up to reality and take tough decisions about products, costs and people in order to deliver sustainable results.

continued

- Ideas: Insatiable curiosity to seek out and develop new opportunities. The ability to use knowledge across a wide range of applications.
- Living values: Demonstrating behavior that will build a strong business culture and deliver sustainable performance.

Initially, the system was only being used in the UDV business in North America and was also e-enabled. This experiment was intended to bring about a radical change in the culture of Diageo. It had the potential to transform the way that staff thought about managing people. The online performance management process was based on a series of capabilities (competencies) that had been identified through a strategic management process across Diageo. The experience that was gained from North America was to be used as a basis for developing the approach and using it across the other businesses worldwide.

Source: Braun *et al.* (2003a)

It is of interest to note that one of the capabilities built into the UDV North America People Performance Management system was called Rapid Capability Building. This is an example of the HR function internalizing concepts derived from marketing and strategy experts into the HR architecture of the organization. Different levels of capability were articulated, with mastery including the following:

- creating a sense of readiness and mobilization of the organization to build capability at a rate considered to generate competitive edge;
- anticipating the scale and demands of strategic options and taking preventative action to build capability;
- assembling an optimum balance of internal and external resources and using them flexibly and innovatively to bridge capability gap; and
- executing, communicating and measuring capabilities within the organization.

This initiative can be linked to the previous discussion of rapid capability building in Chapter 2. By internalizing it into such a central part of the HR architecture across merged businesses it became one of the "superordinate" global themes discussed in this chapter. In practice the implementation of the People Performance Management system showed that there were quite different levels of HR sophistication across the businesses and this limited the pace at which such themes could be deeply applied. In Pillsbury and Burger King – which were subsequently divested by Diageo – the system was not adopted as keenly. Two of the businesses – Guinness and UDV – were however relatively comfortable with operating a performance management system that measured key capabilities.

Clearly, the system at Diageo was an initiative that grew out of the necessity to bring the diverse businesses more strongly together in the initial years after the merger. It highlighted the perceived need within the company to *centralize* some of the core HR processes in order to bridge the diversity between the merged businesses. It had the potential to be transformational for the following reasons:

1 It drove at the core way in which business was carried out by focusing on organizational and leadership capabilities.
2 It could introduce some consistency across the four businesses in terms of performance management and related people management processes.
3 It was driven by the individual and their manager, providing them with the opportunity of gaining some control over the monitoring and tracking of performance.
4 The continuous nature of the process could overcome the limitations of a ritual annual review.
5 It was a technology-based approach, which enabled frequent live interactions between manager and employee.

Employer branding

We move now into a discussion of the second of the global themes being used to integrate HRM, namely employer branding. The power of global brands is well understood. For example, Nike focuses on the values of "authentic sports," "innovation" and "inspiration" in its advertising. It operates in a demand-pull business environment in which the $1 billion a year it spends on advertising is considered to generate $11 billion a year in revenue. The brand management function is extremely important. In Starbucks, by contrast, it is the HR function (actually – another triumph of marketing – called Partner Resources rather than Human Resources) that plays a central role. It attempts to develop values based on being "a great work environment," "embracing diversity" and "pleasing customers." It has a "developing local talent" initiative in which young managers are in-patriated to Seattle. Developing talent is important to it because a typical store manager is aged 21 to 23 and runs a $1 million business. It develops a strong sense of its values through a 2-month "immersion" process where managers work in-store learning every part of the business (Kuchinad, 2003).

Employer branding represents an extension of brand management and is another development whereby HR thinking has been influenced by that of the marketing function. Building or defending the corporate brand or reputation has become a major concern in many industries (de Chernatony, 2001; Davies *et al.*, 2003). A vast marketing literature has established the connection between brand advantage, customer service and the style of people management in the organization. The increased importance of corporate and global brands has forced organizations to think more closely about their external brand image and how their employees can actively support the brand. Employees sit at the interface between the internal and external interface of the organization with its environment and can, through their actions and behaviors, exert a powerful influence on the perception of the brand offering and the corporation (Harris and de Chernatony, 2001). Attention has therefore been given to how they can become ambassadors for the organization. It is implicit that employer branding – the image of the organization as seen through the eyes of *external* stakeholders – actually requires consistency and uniformity in delivering the brand identity by all *internal* stakeholders, including employees.

However, currently, we still know little about the linkages between HR and marketing in the brand management process, despite increasing awareness that the HR function is now becoming involved in this work on an international scale.

Theoretical approaches

Before examining the evidence that we found about the role of employer branding in relation to global HRM we first lay out the main theoretical frameworks that underpin discussions of employer branding. We rely strongly here on the recent excellent summary provided by Martin and Beaumont (2003). There are four strands within the management literature that have most shaped recent thinking about employment branding.

Box 6.1 Four perspectives on employer branding

Culture Excellence: Started perhaps from *In Search of Excellence* by Peters and Waterman (1982) and more recent academic work on the management of culture (Hatch and Schulz, 2001). This argued that organizations could best deliver advantage by focusing on changes from an inside-out perspective. Internal images of the organization mattered most; for example, did the organization have a strong emphasis on the customer? So too does the alignment of the internal and external images (the perceptions of customers, shareholders, the media and the public). Hatch and Schultz (2001) argue that three gaps must be eradicated within the organization: the vision-culture gap (the gap between vision as expressed by corporate functions and traditional culture values as experienced), the image-culture gap (evidenced when employees' views of the company are quite different to those held by outsiders such as customers or potential employees) and the image-vision gap (when there is a mismatch between the external image and senior manager's aspirations for it, as with British Airways' attempt to globalize its image by removing the Union Jack from the tail fin).

Resource-based view of strategy: Focuses on the relationship between competitive advantage for the organization and intangible assets such as people and knowledge (Barney, 1991; Grant, 1991; Boxall, 1995). This argued that sustainable competitive advantage only arises when an organization can put together a unique and enviable combination of internal resources. These resources include the people and their relationship to key systems in the organization such as knowledge and information. The management of organizational culture and processes of employee selection, development and reward reinforces this uniqueness. The Sears employee-customer service chain is an example of a cause-and-effect linkage assumed to operate across several business strategy functions (Heskett *et al.*, 1997).

Employer of choice: Development of new strategies to become an employer of choice because of the emergence of a new psychological contract at work and the erosion of trust, commitment and identity necessary to maintain a connection between employee satisfaction, customer satisfaction, branding and financial performance (Rousseau, 1995, Cappelli, 1999; Sparrow and Cooper, 2003). Following an employer of choice, strategy ranges from adopting sophisticated and more two-way recruitment processes, a focus on internal talent development, through to the development of a more relational rather than purely transactional psychological contract (Pfeffer, 1998).

Employment branding: Use of marketing tools, techniques and concepts to align employees behind strong corporate brands, engage their loyalty and build organizational commitment (Dell and Ainspan, 2001; Shackwell, 2002). It involves building layers of information about the organization supported by facts, knowing what is compelling about the organization in the eyes of high performers, linking this to the acceptance of employment offers, understanding the non-negotiable elements of the "brand promise," ensuring consistency in the story as presented by the organization and all intermediaries in the recruitment chain and aligning all subsequent external and internal interventions to the message about the employment brand (McKenzie and Glynn, 2001).

Source: adapted from Martin and Beaumont (2003)

In describing the marketing perspective Martin and Beaumont (2003) note that brands convey a series of strategic advantages for organizations:

- They reduce the effort needed by consumers in their search for high quality products.
- They convey certain psychological rewards such as a sense of belonging and social inclusion.
- They can be infused with emotional values (a personality) beyond their functional benefits.
- They can be used to develop a relationship between the consumer and this perceived personality.
- The clusters of values that they represent can be used to help an organization extend into new international markets with related values.

The use of these concepts is increasingly being used by international HR professionals in their search to create meaningful values that transcend national boundaries.

If one looks at the employer branding approach, it could be seen from a negative perspective as a form of social engineering now simply being practiced on a global scale. There is indeed a danger of this being the case in more unscrupulous organizations. Critical management writers have noted how ethical strategies that do not have a sense of authenticity may be seen merely as "ethical imperialism" in which global culture change messages are exported to all subsidiaries as thinly veiled attempts to create a new "symbolic architecture of control" (Clegg *et al.*, 1999).

The management of values in global HRM

However, from our case studies it was clear that in most cases organizations only made significant investment in this form of global coordination when they were convinced that they could do so with a sense of "authenticity." Employer branding is about engaging with people's values. It is, in this sense, an example of Ghoshal and Gratton's (2002) emotional integration. By making values more visible, organizations attempt to manage them in the desired direction. In practice, global organizations tend to pursue values-based HR strategies for three reasons:

1 They are implicit in the successful execution of strategy, that is, the organization considers that it has to live the values in order to deliver performance (for example, Diageo).
2 The values serve an important part of the proposition made to talented and scarce employees (for example, Shell).
3 The values represent a clear ethical stance inherent in the nature or role of the organization (for example, ActionAid).

An example of the last motivation is seen in ActionAid. As ActionAid enters its thirtieth year, it continues its steady transformation into a truly international organization – working with local partners and in national and international coalitions to empower poor and marginalized people. Developing organizational capability in a primarily field-based and geographically dispersed environment requires skillful interpretation of strategic goals to both empower and motivate staff at all levels and in all locations. For ActionAid, commitment to the organization's values provides a powerful lynchpin against which individual managers throughout the world can check the appropriateness of policy and practice initiatives (see case example).

Developing the values at ActionAid

Case Example

"Fighting poverty together" is the simple, but powerful vision of one of the UK's largest development agencies. But how does this statement translate into practical action plans and how can the work of an international HR manager help deliver the mission? ActionAid focuses on long-term development, rather than short-term relief. The 1980s saw a period of consolidation of the wider work originally started to support children's education. Under the title "tackling the root causes of poverty," ActionAid's activities evolved to include programs in agriculture, health, water, skills training and helping poor people borrow and save money. ActionAid is one of the UK's largest development agencies, working in more than thirty countries in Africa, Asia, Latin America and the Caribbean. The head office is in London, with an office in Washington for fundraising and influencing.

For the Global HR/OD Director, the greatest task is inspiring a common values-based culture throughout the dispersed and highly diverse workforce, through a network of regional and country HR professionals. She lives the "global versus local" dilemma every day and devotes much of her time to working with her HR colleagues around the world, developing and implementing policies and practices that will take the ActionAid agenda forward. In many countries the fear of government repression for local nationals is a real and serious threat. Recruiting and retaining people with a strong commitment to ActionAid's values is therefore a key concern. As all of ActionAid's work is in the field, motivating the regional and country management teams to deliver the mission is a critical success factor. Empowerment within a values-based framework is the chosen way forward for ActionAid.

ActionAid adopts a values-based selection process and places heavy emphasis on its values and principles during induction. A large part of the Global HR/OD Director's time is devoted to selecting and developing ActionAid's top 100 senior managers. Getting "new blood" into the organization is a key part of the new strategy. Having recruited talented and committed people, a critical component of HR's task is also to retain and develop these individuals into a highly professional managerial cadre. Within ActionAid, as with most other international charities, choices need to be made as to the relative proportions of international and national staff. Employment of national staff closes international mobility options, however, there are many pressing needs for excellent national staff. Mobility and succession planning are therefore critical components in ActionAid's management development activities and a new process of assessment of the top 100 managers has recently been introduced which is jointly carried out by the Global HR/OD Director and the International Directors once a year.

Source: Hegewisch *et al.* (2003)

Issues of Employer Branding and Talent Management, which we will discuss shortly, are intimately linked for most global organizations. Global HR professionals are concentrating on what they have to do to retain staff. In order to develop a global recruitment strategy the organization needs to understand the issues that they are trying to resolve. For recruitment this might be that it is taking too long to fill jobs, people are joining the company with mixed experience, there is fairly high turnover, or costs are not really understood. In short, there is no guarantee that HR can help the businesses fill the critical positions with the high calibre people that they seek. When global HR functions have tried to find out how they can help guarantee this to the businesses – both now and over the next few years – then they have realized that as the world gets smaller, they need to make sure that the way in which they are perceived as a company is similar wherever they go. What do their consumers want from them, what do current employees think?

For global organizations this involves constantly reselling the proposition to employees as to why their organization is the place they should work. The challenge then is to understand what makes a really good person want to stay with them *globally*. The answer tends to impact on both the development of people, which is a key driver of retention, and how the organization recruits. It affects how the organization approaches the media, how it conducts its investor relations, how it designs compensation and benefits and how it designs performance management systems. In other words, it informs all the policies and procedures. These messages cannot be aspirational – they have to be grounded in what the organization really offers and what potential employees really want. The processes must back up what the organization says it is. The key messages to potential employees also must make sense in all the organization's markets worldwide. The organization has to pick out which messages they can match and where they are able to give out a message that can be fulfilled. Each market has cultural differences but also similarities.

Talent management

All this brings us to the issue of talent management. This concept can be traced back to 1997 when a group of McKinsey consultants asked organizations how they built a strong managerial talent pool and whether such talent helped drive organizational performance? The title of the report – *The War For Talent* – vividly captured the realities of the US talent market that was then at the height of the economic boom. However, even when the economic bubble was over, the authors argued that the drive to attract and retain individual talent had not diminished. Michaels *et al.* (2001) subsequently reported on this study, which involved a survey of nearly 6,000 managers from twenty-seven large companies, eighteen case studies in major US organizations with later follow-up work including another thirty-five. They used a criteria-based approach, looking at what differentiated the top performing firms from the average (based on total shareholder return). They argued that it was not sophisticated HR processes concerned with succession planning, recruitment and compensation that made the difference in this type of labor market. Rather, it was the mindset of leaders throughout the organization. They held, it was argued, a fundamental belief in the importance of individual talent. This talent is typically identified as abilities that "add immediate or future value to any prescribed activity, discipline or enterprise" (*People Management*, 2003: 59) often through the development of capability or competency-based HR systems. The purpose of a successful talent management system is to attract, retain, develop and utilize employees in ways that create:

- sustainable commercial competitiveness through the alignment of employee competence, behaviors and intellectual energy with business activity;
- higher levels of focused innovation;
- improved staff engagement and commitment;
- lower loss rates of knowledge and experience; and
- lower external resourcing costs.

There is little evidence that many organizations do this well. Michaels *et al.* (2001) reported that only 19 percent of senior managers strongly agreed that their organization brought in highly talented people, 8 percent believed that they retained almost all of their high performers, and only 3 percent considered that the organization developed people quickly and effectively, or removed low performers. One of the central tenets of "war for talent" thinking was the *employee value proposition* (EVP). This idea touches upon the psychological contract in that it conveys a clear statement of some of the more explicit obligations that the organization commits to.

> it is a human resource management policy influenced very much by marketing thinking that cuts across the whole of the employment experience and applies to all individuals in the organization. It is the application of a customer value proposition – why should you buy my product or service – to the individual – why would a highly talented person work in my organization? It differs from one organization to another, has to be as distinctive as a fingerprint, and is tailored to the specific type of people the organization is trying to attract and retain.
>
> (Sparrow and Cooper, 2003: 160)

Talent management in a global context

In the few years since the emergence of this work, building an EVP has become a central focus of HRM in many global organizations. Scullion and Starkey (2000) have argued that talent management is important in both centralized and decentralized international organizations. They based this observation on a study of thirty UK organizations in which they drew attention to the importance of senior management development activity, succession planning and the development of an international cadre of managers. They concluded that "[there is a] growing recognition that the success of international business depends most importantly on the quality of top executive talent and how effectively these critical resources are managed and developed" (Scullion and Starkey, 2000: 1065).

However, talent management on a global basis is a far broader concept than plotting a series of international assignments for young high potentials and an international cadre of managers (Harris *et al.*, 2003). As has been evidenced throughout this book, when global lines of business are introduced there is a more immediate relationship between the international HR professional and the global leadership teams within major business functions or markets. International organizations want to know who are their top people and what are the key roles within the business that they need these people for. They want to know how they can develop them and then get them to key positions, then how they can build succession cover for these key positions. In order to do this, they have to develop a much deeper level of understanding about the links between the business agenda and the capabilities of the most talented people in the organization, and also understand the potential for mobility around these people. When they conduct such a "calibration" of talent on a global basis, they have to ask what this suggests for the planned business development. Yet, as we saw in the section on Employer Branding, the real challenge for global organizations in terms of even initiating their hunt for talent is to decide what is the overriding message to talented people in terms of "who they are" as an organization and also "what they stand for." This challenge inevitably leads organizations to think about talent on a more global basis. There has been a fairly common response to the challenge, which has included the following:

- researching into "consumer insights" with current and potential employees, sister companies, external agencies and benchmarking with external companies;
- managing the "talent pipeline" – trying to recruit "ahead of the curve" instead of the more traditional vacancy-based recruitment;
- communicating an awareness in graduate schools and businesses to get the people they need;
- developing internal talent pools around the world;
- creating skilled and competent teams of assessors in different regional geographies;
- managing recruitment suppliers on a global basis, introducing speed, cost and quality controls, establishing master contracts to coordinate the messages conveyed and the use of preferred partners, ensuring audit trails to protect against legal issues associated with global diversity; and
- e-enabling jobs notice boards, redesigning web sites to convey important messages about the employer brand.

For example, Diageo set up a global network project around recruitment and talent development, to be led by the HR community in the US given the learning that they had developed about the recruitment issues after the integration of Seagram into Diageo operations. This network did not look at issues in the old HR way – considering whether the ideas were technically great. Its very existence – and the endorsement for any projects undertaken – depended on the ability of the HR leader to write a strategy paper that stood up against a brands strategy or other business strategies. The network then had the endorsement to look at key issues globally, not just locally, consider the learning HR could take from initiatives such as setting up a global brand team, and then consider how HR could add value. Evaluation was based not just on the success of implementation but also on the extent to which ideas were embedded within the businesses (see case example).

Talent management at Diageo

Case Example

In 2001 Diageo established a global HR network initiative around talent management and capability development. The network was driven through functional channels and functional leadership groups. These leadership groups took on sponsorship for the talent agenda for each function across the global operations. It was also these leadership teams that made the decision on which core people from the markets were to be involved in the HR network and how to define both global and internal benchmarks for the initiative. It needed to get to a level where if someone considered that a manager was "good" in one country, this judgment matched the way that managers were calibrated in other parts of the global business. This process of equalizing calibration of managers took quite a lot of effort, in terms of building up levels of trust, respect and knowledge of what the network was doing. The network had to liaise with the various "markets" in terms of making sure that key positions and key succession plans were in place and ensure there was a global pool of talent. It was recognized that each market represented its own idiosyncratic context. Yet, Diageo is also a global brand name. The Resourcing Director explained:

> "As the world gets smaller, we need to make sure that the way we're perceived as a company is similar wherever we go. The name is important . . . The company is global and will be able to offer some things the same across all markets. We need to focus on similarities and not get bogged down in differences . . . We won't come up with things that mean the same in all parts of the world as it's impossible but we can come up with something unique to us that resonates with people throughout the businesses."

An important initiative was the development of an employee value proposition that Diageo wanted to put forward on a global basis. There were attempts to use the marketing skills and competencies that were core to a leading consumer goods company like Diageo in order to build a better understanding of its employees. The global HR network looked at the issue of "employer branding." There was a strong belief within the company that the skills present within the marketing side of the firm could be tapped into to help the HR function in its thinking about this theme. The question they wanted to explore was what message did Diageo want to send to its potential "consumers" (i.e., its employees). Of course each market had its own specificities in terms of recruitment activity. On the other hand, Diageo saw the need to decide on the overriding message that they wanted to put forward to future employees. This needed to be a message about "who Diageo is, and what does Diageo stand for?" The organization was aware that it had to raise awareness in graduate schools and businesses in order to get the people it was looking for. The company also knew that it had to recruit people towards what it called a "mobility attitude." It was believed that levels of mobility needed to be raised within the company. Therefore, key messages about the employee value proposition had to make sense in all the markets that formed part of Diageo's operations.

Work has been carried out to examine the "employer brand" – finding out the message that was sent to potential consumers (i.e., employees), and whether the type of people they were after had brand awareness and could quote what the brand benefit statement was. They examined what the population thought of them in their major markets such as the US, UK, Ireland and Spain. Creating a career site and an employer brand was considered to be critical to the messages given to consumers.

Operational integration becomes important in this context and as part of this process the global network worked on a global career web site. Diageo's web site was believed to be useful for investors, but was considered to be less useful for employees. Clearly it could be mobilized to help create an employer brand. The web site tied into several other initiatives in Diageo. It was linked with the management of internal talent pools around the world by advertising jobs worldwide internally. It was also linked with attempts to deal with external recruiters more consistently.

A wide range of initiatives (the how of the HR strategy) ended up following the early work on employer branding. These included designing and embedding a more effective global HR operating model and deploying global recognition and reward and performance

continued

management processes linked explicitly to performance. It also involved incorporating the principles into recognition and reward systems, embedding leadership behavior and communication programs, differentiating an authentic employer brand that was compelling to internal and external talent, ensuring succession cover and a strong pipeline of talent and implementing a model for leading and managing change that would inspire employees globally.

Source: Braun *et al.* (2003a)

From a pragmatic perspective it must be noted that many key "enabling" approaches to change such as those discussed here under the topic of talent management, operate in an environment of volatility. Despite the best intentions, many organizations find it difficult to maintain a focus on such initiatives on a global scale. One organization that had pursued work based on the prescriptions of a War For Talent and had seen itself as having made effective gains in this area experienced a 70 percent loss of business within a year. In such circumstances it was difficult to keep a focus on the good work that might have been achieved around talent management.

Concentrating on the talent pipeline

This chapter has concentrated on some of the most important themes that global organizations put in place. Recruitment has become one of the most global of all the HR processes and the talent pipeline – the internal talent pools and the process of bringing people in from the outside – is crucial to any resourcing strategy.

For all global organizations there is an understanding that marketing strategies quickly become outdated and the pecking order of the most desired employers changes. The Most Wanted employer of yesterday may no longer be so today. Moreover, there is an understanding that their brand can be very valuable. Shell's logo is for example one of the top four best known in the world and Shell's brand image alone is valued at $2.98 billion (*Business Week*, 2003a). Global HR managers in such organizations have a natural reluctance to "tweak" or play around with the outside recruitment images associated with such logos. They adhere to global rulesets surrounding the use of this logo. Considerable care and attention is taken, with every image analyzed and scrutinized. It takes a long time to create a new brochure for such reasons. However, this slowness in some areas of the HR service is counter-balanced by tight performance standards applied to the areas that can be delivered speedily whilst still to a high quality specification. Shell for example applies a global standard of 10 days from application to offer in open recruitment situations.

As we saw in the example of Diageo, superordinate themes were used to help establish a sense of operational integration at a global level. An example could be seen in the

Box 6.2 Key indicators in talent management

The typical metrics or key indicators used to evaluate the success of talent management systems include:

- *Added value per employee*: is the organization in the top decile of like organizations on a measure of money added per monetary unit cost?
- *Recruitment:* do talented recruits make up at least 5 percent of total recruits?
- *Graduates:* Do 95 percent of graduates stay with the organization for longer than three years?
- *Development*: Does the organization provide at least 22 hours of training per employee per year?
- *Internal appointments*: Are at least 72 percent of vacancies filled internally?
- *Retention*: Is the level of resignation by identified talent less than 3 percent each year?

Source: *People Management* (2003)

thought process around the use of partnership arrangements with headhunters and recruitment agencies. There had been much contemplation around the establishment of preferred partner arrangements with recruiting companies across several countries for many years. As part of the early integration efforts, when Diageo had consisted of four businesses, moves had been made towards introducing partnership arrangements with headhunters on a global basis. Now, however, the general feeling was that the quality within specific recruiting companies varied markedly between locations and such deals could only be reached with difficulty. Nonetheless, consistency with regards to recruitment companies was still of high importance to Diageo because 70 to 80 percent of the recruitment within the company was conducted through outside agencies. This called for consistency in terms of the requirements for the selection of recruiters because the recruiters represented Diageo to clients and clients to Diageo. The global HR function in Diageo set the standards but did not apply a global "one size fits all" requirement for partnership agreements. However, specifications for recruiters were applied worldwide. On the basis of this specification local Diageo businesses could choose with whom they wanted to work. It was considered that preferred deals for recruiting companies should only start if three countries used one recruiter. However, a more global perspective on resourcing had brought with it the need for appropriate control measures to be put in place, and also a need to focus on issues of speed, cost and quality. Instead of concentrating mainly on negotiating to reduce recruiters' fees the approach shifted attention to ensuring that recruiters signed up to contracts that delivered against these new priorities.

Although talent markets still operate in very national ways and even global organizations can find that their relative positioning varies markedly from one country to another those organizations that are consistently in the top ten tend to maintain local recruitment strategies (Brewster *et al.*, 2002). They mix this with more global transfer of information and best practices. Why are organizations coordinating their talent pipelines more on a global basis?

1 Talent itself has become more mobile. At first organizations found this with graduate job seeking behavior, but now they experience it with more and more types of job seeker.

2 Competition with other employers has also become more generic. This competition was country specific at first, then regional and then global.

3 The desire for more gender and nationality diversity generally requires that managers need to be shepherded away from applying an HQ mindset, and this requires that they follow formal processes.

4 Economies of scale are important. To build excellent talent pipeline processes for each country would require huge funding. It is easier to concentrate on their demonstrated capability in a few countries or regions and then build a network to transfer best practice around that.

There is a downside to creating common recruitment processes. An obvious example is the consequence of e-enabled recruitment on a global scale, which means that large organizations have thousands of people who have sent in their CVs who must be screened before a decision to proceed. The flip side is that the 90 percent of the world's population who have no access to computers, but who include many talented people, are excluded from applying. Organizations that have common processes also have to have a good audit trail and quality control. In the USA they may end up in court if the process goes wrong and, at a more general level, large multinationals know that they are targeted by people looking for money. Consequently, providing a global process in this area, with a common language as to how they define talent, and increasingly standardizing rules for processes such as assessment centers, is a complex role. Global organizations do not just compete with the best local employers but also with each other.

Managing the Talent Pipeline at Shell

Case Example

One of the seven core HR processes at Shell is called the Talent Pipeline. This organization provides three groups of people to the organization:

1 top graduate talent;
2 experienced people;
3 executive and MBA level.

The labels are actually based on the amount of talent that candidates have and the assessment centers relate both to the level that they start at and where they have the potential to go to. Potential is graded in bands, with each level classified, so there are for example top leadership roles or country chairmanship roles. Shell estimates that only

5 percent of students at university have this potential, which is why they consider their efforts to attract top graduate talent part of a "war for talent."

The role of the Center of Excellence Coordinator is to identify the best practices that can be used for attracting, selecting and "on-boarding" these individuals. There are a lot of best practices around and they change constantly. Shell put considerable effort into developing an employee value proposition by identifying the most important features of working for Shell. The career opportunities section of their web site http://www.shell.com is managed by the center of excellence coordinator. It has five themes, which are all about the general nature of working for Shell (called employment attributes). For each attribute you see a live example. A lot of information is made available and shared about the assessment centers. Part of the CEC role is therefore about conveying information to the outside.

The issues are different however for the recruitment of experienced people. Here campaigns are run through the Web and other media for low volumes of people – usually around ten to twenty. There are common "branding" roles for the adverts, such as "let's think about a better future" and these are used to create an image again of a real life character who provides insight into life at Shell. Best practice networks are used to garner common experiences, distil examples and then disseminate learning. In Exploration and Production in 2001 for example there were twenty people in the USA, twenty in Europe and ten in Asia Pacific involved in this network and the whole Talent Pipeline process was captured in an annual booklet.

A natural consequence of this need for more operational integration is to consider the cross-cultural relevance and fairness of the tools and techniques. As can be seen below, globalizing the capabilities of the HR and line community involved in the talent management process is critical and some organizations devote a lot of attention to it:

> We have a very diverse set of assessors. The exercises are not the problem – it is the assessors. They have to be able to interpret behaviour. For example, in the Asia-Pacific region we have 70–80 per cent of assessors from that region. We test a new process or exercise with focus groups. We see images of people around the world and we test our image and our message with students around the world.
>
> (Senior HR Manager)

Finally, for many organizations the talent pipeline is considered to start in the vocational education and training system of the countries that they operate in (we outlined the global competition for skills in Chapter 2). They seek to influence this process as part of their talent management strategy. For example, Rolls-Royce puts effort into the way it manages early career development, how they are perceived by universities and their employer branding. As a result of their efforts they have climbed up the "league tables" – their graduate brochure of 2001 was the second most popular in the UK amongst graduates. However, as a technical organization it is also important for them to gain some control over the skill formation process. For example, senior managers are building on their connections and are marketing the organization, becoming more proactive in influencing the national education policy of countries and sitting on government advisory panels, local school boards and technology colleges.

Conclusion

In conclusion, we would observe that the first two global themes noted at the beginning of this chapter (corporate strategy and core competencies) are driven more by the hard realities of the business strategy and an assessment of the resources and capabilities that exist within the firm. The third theme (employer branding) is often based on a more tacit understanding about the organization and therefore requires a degree of exploration and investigation by it. The final theme (talent management) reflects the response to a generic challenge faced by many organizations and threats to its sustainability (i.e., the inability to attract talented employees). Relating back to our discussion of the work of Kostova (1999) on the transfer of global best practice, and the importance that she gave to the need to develop high levels of internalization, many of the approaches that we discussed in this chapter were based on the following thought process:

- Behavioral engineering can be used to overcome the limitations of pursuing a change strategy based solely on the export of programs to subsidiaries.
- Clear frameworks can be created to influence how global strategies are implemented and these tend to transcend national boundaries more easily when they are tied into a shared and accurate view of the capabilities and resources available to the organization.
- Principles, such as self-interest or the desire to feel a sense of belonging, can be used to better engage employees.
- Self-interest might be served by the categorization and treatment of employees as talented resources and the development of a proposition reflecting this.

In any event, there is often a process of self-selection in MNCs through which "like will attract like" and this ultimately embeds shared values more deeply into the character of the organization. However, the challenge to embed a more international mindset into the organization also requires that organizations internationalize their whole HR systems. In particular, they have to offer more forms of international working and manage international mobility better within their existing workforce. It is to this topic that we turn now in the next chapter.

7

Managing international mobility

Introduction

One common feature of organizations operating in international arenas is the need for increased mobility of staff. The strategic and practical aspects of expatriation have been a favored topic of study for many IHRM scholars. Indeed, at one time, the topic of IHRM dealt mainly with the management of expatriation. Yet, amongst the larger and more established international players there have been significant changes, notably a much more competitive environment (D'Aveni, 1994) forcing an increasing attention to cost reduction and cost-effectiveness. Since expatriates are amongst the most expensive people any organization employs, and the measurement of expatriate performance is, to say the least, uncertain, this has had a direct effect on the way organizations view their expatriates and the challenge of international mobility. This has been made more problematic by the reorganization of MNCs in Europe and the consequent reduction in the size of headquarters (Scullion and Starkey, 2000). The strong trends towards decentralization and downsizing over the last decade, mean that many MNCs have lost the central expertise in the management of expatriates built up over many years, as the numbers of expatriates increases (Scullion and Starkey, 2000). New approaches are required that

- link developments in the management of expatriation with the broader international strategy
- look at the strategic positioning of mobility in international organizations and the implications for individuals of various forms of this mobility.

From a strategic perspective we have already noted the role of expatriates as one vehicle for global knowledge transfer in Chapter 5. The international assignment is also seen as the main process through which organizations can develop global leadership. For example, Novicevic and Harvey (2001) cite the example of Gillette where 85 percent of its global assignees come from twenty-seven countries outside the US and the implicit policy is that 80 percent of its top management team have extended international experience. However, it is important to take a wider view of mobility. Nowadays, mobility takes many forms, including short-term and commuter assignments and frequent flying. Managing both the organizational and the personal implications of mobility is a critical task for both HR and line managers.

A process model

Schiuma *et al.* (2001) have explored the changing nature of managing international staffing via a processual model that highlights the holistic nature of this activity. In particular, it emphasizes the link between international staffing and overall corporate strategy. This model identifies six key stages for the implementation of an international assignment. The six stages comprise:

1 stakeholder satisfaction and contribution identification;
2 strategy definition: targets and objectives definition;
3 assignment planning: process analysis and capabilities identification;
4 international worker profile definition;
5 the global assignment cycle;
6 repatriation or new assignment.

The model adopts a stakeholder centric view. According to this approach the objectives of each assignment must be derived from a clear identification and definition of stakeholder needs/wants. In the case of international assignments, five main categories of stakeholders can be identified in both the host and home country as follows:

- shareholders;
- customers;
- suppliers;
- regulators and governments;
- employees.

Changes in the needs and expectations of each of these stakeholders dynamically impact on the management of international staffing.

Shareholders

Shareholders are mainly interested in the financial value of a company as evaluated by share price or rates of return. Other important shareholders' wants include operational performance, for example, quality, productivity, standardization, innovation. Expatriates are often seen to be amongst the most expensive people any organization employs, with their whole compensation and benefits package costing three to four times that of a normal salary. The need for tight financial control has led many organizations to focus on trying to reduce the size of the expatriate compensation and benefits package (ORC, 2001). This in turn will impact on the motivation of individuals to accept international assignments as we will discuss in the employee stakeholder section. Shareholder pressure is also driving much of the interest in being able to measure the value of international assignments. Features of measurement systems are discussed in Chapter 8.

This focus also brings with it the need for a clear identification of the objectives of international assignments and how they link with organizational strategy. In a broader, organizational context, shareholder pressure to reduce costs and streamline processes has led to a move towards organizing on the lines of business streams. In addition, there has been pressure to reduce the number of people in corporate international human resource management departments, which means that more than a few MNC s have lost the central expertise in the management of expatriates that they had built up over many years.

Customers and suppliers

Customers are looking at features of the products/services, for example, quality, costs, design, technology content and so on. *Suppliers* are interested in the suitability and stability of the relationships with its customer company. These two stakeholders have been driving the pace of change in international business, with an increasingly global marketplace and the growth of international joint ventures and alliances as a dominant mode of business. This has impacted on international staffing in a number of ways.

First, in the increasing number of trading blocs throughout the world, and most obviously in the European Union, the growth in international assignments is less amongst the giant "blue-chips" (which are often reducing their numbers of expatriates) than in smaller or newer organizations in the international arena (Scullion and Brewster, 2001). We can see this in the case of Pacific Direct and Stepstone. In both cases these companies had to become international in the initial stages of their existence. Neither of these companies had any history or experience of internationalization to guide them and took very different routes to achieving their goal. Pacific Direct adopted a franchised approach, whilst Stepstone had to deal with recruiting and socializing substantial numbers of staff in many different international locations in very short periods of time. International managers from existing Stepstone operations needed to be able to quickly and efficiently instil a corporate culture and adherence to company methods.

Second, the unique issues relating to expatriation in international joint ventures (IJVs) have only recently been the focus of attention by researchers (Schuler 2001, Schuler *et al.*, 2003). We noted the importance of organizational learning in IJVs in Chapter 5. However, the differing forms of control structure and intent in these forms of international organizations also creates additional complexity for the role of the expatriate. Many of the failures of IJVs have been attributed to HR issues, such as staffing, communication, delegation of authority from parent firms to the IJV and difficulties in adapting to a host country (Albrecht *et al.*, 1996). The same authors argue that, as the key HR issues in IJVs include selection and recruitment, training and development, spouse and family considerations, performance appraisal, compensation and reward systems and career and repatriation needs, the HR function should have a critical role when firms decide to enter an IJV. Rolls-Royce had more experience in sending technical expatriates abroad, but was relatively inexperienced in using these people to work within their international joint ventures and alliances.

Third, developments in world trading, most noticeably the extensive European and Japanese investments in the USA and the cross-border developments in new world trading blocs, particularly, of course, in the European Union, have led to a substantial increase in transfers between developed countries. Figures from Organization Resource Counsellors (ORC)'s (2000) latest survey of expatriate management trends shows the most popular regional destinations for expatriates as being, Asia (33 percent), Western Europe (26 percent) and the United States (16 percent). Expatriate managers working in countries with highly educated and professional employees can no longer adopt an autocratic approach without any regard for the outcomes. Equally, motivation and development of local country nationals is an integral part of creating a truly global operation and as such should be reflected in performance measurement of expatriate managers.

Empowering local nationals at ActionAid

Case Example

Mobility is a central plank in ActionAid's efforts to improve communication and organizational learning. In addition to long-term assignments, most of the senior managers in ActionAid travel extensively either across or within regions. The eight regional functions (which include HR/OD, IT, finance, gender coordinator, HIV coordinator and sponsorship coordinator) are geographically dispersed: each attached to a different country office and hence on local terms and conditions. The reason for this is both cost effectiveness, and to ensure for example, that the Harare HQ of the Africa region does not sit in an ivory tower or become too isolated. These people spend approximately 35–40 percent of their time traveling. The role of regional staff is a mixture of technical support and quality control. The HIV role also includes actual operational responsibility but this is the exception. These people act both as disseminators and gatherers of localized expertise.

"We have talked a lot about being 'leaders' rather than managers – empowering the community; believing in people and trusting them. There has been a change from having quite a few vertical structures and being quite hierarchical to flatter structures. As part of this, within Africa, regions and regional directors have been given much greater powers: there is an element of letting go – trusting people to make the right decisions. Making people feel valued to get the best out of them; let them develop confidence – let them learn from mistakes. Of course there is also a need to establish some guidelines – there is a need for leadership – but more a concept of peer leadership" (HR Country Manager, Africa).

The approach at ActionAid reflects both the organizational values and the global strategy. Rather than being explicitly spelt out it is implicit; that is, if you want to have flatter structures by implication you need to trust people. Similar thinking applies to the behaviors that ActionAid seeks from staff. Its values are to be an organization of integrity and fairness. To be convincing and authentic in this it has to start internally and treat its own staff according to those principles.

Source: Hegewisch *et al.* (2003)

Regulators and governments

Regulators and governments look at the behavior of a company against local legal, socio-cultural and environmental norms. In terms of legal implications, we see fewer expatriates going from the developed world to the developing world in commercial organizations. This is partly because there are fewer profits to be made from poor countries and partly due to an increasing unwillingness on the part of the poorer countries to continue taking foreign expatriates instead of using local nationals. Restrictions on work permits for both expatriates and accompanying spouses are forcing more and more organizations to look at alternative staffing methods. This approach falls short of a truly global orientation to staffing, as discussed later, and is often more a reactive response to individual country conditions.

The impact of differing socio-cultural norms has been particularly evident in research into women in international management. In a survey of sixty major North American MNCs, carried out 20 years ago, more than 50 percent expressed reluctance to select female managers for foreign assignments. One of the major reasons given was that foreigners are prejudiced against female managers (Adler, 1984). This "myth" was shown to be questionable by research carried out by Adler in 1987 amongst fifty-two North American female expatriates in Asia. Of this sample, 92 percent self-reported their assignment as being successful, backed up by supporting organizational evidence. Adler concluded that this finding revealed that the female expatriates were seen mainly as foreigners (who happen to be women) and were not therefore subject to the same cultural constraints as local women (Adler, 1993a, 1993b). Subsequent studies reinforce the need to question the blanket refusal to send women to certain countries on the basis of socio-cultural norms alone (Harris, 1999; Jelinik and Adler, 1988, Westwood and Leung, 1994). Caligiuri and Cascio (1998) attribute such a phenomenon to the cognitive process of stereotyping subtypes (Brewer *et al.*, 1981; Kunda and Thagard, 1996). They argue that according to this theory, Asian host nationals in Adler's study would have a substereotype of "Western working women" and a very different substereotype for "Asian working women". Reactions to the two groups can therefore be very different.

Employees

The final category of stakeholders is the employees themselves. Here we see major changes in terms of the profiles of individuals undertaking international assignments and their expectations. The traditional expatriate profile is changing. We are moving away from the traditional career expatriate model, usually filled by white, middle-class, male employees from headquarters. Key features of the expatriate population include:

1 *More third-country nationals and inpatriates (i.e. people brought into headquarters) as part of a more geocentric staffing policy:* For example, one major UK-based retailer has just instituted a one-year inpatriate program for young managers from international subsidiaries with director-level potential.

2 *More women:* The number of female expatriates is low in relation to the overall size of the qualified labor pool, with proportions ranging between 2 percent and 15 percent, depending on date and country (Adler, 1986a; Caligiuri and Tung, 1998; Harris, 1995, 1999; Linehan and Scullion, 2002). This is despite evidence that women may well be suited to the needs of international management because of their interpersonal skills (Tung, 1995; Jelinek and Adler, 1988; Mayrhofer and Scullion, 2002). Numbers of women are increasing slowly (Tung, 1998) and there is some evidence that numbers of women expatriates are particularly high in some Nordic MNCs (Suutari and Brewster, 1999). However, the preponderance of "informal" selection mechanisms for international assignments is seen to reinforce barriers to women's selection (Harris, 1999). Linked to this, recent research has identified the lack of networking facilities and mentoring as further informal barriers for women in international management (Caligiuri *et al.*, 1999; Linehan and Scullion, 2002).

3 *More dual-career couples:* There have also been increases in the numbers of dual-career couples (Caligiuri, 1998; Harvey, 1995, 1996, 1997, 1998). Harvey (1996) identifies five potentially problematic outcomes of international transfers to both partners in dual-career couples. These include the following:

(a) the expatriate manager not successfully completing the foreign assignment, therefore having a negative effect on career path;

(b) the trailing spouse having to abandon his/her career;

(c) the dual-career couple attempting to maintain both careers by the expatriate commuting back and forth between the home and host countries;

(d) inability to replace trailing spouse's income during expatriation; and

(e) potential candidates for expatriation refusing to relocate due to dual-career family considerations.

4 *Career expatriates:* The traditional lifelong appointment is still in evidence amongst European MNCs (Suutari and Brewster, 2001; Petrovic *et al.*, 2000). However, many expatriates now undertake either a single or a series of assignments, returning to their home country in between times. The increasing number of young, highly educated expatriates means that the psychological contract with this population is changing.

The Permits Foundation: advocate for expat spouse employment

Case Example

Interview with Kathleen van der Wilk-Carlton

The Netherlands-based Permits Foundation was established in 2001 as an international corporate initiative to improve work permit regulations for the spouses of expatriate employees. More than twenty multinationals from Europe and the United States set up the foundation to push local governments to relax work permit regulations that make it difficult for spouses to work in many countries. The organization believes dual careers, a need for employee diversity and an increased need for international employee mobility make it imperative for multinationals and governments to address the issue of work permit barriers for spouses. The Permits Foundation takes a concerted worldwide approach to raising awareness about work permit difficulties. And there are several signs that this issue is being recognized and change is starting. In the USA, for example, as a result of lobbying by an employer's coalition MEWS (Multi-national Employers for Working Spouses), supported by the Permits Foundation, two Spousal Work Authorization bills – which allow spouses of L and E visa holders to obtain work authorization, under certain conditions – were introduced in June 2001 and subsequently became law in January 2002.

Source: after Expatica.com 13/03/03

The boundaryless career

A key change in terms of employee expectations is the fact that going on an international assignment no longer ensures career progression, in line with changes in the psychological contract (Welch, 1998). So why do managers continue to accept offers of international assignments? Some initial research suggests that managers increasingly view an international assignment as enhancing their internal, rather than external careers (Tung, 1998, Black, 1999). According to Schein (1996), the "internal" career involves a subjective sense of where one is going in one's work life, whereas the "external" career essentially refers to advancement within the organizational hierarchy. The emerging notions of "internal" or "boundaryless" careers (Arthur and Rousseau, 1996; Parker and Inkson, 1999; Suutari and Brewster 2003) suggest that managers value an international assignment for the opportunity it brings for skill acquisition, personal development and career enhancement, even though it may not help them advance within their current company. This trend has major implications for organizational policy and practice in terms of repatriation and career management.

A recent study of French and German expatriates (Stahl and Cerdin, forthcoming), corroborated findings on the implications of boundaryless careers, particularly in relation to the fact that many repatriates deliberately choose to leave their company and do not perceive the organizational exit as a negative career move. More than half the German expatriates and one third of the French expatriates in the study said they were willing to leave their company upon return, and an additional one fourth of expatriates in both samples were neutral, meaning that they could be persuaded to leave with the right conditions. Although it is impossible to predict how many of them would actually leave the company upon return, these findings illustrate that companies risk losing large numbers of internationally experienced managers and professionals. As a result, the authors stress the need for organizations to integrate international assignments into logical career paths. This advice, however, runs counter to the trend in many organizations for more self-managed career progress, including open posting of jobs.

Strategy definition: targets and objectives definition

All the organizations in the CIPD study (CIPD, 2001; Brewster *et al.*, 2002) were aware of the need to align overall corporate, regional and country strategy with their key stakeholder groups' expectations. Almost inevitably, this leads to conflicts of interest. This may be between the same groups of stakeholders in different countries, for example, host country governments that try to impose barriers to entry to expatriates and spouses, whilst home country governments may be actively encouraging international mobility. It may also be between differing groups of stakeholders, that is, between shareholders who are looking to cut the cost of labor by relocating production to low-wage areas of the world, and employees in higher wage areas who feel their jobs are threatened. This excerpt from a recent article (Crabb, 2003) highlights the scope of the issue in relation to outsourcing to India by financial companies (see the discussion about the transfer of high-skilled jobs in Chapter 2).

Box 7.1 East India companies

In January 2003 the *Financial Times* held a conference in London entitled "Outsourcing to India." The event was massively oversubscribed and the attendance list looked like a *Who's Who* of the UK's financial services sector. These household names are either already shifting work overseas or they are seriously thinking about it. Addressing the conference, Chris Gentle, director of research (Europe) at Deloitte Touche Tohmatsu, said: "We're on the cusp of a revolution". The top 100 financial services companies could save between $700 million (£432 million) and $1 billion (£618 million) apiece over the next five years if they switched their operations to the developing world, he said. And a recent Deloitte's survey of twenty-seven of the biggest financial services companies had indeed found that most were planning to export many of their business processes. In 2003, for example, Powergen announced plans that could lead to more than 300 call center jobs transferring to India. BA, Prudential, HSBC, Axa, Bupa and Royal and Sun Alliance are already established there. Stephen Roncoroni, an independent consultant, estimates that an outsourced call center in the UK costs a minimum of £16 to £17 per "man hour" to run, with the average closer to £20; in India the average figure is closer to £9.

Source: adapted from Crabb (2003)

In Chapter 3 we noted the different approaches to staffing identified by Perlmutter (1969). One of these was a geocentric approach, considered to be the most appropriate for transnational organizations. An example of the shift from a traditional reliance on expatriates towards a more geocentric approach is provided below based on changes taking place within BOC.

Shifting from expatriation to a geocentric approach at BOC

BOC used to manage through a standard regional structure. Highly autonomous country managing directors reported to regional directors. Results were collated in these regions and regional directors ran each one with immense autonomy. Four years ago they began a move towards a new business structure based on a global line-of-business model. By late 2001 BOC considered that it had made the transition from being essentially a regionally based organization to one that was structured around global lines of business. Such a strategic change in the business model implied a completely different approach to staffing, including international mobility. Asia was the last region to transfer to a global line of business. HR had to help the business manage the risk of taking out expatriates and putting local people into bigger positions, whilst also supporting the new managers and structures to help them succeed. The Asian organization had not been as "structurally evolved" as other geographic areas. Therefore, the organization capabilities in BOC were derived from "steady, stone-piped and seniority-driven" structures. The managing directors had been the only integrating point within the organization. The new global structure meant that even the country experience and insight of senior managers was not necessarily valuable: "They can't apply what they have learned from similar jobs in countries because the jobs are slightly different." Therefore, those individuals below managing director level would now face real business management exposure, whilst also having global support and development. The country managing directors would slowly let go of control and would be gone within a couple of years.

Operationalizing strategy in international staffing

Discussions of overall orientations to internationalization and their impact on staffing practices provide the context for a more detailed formulation of strategic operational goals and their link to international assignments. Ideally, strategy should explain both the goals of the organization and a plan of action to achieve these goals. This definition is still useful to describe how strategy outlines the targets and objectives to be reached both at corporate level and at business level. The literature identifies five main strategic reasons for sending employees on international assignments: professional development, knowledge transfer, transfer of scarce skills, control and coordination. From the CIPD Benchmarking Study of sixty-four organizations (CIPD, 2001; Brewster *et al.*, 2002), the relative importance of these factors can be seen (see Table 7.1). It is important to note that whilst 59 percent of the HR directors thought that international assignments were perceived as providing some useful experience within their organizations, only 8 percent considered that they were well regarded and critical to career success. In 40 percent of cases vacancies were filled on an *ad hoc* basis, but then in another 40 percent of organizations they were filled as part of a global HR planning system.

Table 7.1 Main organizational reasons for sending expatriates on assignment

Main reasons for assignments	Percentage
Career development	57.8
Local expertise not available	56.3
Transfer of expertise	53.1
Creating international cadre of managers	37.5
Control of local operation	20.3
Coordination of global policy	7.8

In practice, there may be few "pure" cases – many assignments will have more than one rationale. In addition to agreeing the objectives of the assignment, the organization also needs to make strategic decisions as to the type of assignment and assignee. This will be affected by both practical considerations and overall orientation to the management of human resources as illustrated in the previous section.

International worker profile definition

Both the cost of expatriate assignments and the problems associated with them, such as dual-career and family issues, have led organizations to investigate alternative forms of international working. A move away from reliance on long-term assignments increases the complexity of strategic decision-making in this area. International HR professionals now need to decide which type of international assignment might be better for

- developing an international managerial cadre
- skills and knowledge transfer
- control and coordination of operations.

Four main forms of assignee can be identified as follows.

1. *Expatriate assignments* are long-term assignments where the employee and typically their partner/family, if they have one, move to the host country for a specified period of time, more than one year.
2. *Short-term assignments* are those with a specified duration, usually less than one year. The family may or may not accompany the employee.
3. *International commuting* involves an employee transiting regularly from their home country to a place of work in a specified other country, usually on a weekly or bi-weekly basis, while the family remains at home.
4. *Frequent flyers* are those employees that undertake frequent international business trips but do not relocate.

Survey data indicates that there is increasing use of all types of assignment (Pricewaterhouse Coopers, 1999, 2000; Petrovic *et al.*, 2000). The latter CReME survey

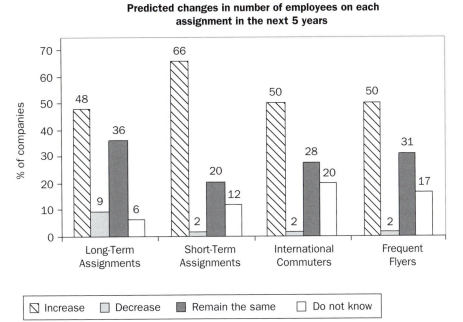

Figure 7.1 Predicted changes in different forms of international working
Source: Petrovic *et al.* (2000)

shows the following proportion of organizations anticipate an increase in the use of all four types of assignment (Figure 7.1).

Findings from the surveys reveal that alternatives to expatriation do not necessarily avoid the problems experienced with this traditional form of international staffing. Work/life balance issues are seen as problematic for all the alternative forms. In addition, stress, burnout and travel fatigue feature heavily as issues in relation to international commuting and frequent flyer assignments. From an organizational perspective, controlling alternative forms of international working is problematic with more and more deregularized approaches to policy and practice moving from long-term through to frequent flyers. Indeed, many companies are unable to identify frequent flyers within their workforce – due to the absence of a policy for this type of international assignment (Pricewaterhouse Coopers, 1999, 2000; Petrovic *et al.*, 2000).

The problems facing international HR professionals trying to manage differing forms of international working are significant. In particular, few organizations have any real grasp of costs – and almost no idea of the benefits to the organization of each form of international working. The CReME survey revealed that whilst two thirds of larger international companies prepared a cost analysis for long-term assignments, only a half did so for short-term assignments. Less than 40 percent prepared a cost analysis for international commuters and only 23 percent did so for frequent flyers.

Willingness to move internationally

Following initial attention to international careers by Adler (1986b), the willingness to move internationally – whether this means relocating employment, accepting an overseas assignment or indeed just initiating international experiences – has received considerable attention in recent years (Scullion, 1992; Solomon, 1994; Brett and Stroh, 1995; Aryee *et al.*, 1996; Forster and Johnsen, 1996; Inkson *et al.*, 1997; Lowe *et al.*, 1999; Suutari and Brewster, 2000; Feldman, 2001). Understanding the receptivity to working abroad of young graduates is important for a number of reasons (Tharenou, forthcoming):

- It assists organizations in their quest for talent (see Chapter 6). Many young employees will self-initiate an international move rather than waiting to be expatriated.
- Many firms, however, do expatriate young employees with only 2 or 3 years of work experience.
- It therefore provides insight into the mindset of the next generation of international managers.

Understanding the factors that make people more receptive to international mobility is then very important. In practice, international organizations have to make a trade-off in their recruitment and selection between competence for international work and willingness/commitment to it (Sparrow, 1999). Psychologists consider that this is a moderately stable attitude or career interest that individuals hold, but how does it develop and are certain groups more predisposed to hold it?

Box 7.2 Receptive attitudes to international work. The case of Australia

Young Australian managers and professionals are relocating abroad more than any other age group and more than ever seen before (Hugo *et al.*, 2001). In 1998–99 19 percent of all Australians relocating abroad were aged 15 to 24 and 34 percent were aged 25 to 34. Australian students have been found to be more receptive to international careers than their US counterparts (Cianni and Tharenou, 2000). A longitudinal study of 213 Australian business graduates over the first two years of their careers found that receptivity to international careers and willingness to relocate to developing countries were separate dimensions, though both developed from a combination of factors including personal agency, home barriers and work experiences. Perceptions of "self-capability" also predicted willingness to relocate. However, organizations could do much to influence receptivity at an early age. The higher their international focus the more receptive were younger graduates (this link was not found in older graduates). Receptivity to international careers was found to be moderately stable and therefore considered as a potential selection measure for expatriates.

Source: after Tharenou (forthcoming)

Fostering diversity in the expatriate population

In addition to strategic decisions in terms of the type of international assignment, organizations need to consider *who* they should be using to fill these positions. In general, these types of decisions reflect the overall orientation of the organization in relation to internationalization, as discussed previously. A commitment to a geocentric approach would indicate equal gender representation amongst the international worker population and a proportional representation of managers from the countries and regions covered by the organization.

From a gender perspective, as mentioned earlier, despite an increase in demand for international assignees, the numbers of women in such positions remains stubbornly low. Such statistics question the assumption that diversity is being acknowledged and incorporated in the development of a geocentric mindset. It is particularly worrying to see that the representation of women on international assignments is increasing at such a slow rate since Adler's (1984) study.

Geographical diversity amongst expatriates is even more problematic in that there is almost no research in this area. Anecdotal evidence, however, suggests that many multinational organizations still have a predominance of expatriates from the home country/region. This situation is problematic if organizations wish to attain "transnational" or geocentric status (see Chapter 3 for an outline of these international stances). Bartlett and Ghoshal (1989: 212) explain the objectives of a "transnational" mindset:

> the development of a transnational organization requires more than multidimensional capabilities and interdependent assets. It is crucial to change the mentality of members of the organization. Diverse roles and dispersed operations must be held together by a management mindset that understands the need for multiple strategic capabilities, views problems and opportunities from both local and global perspectives, and is willing to interact with others openly and flexibly. The task is not to build a sophisticated matrix structure, but to create a "matrix in the minds of managers."

We discussed some of the assumptions made about the development of this mindset in Chapter 5. Kobrin (1994) defines this geocentric mindset in terms of a global systems approach to decision-making in which superiority is not equated with any nationality and ideas and resources, including human resources are valued according to their worth for the global entity, no matter where their source of origin might be. Managers have to frame problems in different ways, which in turn requires a change in their "cognitive processes" (Murtha *et al.*, 1998). In other words: "global thinking places high value on sharing information, knowledge, and experience across national, functional and business boundaries and on balancing competing country, business and functional priorities that emerge in the globalization process" (Pucik, 1998: 41).

This forces organizations to make some important distinctions, notably between an expatriate and a global manager. The term "expatriate" or "international manager" defines an executive who is able to assume a leadership position fulfilling international assignments across countries and cultures. The term "global manager" (sometimes also called transnational manager) refers to an executive who is assigned to a position

> with a cross-border responsibility, who has a flexible and open mind, with a well-rounded understanding of international business and an ability to work across cross-cultural and cross-functional boundaries . . . some global managers may be expatriates; many, if not most, have been expatriates at some point in their career, but probably only few expatriates are global managers.
>
> (Pucik, 1998: 41)

Although there is considerable overlap in the attributes associated with success of expatriates and global managers, for the latter as much emphasis has to be placed on cultivating (and in the context of selection also assessing) the manager's mind as opposed to traditional concerns about relevant behaviors and competencies.

However, by its very nature, the development of a global mindset can only be achieved through exposure to diversity. It is hardly likely that a homogenous group of managers will develop a global mindset unless the composition of the group is changed to reflect the diversity within the organization and potentially within its client base. In many organizations a complex set of changes to existing HR programs have to be set in place in order to build this international mindset.

The ultimate challenge is to slowly internationalize the whole management development process. Consider the response that Rolls-Royce made to its internationalization process. It would consider itself to be different to many MNCs in the way that it handles its international resourcing. The organization looks to high levels of international mobility and relies less on local hires than many MNCs. In part this is because they are a high-technology company, relying on world-class engineering knowledge and also because they are highly vertically integrated in terms of products, with self-standing business units built around customers. With such vertical integration of products there is considerable advantage in moving people around the company to understand the different business units and pressure to make use of the advanced technical skills, competencies and capabilities that the managers have in more than just one unit. Senior managers need cross-cultural awareness because the customers for these business units come from all round the world. International mobility is therefore encouraged from an early age in Rolls-Royce careers. International career development in such organizations represents a major challenge. However, the reality is that managers can develop parochial attitudes to international moves because at business unit manager level understandably commitment to the general good of the company can be weaker than commitment to the immediate needs of their business unit. It is difficult enough to plan for inter-unit technical moves, let alone international moves. So what is the solution? It has to be to internationalize the whole management development process so that even with constrained moves managers already have an international mindset.

The impact of internationalization on career development processes at Rolls-Royce

Case Example

In order for Rolls-Royce to develop the well rounded people that its business strategy and organization structure required, then its mobility policy had to work effectively but it also needed to internationalize its management development processes by either adapting existing HR processes or creating new ones. This is a slow and arduous task for international HR functions.

The foundation of the management development process in Rolls-Royce was the Development Cell process. This was a managerial meeting focused on the development of the high performers. It focused on succession issues and the key players as seen against the strategic priorities. The cells started with the CEO cell, then moved down into functional cells. Rolls-Royce operated these on a matrix basis, so there were also a series of Business Development Cells which looked after the management of talent within IJVs. Development Cells were also linked to a "Skill Ownership" system, which articulated the detailed competencies and the subsequent career paths needed to develop these. As the Development Cell process began to "perculate through the company globally" it looked at management development issues worldwide. The definition of skills and competencies needed throughout career paths began to absorb the competency-specifications for more internationally exposed role requirements.

Another adapted process was the Accelerated Leadership Programme. This had been created in 1999 out of the belief that Rolls-Royce needed to shift the focus from external recruitment to internal development. There had been high levels of external recruitment at senior levels in some parts of the business as part of a deliberate policy to change the culture and bring in new commercial skills but the organization considered that it now needed to look at its internal processes to develop youngsters and bring them through a fast-track route. The ALP operated like most fast track schemes, but individuals nominated themselves rather than having to be put forward by a committee. The scheme helped them look at their capabilities and was run on an assessment center basis. There was a 3-day AC event, after which those selected (around seventy) went onto a development program and were afforded extra opportunities. As part of the internationalization process this scheme was opened up to the whole company, and was publicized internationally. There was a broadened international population in RR terms. Changes were made to the delivery process to match the expectations of this more internationalized population. Similarly,

continued

Rolls-Royce had introduced a behavioral improvement plan called One Small Step, with Phase 1 starting in 1997 in its Aerospace business. All 14,000 employees were taken through the program, which took them away from the business for a day, working through businesses in a period of 1 month with small groups of twenty cross-functional staff. They were exposed to the business problems, customer views and examined how they could change the performance of their unit. Rolls-Royce also introduced a Taking the Lead program to respond to a need for good quality leadership. This program was run in the UK, North America and was then worked through India, Germany and Scandinavia. Around 5,000 managers around the world were put through these programs, which included 360-degree feedback. Rolls-Royce management development staff monitored the cross cultural issues that surrounded an intensive behavior change process in different parts of the world, making minor changes to the process and using more international assessors as the program developed.

Another challenge was to build awareness about international business into first line management level. Rolls-Royce ran a 2-week residential International Business Awareness program for twenty people at a time twice a year. This was for people with 3–4 years' service. They were high performers nominated for the process. The program was purposely run in a culture that was alien to the participating managers – for example it had been run twice in China, twice in Brazil, once in India and once in Malaysia. The program was generally sited in a strategically important area for Rolls-Royce in terms of global customers. The managers were thrown into the culture, there were staged visits to customers and a business simulation was run. They were counselled by senior HR staff. This took them through a process which outlined the expectations that Rolls-Royce had of them as their accountabilities increased.

Rolls-Royce also worked on international graduate programs. It initiated a lot of work with staff in terms of early career development in the organization – how they were perceived by universities, had they got good employer branding? Rolls-Royce in fact spent a lot of time and money on building this. Their 2001 graduate brochure was the second most popular amongst graduates. Senior managers were tasked with building their connections and with marketing Rolls-Royce. They became more proactive in influencing the national education policy of countries. Senior managers sat on government advisory panels, local school boards, technology colleges, through which they could influence the training and development policies of schools and universities. It was clearly important to Rolls-Royce that they extended this activity internationally. They did this in North America and were also operating this influence on the skill formation process in Europe. Although much of the entry-level resourcing was still domestic, Rolls-Royce set up visiting lecture programs around the globe and set a policy of taking on graduates from wherever around the globe.

Managing the global assignment cycle

As the above example shows, internationalizing the mindset of a workforce involves far more than just managing global assignments more effectively. However, global

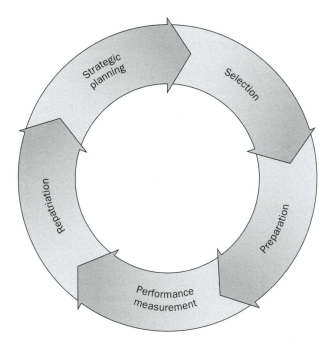

Figure 7.2 The global assignment cycle

assignments are central to this process. Effective management of international mobility entails the need to take an holistic approach to all aspects of the assignment process. The Global Assignment Cycle (see Figure 7.2) identifies the key components of this approach.

The complexities of managing this cycle have been the focus of sustained academic research over many years. Despite this focus, key challenges still remain under each of the cycle components.

Recruitment and selection

Research into selection criteria for international assignments shows a split between theory and practice. The literature on the criteria used for expatriate manager selection also has a tendency towards prescription and a heavy North American bias. There have been several reviews of this literature (Mendenhall and Oddou, 1985; Dowling *et al.*, 1994; Harris and Brewster, 1999). Reflecting the discussion of expatriates and global managers earlier in this chapter, important distinctions have been made with regard to the selection criteria for each (Adler and Bartholomew, 1992; Pucik, 1998).

From the more abundant literature dealing with selection of the *expatriate* or international manager, a key observation is the emphasis on interpersonal and cross-cultural skills as determinants of success for international assignments (Barham and Wills, 1992; Forster,

1997; Sparrow, 1999; Caligiuri, 2000). The stress on "soft skills" reflects a more general departure from reliance on traditional "hard" skills for successful management. A major drawback of these lists, however, is that few of them are drawn from empirical data.

In practice, however, the key selection criterion for most expatriate assignments is technical competence. This is hardly surprising; sending a technically incompetent person is a recipe for disaster. More worrying is the lack of inclusion of intercultural and interpersonal skills as criteria for selection. This would suggest the continuing existence of an underlying assumption of the universal nature of managerial skills, as first identified by Baker and Ivancevich (1971).

International management selection systems

The impact of the type of selection system for international management assignments on the composition of the expatriate population has received limited attention. However, Harris (1999) found a significant link between the type of selection process used and participation rates of women. Organizations operating open, formal systems were much more likely to have more equal representation of women than those operating closed, informal systems. Drawing from both the sociological and social psychological literature on "fit," Harris argued selection processes are inherently geared to assess acceptability rather than suitability and where there is a dominance of one gender in a particular role or occupation, selectors will include gender as part of their "schema" of ideal job holders. Her research found that a majority of UK-based international organizations were operating closed, informal systems (see Table 7.2).

Table 7.2 Types of international manager selection system

	Formal	*Informal*
Open	• Clearly defined criteria • Clearly defined measures • Training for selectors • Open advertising of vacancy (internal/external) • Panel discussions	• Less defined criteria • Less defined measures • Limited training for selectors • No panel discussions • Open advertising of vacancy • Recommendations
Closed	• Clearly defined criteria • Clearly defined measures • Training for selectors • Panel discussions • Nominations only (networking/reputation)	• Selectors' individual preferences determine criteria and measures • No Panel discussions • Nominations only (networking/reputation)

Source: Harris (1999)

Recent evidence does, however, show a move towards the use of more sophisticated selection methods by some leading international organizations. The CIPD Guide to International Recruitment, Selection and Assessment (Sparrow, 1999) notes the increasing use of assessment centers and psychological testing as part of the selection process for people working in international contexts. The need to ensure that such testing is appropriate across different cultural contexts is a key factor in most of the developmental work associated with setting up the processes.

Assessing sensitivity to multicultural issues at EMI

Case Example

Psychological testing forms one part of the recruitment and selection process for managers in the main functional areas. Typically, managers meet a group of managers or clients that they might be working with, perhaps at a local event or just as a team meeting. This is intended to imbue them with the EMI culture. Self-selection is an important part of the selection process. Candidates then undergo a psychological assessment process. This selection process is used for a pool of internationally mobile managers. Many of these candidates are "in transit" and have no particular home base or nationality – an example might be an American manager working in Hong Kong who is being recruited for a position in Japan. The testing is oriented towards social interaction and relationship skills. It is meant to look at the candidate's ability to integrate, learn and receive feedback. A popular tool is FIRO-B. EMI stresses that it does not place value on the results of the tests *per se*, nor look for a simple clinical assessment. The value lies in having independent assessors who can rapidly evaluate the candidate's maturity level and readiness to do business. The testing precedes a detailed follow-up feedback session, which EMI insists all candidates should receive regardless of the outcome. It is thought that candidates who are ready to receive feedback about themselves are also ready to learn about themselves, and to develop their own sensitivity to other people, cultures and customers.

Source: after Sparrow (1999)

We noted earlier in the chapter that receptivity to international careers has also been considered a potentially useful selection criterion for expatriation (Stone, 1991; Pricewaterhouse Coopers, 1999, 2000).

Expatriate adjustment

The factors influencing the successful adjustment and performance of international assignees have been the subject of intense research interest and debate over the last three decades.

The term "adjustment" has varying meanings. It can be defined either as a process or a state (Haslberger, 1999). For example, Berry (1992) defines adjustment as "a state whereby changes occur in the individual in a direction of increased fit and reduced conflict between environmental demands and the individual attitudinal and behavioural inclinations". On the other hand, Brewster (1995b) defines adjustment as "the process of behaviour modification by the expatriates so their behaviours are in accordance with the accepted behaviour of the host culture".

Hechanova et al., (2003) in a recent review of research into adjustment, give a sense of the confusion reigning in the field. They argued that the term "adjustment" has been used in a general sense to indicate a number of things, including the following:

- feelings of acceptance and satisfaction (Brislin, 1981);
- acquisition of culturally acceptable skills and behaviors (Bochner et al., 1977);
- the lack of mental health problems such as stress or depression (Berry and Kim, 1988); and
- the psychological comfort that an individual feels in a new situation (Gregersen and Black, 1990).

The majority of research on expatriate adjustment has also generally focused on three specific facets (Black, 1988; Black and Stephens, 1989):

- *General adjustment*, which refers to the degree of comfort with general living conditions such as climate, food, housing, cost of living, transportation, or health facilities.
- *Interactional adjustment*, which involves comfortably socializing and interacting with host nationals.
- *Work adjustment*, which relates to specific job responsibilities, performance standards and expectations and supervisory responsibilities.

Hechanova et al. (2003) applied meta-analytic methods to research on these three forms of expatriate adjustment. Based on forty-two empirical studies covering 5,210 expatriates, the most important and consistent predictive relationships were identified. These are shown in Figure 7.3.

Expatriate preparation

In view of the complexity of factors determining expatriate adjustment, Harris and Brewster (1999) argue that organizations should take a more holistic approach to pre-departure preparation for expatriates. A survey of 205 expatriates in a variety of countries around the world about their pre-departure training needs found that half had little or no knowledge in terms of practical items or social and family issues. Seven out of ten indicated that they had little or no knowledge in the area of business relationships. The results from the survey led the authors to argue for a more tailored approach to pre-departure preparation (see Figure 7.4).

The integrative framework takes into account job variables at the home and host country level, including the nature of the international operation, size of home country

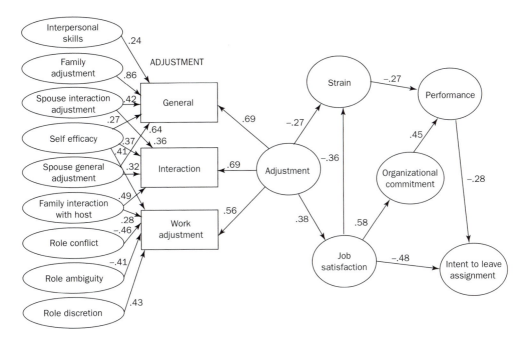

Figure 7.3 Model of expatriate outcomes
Source: Hechanova *et al.* (2003)
Note: Figures denote size and direction of correlation

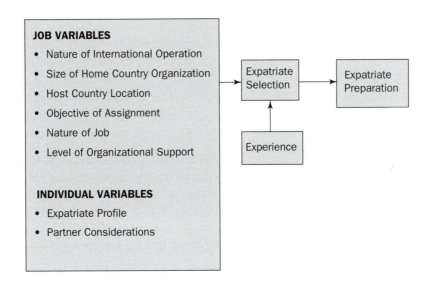

Figure 7.4 Integrative framework for pre-departure preparation

organization, host country location, objective of assignment, nature of job and level of organizational support, together with individual variables in terms of the expatriate profile and partner considerations. These antecedents are considered alongside an assessment of the individual's existing level of competency before deciding on an appropriate preparation scenario.

Performance measurement

The last section on adjustment has highlighted the critical variables linked to expatriate adjustment. As yet, however, no definitive causal links have been established between adjustment and performance.

Fenwick *et al.* (1999) present a theoretical model that explains the way in which international organizations can use expatriates and their performance management as a form of both cultural and formal, or bureaucratic, control mechanisms. In terms of cultural control, assignees from HQ are used to "socialize" subsidiary employees into the values, expected behaviors and social knowledge required to become fully integrated members of the organization. The outcomes of such socialization are expected to be shared values and organizational commitment. Problems with this type of cultural control include uncertainty as to the extent of socialization and commitment to the organization on the part of the expatriate. The authors argue that the use of performance management is a viable component of bureaucratic control. Control is often exercised through the way in which organizations select, train and monitor the behaviors and output of staff. The characteristics of an HRM performance management system are as follows: links to organizational strategy; setting individual performance goals; providing feedback on progress towards goal achievement; providing opportunities for improvement through appraisal feedback; training and development; and links between results and rewards. The authors conclude by saying that it is not enough for organizations to rely on informal control mechanisms as a flexible way to achieve desired outcomes. The use of expatriate assignments as a primary form of cultural control should be combined with an integrated performance management system.

Repatriation

In a recent study of the career progress of Finnish expatriates, Suutari and Brewster (2003) noted that although the respondents (individual repatriates) reported mainly positive career outcomes, 59 percent of those who stayed with the same employer had seriously considered leaving. In total, about one third of the repatriate group had changed their employer. From those, one third had done so while they were still abroad. The timing indicates that they had changed employer earlier than the average repatriation job negotiations started.

One of the key elements in return on investment in relation to international assignees is the ability to be able to use the skills and experience they have gained whilst working internationally to help improve overall organizational capability. Indeed, "[MNCs] such as Coca Cola, will not repatriate managers until there is solid evidence that they have had an impact on overseas performance and that they have developed a global mindset" (Novicevic and Harvey, 2001: 1252).

In view of evidence showing that managers view international assignments more as a way to increase their own internal capital, than as a way of progressing up the organizational ladder, making sure that key managers do not leave before or after repatriation is a critical concern.

The situation is difficult on both sides. A majority of organizations nowadays do not provide post-assignment guarantees (GMAC GRS/Windham International, 2000; ORC, 2000). From the repatriate perspective other problems associated with reintegrating into the home country are as follows (Johnston, 1991):

● loss of status
● loss of autonomy
● loss of career direction
● feeling that international experience is undervalued by the company.

A critical issue in repatriation is the management of expectations (Pickard, 1999: Stroh *et al.*, 1998; Welch, 1998). Work-related expectations of repatriates can include the following:

● job position after repatriation
● standard of living
● longer-term career prospects
● opportunities to utilize skills acquired whilst abroad
● support and interest from supervisors and colleagues in the home country.

Despite these reservations, most studies of repatriates report quite positive expectations prior to the return home. One study of English expatriates reported that 69 percent of them expected the return to enhance their career prospects and 55 percent of them expected their return to be exciting and/or challenging (Pickard, 1999). Similarly, studies of US expatriates (Tung, 1998) and Finnish expatriates (Suutari and Brewster, 2001) have found a majority to be positive about career development.

Ensuring positive repatriation experiences and the retention of key talent is therefore a critical task for most organizations. A review of positive company practices in this respect include the following:

● pre-departure career discussions
● named contact person in the home country organization
● mentor at host location
● re-entry counselling
● family repatriation programs
● employee debriefings
● succession planning.

In light of research evidence mentioned earlier in this chapter, highlighting the growth of the "boundaryless" career, the need to handle the repatriation process in a proactive manner becomes a critical imperative for organizations in order to retain their key talent for the future.

Conclusion

This chapter has explored the strategic and contextual influences affecting the strategic management of international mobility. A clear finding from research in this area is the need to align decisions regarding international assignments with the broader international strategy of the organization. This will include its overall orientation to international staffing as well as the constraints and obligations imposed on it by host governments. The holistic nature of the global assignment cycle highlights the need to take a strategic and integrated approach at each stage of the process in order that the management of international mobility becomes a critical component of an organization's global HR approach.

8 Measuring the contribution of the corporate HR function

Introduction

The how, who, what and where questions usually raised when addressing the issue of measuring the contribution of corporate HR, becomes increasingly difficult at the international level. Complexities of scope, authority level, cultural, political and legislative barriers are just some of the issues which might impact on being able to trace direct causal links between HR input and organizational performance. The following two distinct approaches can be identified in this area:

1 attempts to prove a link between people management practices and organizational performance; and
2 methods of evaluation of the contribution of the HR function itself.

Although there is obviously some overlap here, most of the research into the first approach consists of identifying the type of people management practices adopted and assessing these against published organizational performance figures. The initiators of the practices may not be HR professionals, but rather line managers. In contrast, the second approach focuses on the processes and delivery mechanisms by which the function delivers value in an organization. Much of this chapter details the main evaluation options open to the corporate HR function. We shall examine the following:

- service-level agreements
- evaluating high-impact projects
- balanced scorecards and HR scorecards
- perceptions of effectiveness
- measuring the value of international assignments
- audits of strategic aspects of global HRM
- diagnosing global HR positioning.

First, however, we begin with the links between people management practices and organizational performance. For many years, practitioners and academics have struggled to prove a causal link between various forms of people management approaches and organizational performance. The attention is well deserved as failure to be able to "prove" that a particular intervention has the desired outcome is problematic for both the

HR professionals responsible for designing the policy and the line managers looking for an immediate impact on their organization's or unit's performance. The complexity of human behavior and the many intervening variables that can occur in any operational context, make evaluation of the link problematic. However, the increasing focus on human capital as a key contributor to competitive advantage, makes this area one of the "Holy Grails" of contemporary HR research.

> The economic conditions created by globalization, and the advent of new technologies have combined to make human capital and other intangible assets the major drivers of economic competitiveness . . . [but] without advances in the internal measurement and reporting of human capital, management are unable to fully recognise the value of their employees' competencies and commitment for business performance . . . without advances in the external reporting of human capital, capital markets are unable to allocate capital efficiently to firms whose principal assets are not reflected in their balance sheets.
>
> (Scarbrough and Elias, 2002: ix)

Reflecting what we saw in Chapter 5 when we considered the nature of HR knowledge that has to be transferred within global organizations, Scarbrough and Elias (2002) note that human capital is dynamic, flexible, embodied in people and embedded in tacit knowledge. Moreover, we know that "in the great majority of [UK] firms the systems for evaluating and reporting human capital are either rudimentary or non-existent" (p. 4). This is true both across firms of different national ownership (i.e., in the US, UK, France, Germany and so forth) and within HR functions whether they operate at a national, regional or global level.

Box 8.1 What is human capital?

Some of the best-known definitions of human capital include the following:

- the knowledge that individuals acquire during their life and [then] use to produce goods services or ideas in market or non-market circumstances (OECD, 1996);
- ability (knowledge, skill, talent) PLUS behavior TIMES effort TIMES time (Davenport, 1999); and
- competence TIMES commitment (Ulrich, 1998).

Source: Scarbrough and Elias (2002)

At present, the majority of studies have been domestically based, but even here, three distinct approaches can be identified. Studies have focused on the following:

1 best practice
2 strategic contingencies
3 configurations of practices.

Best practice approaches

The first is the *best practice* approach, most commonly attributed to the work of Pfeffer (1994). This approach advocates that a standard set of HRM practices or high-performance work systems (HPWS), leads to superior organizational performance. The whole debate in Chapter 4 about the use of technology in HR systems to help produce a set of *optimized HR practices* is based on the premise that there is such a thing as best practice on global scale. Pfeffer (1994: 64) identifies a list of seven HR practices of successful organizations.

- employment security;
- selective hiring of new personnel;
- self-managed teams and decentralization of decision-making as the basic principles of organizational design;
- comparatively high compensation contingent on organizational performance;
- extensive training;
- reduced status distinctions and barriers, including dress, language, office arrangements and wage differences across levels; and
- extensive sharing of financial and performance information throughout the organization.

Pfeffer illustrates the benefits of each of the seven practices with case examples (mainly from North American firms). The best practice approach has been widely tested by American scholars and generally supported (Arthur, 1994; Huselid, 1995; MacDuffie, 1995; Delaney and Huselid, 1996; Ichniowski *et al.*, 1996). The applicability of this set of high-performance working practices in all contexts is, however, questionable. The success of the practices described will depend, to some extent, on both the economic and the cultural conditions in which they are applied.

Pfeffer's set of practices are contingent on economic conditions of relative prosperity and growth in which organizations can offer permanent employment, long-term career practices and generous reward practices. Writing only five years after Pfeffer's book, Cappelli (1999) painted a very different picture of the world of work. A clear delineation is made between the "traditional" employment contract and the "new employment relationship." The growth of the traditional employment relationship, consisting of long-term relationships and systems of internal development, was a response to the need to coordinate more complex organizations and to ensure that the skills were there to make that happen. This new relationship is creating a series of generic challenges for HR functions in many parts of the world (Sparrow, 1998; Sparrow and Cooper, 2003). Cappelli (1999) argues that this form of employment relationship is proving to be of less benefit to organizations for several key reasons.

Bringing the market into the firm means, amongst other things, the end of employer and employee loyalty and the systematic dismantling of the HR processes underpinning the traditional model of long-term employment with progressive career development. The new model does call for selective hiring, and compensation processes are even

> ### Box 8.2 Drivers for change in the employment relationship
>
> - More competitive product markets that not only created pressure to cut costs, but, more important, reduced time to market and pursued differentiated market niches. These changes made long-term, fixed investments – in people as well as in capital – problematic because they became obsolete much more quickly.
> - Information technology that could take over the functions of coordinating and monitoring, tasks traditionally performed by middle management. With these technologies in place, outside suppliers could easily be monitored and integrated into an operation. No corporate staff was necessary to manage them. As a result, a huge range of functions could now be outsourced. For those employees who remained within the company, the threat of being outsourced was always present
> - New arrangements that have made it possible for the financial community to advance the interests of shareholders far ahead of other traditional stakeholders within publicly held companies. Pressures to increase shareholder value put the squeeze on costs, especially fixed costs.
> - New management techniques – profit centers, outside benchmarking, core competencies – that brought the discipline of markets inside the firm and exposed every aspect of the business and every employee to market pressures.
>
> Source: after Cappelli (1999)

more critical as a mechanism to try to gain commitment of employees in the absence of employment security. The interlinked nature of Pfeffer's seven practices is no longer defendable. Later in the chapter we highlight work that also questions the cross-cultural validity of much best practice research. However, we now move onto the second generic evaluation approach, which has been to take a more contingent approach.

Strategic contingency approaches

In line with arguments that the "best practice" approach is impracticable in an international context, the *contingency* approach states that the particular set of HR practices that an organization adopts must fit with other organizational factors in order for it to be effective. Again, the majority of this work has been conducted from a domestic perspective. For example, Schuler and Jackson (1987) identified sets of HR practices that would be appropriate for differing competitive strategies. They based their model on the type of employee role behaviors that would be needed for each of the three classic generic strategies businesses were supposed to pursue at that time and identified the corresponding HRM policies that would deliver those behaviors. The three strategies were innovation, cost reduction and quality enhancement (see Tables 8.1 and 8.2 for two examples).

Table 8.1 Role behavior model – innovation

Strategy	Employee role behavior	HRM policies
Innovation	• A high degree of creative behavior • A longer-term focus • A moderate concern for quantity • An equal degree of concern for process and results • A greater degree of risk taking • A higher tolerance of ambiguity and unpredictability	• Jobs that require close interaction and coordination among groups of individuals • Performance appraisals that are more likely to reflect longer-term and group-based achievements • Jobs that allow employees to develop skills that can be used in other positions in the firm • Compensation systems that emphasize internal equality rather than external or market-based equity • Broad career paths to reinforce the development of a broad range of skills

Source: Carter and Robinson (2000); after Schuler and Jackson (1987)

Table 8.2 The role behavior model – cost reduction

Strategy	Employee role behavior	HRM policies
Cost reduction	• Relatively repetitive and predictable behavior • A rather short-term focus • Primarily autonomous or individual activity • Moderate concern for quality • Primary concern for results • Low risk-taking activity • Relatively high degree of comfort with stability	• Relatively fixed and explicit job descriptions that allow little room for ambiguity • Narrowly designed jobs and narrowly defined career paths that encourage specialist, expertise and efficiency • Short-term result oriented performance appraisals • Close monitoring of market pay levels for use in making compensation decisions

Source: Carter and Robinson (2000); after Schuler and Jackson (1987)

In the first example, the organization will want to measure the extent to which the HR practices outlined are actually delivering the required behaviors of creativity and it will also want to ensure that although it pays above the normal rates, there is internal equality amongst equally qualified team members. Attitude and satisfaction surveys can assess the first target, whilst compensation targets can be assessed by careful monitoring of equity across teams. In contrast, the second example is focused on cutting costs through controlling risk and increasing efficiency in all jobs. An assessment of performance appraisal content and results, together with appropriate questions on attitude and satisfaction surveys can be used to measure the effectiveness of the HR practices outlined.

This approach, if applied to international strategies, of course assumes that a German MNC would deliver innovation, for example, in the same way as a Japanese MNC or a British MNC. Chapter 2 has shown that this is unlikely to be the case. However, once the challenge of conducting this kind of research on a wider cross-national population of firms has been undertaken, then it would likely offer a better source of evaluation of IHR contribution than a pure best-practice approach.

Configurational approach

The *configurational* approach again stresses the need for practices that are contingent with organizational circumstances, but in addition emphasizes the need for horizontal or internal fit. This involves developing specific, mutually reinforcing combinations, or "bundles" of practices. Underlying this approach again is resource-based theory (see Chapter 3 for an outline of this thinking), in that the specific "architecture" or culture that binds the HR practices together provides an HR-based source of competitive advantage (Guest, 1997). This approach still assumes that there exists a set of "best HRM practices." Huselid and Becker (1996) in a panel study, provided a partial test by examining the impact of three separate factors which emerged from their factor analysis of a list of HRM practices. They labelled these selection and development, motivation and HR strategy. Delaney and Huselid (1996) however, failed to find a positive impact for combinations of practices as opposed to the total number of HRM practices. The UK-based study conducted by Patterson *et al.* (1998) researched medium-sized manufacturing firms in the UK. They found that HR practices had a greater impact on productivity and profits than a range of other factors including strategy, R & D and quality. This study has been widely quoted in the media as evidence of the importance of HRM as a driver of improved performance.

Before we even get to the question of replicating these studies in a broader set of countries – a task which is slowly being undertaken – there are questions about the validity of the approach as it has been applied to US and UK organizations. Well-intentioned though most in the field believe this work to be, a number of methodological questions as always tend to arise.

One of the problems of all of these approaches is how to measure performance. Most of the studies noted above have measured productivity and quality at plant level, whilst Huselid (1995) and Patterson *et al.* (1998) measured financial criteria at company level. Guest (1997) argues that outcomes that reflect the balanced scorecard approach (detailed later in this chapter) are more appropriate. Critics of these attempts raise doubts about the practicality of being able to tie down such a nebulous concept as the link between often fragmented HR practices and direct organizational performance outcomes. Wright and Gardner (2003) recently brought many of these concerns together, asking questions about which HR practices should be bundled together, the need to factor different strategies into the analysis (see the previous section), an over-reliance on single raters, gross scaling ("yes, we have pay-for-performance"), the reliance on a "black box" between HR practices and organizational performance to explain the linkage, no agreement on the number of boxes that might be involved, and problems in assuming causal direction. Marchington and Grugulis (2000) similarly highlight some of the key methodological problems associated with the use of data sets trying to identify the effect of HRM on performance. Additional criticisms to those listed above include problems in choosing appropriate measures of performance, contamination from other (non-HR) influences and exclusion of hard-to-measure items.

They cite Purcell (1999: 32) who suggests that it is likely that personnel specialists "have detailed knowledge neither of competitive strategies utilized by their organizations nor of the proportion of sales which are derived from these strategies." As a result they urge that caution is exercised when interpreting conclusions from quantitative studies aiming to link HR practices with firm performance. This note of caution was supported in a recent UK-based study attempting to evaluate the relationship between HRM and performance (Guest *et al.*, 2003). The researchers used a sample of 366 UK companies and took a range of objective and subjective performance measures, together with cross-sectional and longitudinal data. Their results showed the complexity of trying to prove causal links between HR practices and resulting organizational performance. When using objective measures of performance, greater use of HRM was associated with lower labor turnover and higher profit per employee but not higher productivity. However, after controlling for previous years' performance, the association ceased to be significant. Using subjective performance estimates, they found a strong association between HRM and both productivity and financial performance. The authors concluded that the study confirmed the association between HRM and performance but failed to show that HRM caused higher performance. When comparing their results to the more positive ones of previous researchers, they attributed the difference to either the choice of measure of HRM, the sample or the context. Context takes on critical importance in any attempt to measure the link between HR practices and organizational performance at an international level.

Cultural limits to assumptions of best practice?

The limitations of both the best practice and organizationally focused contingency and configurational approaches have been debated by many European scholars. They argue that, at an international level, "best practice" is meaningless. Equally, both the configurational and contingency approaches should reflect the need to adapt HR policy and practice to external factors such as culture, ownership structures, labor markets, the role of the state and trade union organization. In Europe, for example, HR policy and practice is highly influenced by the extensive regulatory framework surrounding the employment relationship (Brewster *et al.*, 1996, 2000; Sparrow and Hiltrop, 1994).

We devoted much of Chapter 2 to discussing the relative merits of the universalist versus institutionalist perspective on HRM and in Chapter 5 we considered the nature of HR knowledge that has to be transferred between international HR professionals. Clearly, the comparative HRM approach argues that the notion of best practice is extremely problematic. For example, the set of high performance work practices identified by Pfeffer (1994) reflects the US positioning on Hofstede's framework. The recommendation of self-managed teams, decentralization of decision-making, reduced status distinctions and extensive sharing of financial and performance information all match the relatively low ranking of the US on both the power distance and uncertainty avoidance scales. In contrast, selective hiring and relatively high pay based on performance match a high score for individualism and a relatively high ranking on the need for achievement dimension. Building models of management based on the cultural specificity of that country are not limited to the US and include Germany (Kern and Schumann, 1984), Sweden (Berggren, 1992) and Japan (Ouchi, 1981; Pascale and Athos, 1982).

From a cultural perspective, the "best practice" approach has also been questioned. The issue of the cultural transferability of HR policies and practices has been the subject of intense debate amongst academics for many years (see, for example, Laurent, 1981; Doz and Prahalad, 1981; Schneider, 1989; Sparrow and Hiltrop, 1997; Sparrow, 2000). Cultural frameworks such as Hofstede's (1980) reveal the extent to which countries exhibit very different orientations on aspects such as power distance (the degree to which hierarchy is accepted within organizations); individualism/collectivism; uncertainty avoidance (the need for rules and regulations in organizations) and the desire for material achievement. These differing cultural orientations create multiple interpretations of motivation and general employee workplace behaviors. Table 8.3 outlines complex ways in which cultural value orientation influence rewards behavior and consequently any evaluation of best practice in this area.

More recently, what has become known as the *new cultural paradigm research tradition* has treated cultural dimensions as quasi-individual difference characteristics (Farh *et al.*, 1997; Clugston *et al.*, 2000; Kirkman and Shapiro, 2000; Maznevski *et al.*, 2003). These individual level data show that whilst people can share or endorse a given cultural value or belief there is enough natural variability within a country for it to be treated as an important individual difference (Earley and Mosakowski, 1995). By looking at

Table 8.3 Cultural value orientation influences on rewards behavior

Differences in the attitudes and definitions of what makes an effective employee and the associated competencies in the recruitment training and development systems	Influences the effort put towards, and value of, specific competencies within the labor market
Different styles and attitudes to the giving of face-to-face feedback and associated behaviors in interview, communication, negotiation and participation processes	Influences the extent to which power and influence over rewards issues will be delegated to individual managers
Differences in internal career anchors	Influences the attractiveness of different advancement and mobility patterns within labor markets
Different expectations of the manager–subordinate relationship and their impact on performance management and motivational processes	Influences the perceived validity and attractiveness of performance-related pay systems and incentive programs
Differential concepts of distributive justice, socially healthy pay and the individualization of reward	Sets many of the expectations around the new rewards equation

Source: after Sparrow (2000)

individuals within organizations, it has been shown how cultural variables significantly impact:

- the effect of established antecedents to HRM-related behavior;
- actual preferences for the design and conduct of specific HRM practices; and
- a range of important HRM-related outcomes such as commitment, or job involvement.

Recent work has therefore focused on trying to establish which aspects of rewards behavior are culture-specific (emic) and which are culture-universal (etic). Specifically, this research has helped answer the following questions:

- Which HRM practices are values-free and which can be significantly predicted by values at the *individual level*?
- With what strength of effect do cultural values predict preferences for HR practices?
- What is the causal order of influence?

The question about which HR practices are values-free or can be predicted at the individual level, put practically, is all about what room for maneuver is there for International HR directors? If the *values* of my workforce significantly predict their preference for the nature of HR, then the organization will have a harder job. I can change attitudes to some extent and I can change mindset by communication and education. Values tend to be more resistant to change. The answer to this question is sobering for international HR directors. In a study of over 400 Taiwanese employees at firms such as Tatung, Mitac and Acer, Sparrow and Wu (1998) found that 75 percent of the "menu" of various HR practices suggested by Schuler and Jackson (1987) could be predicted by value orientations. A similar figure was found in a study of Kenyan employees (Nyambegera *et al.*, 2000).

The next question about strength of effect, put simply, is just how important are cultural value orientations really? Even if they predict the desirability of a wide range of HR practices, there are lots of other individual factors that can shape the extent to which employees will find specific HR practices desirable or not. By looking at various demographic factors (age, service, gender, grade) and a range of ways of fitting the person to the organization (see Figure 8.1), studies have shown that an individual's cultural values by themselves explain from 10 to 16 percent of the attractiveness (or not) of various HR practices to them (Sparrow and Wu, 1998; Nyambegera *et al.*, 2000). That is 10 percent of resistance many international HR directors could do without. Similarly, cultural values explained about 19 percent of variance in job involvement (Nyambegera *et al.*, 2001) and 11 percent of variance in commitment (Wu and Sparrow, 2002). To help scale this impact, where employees worked in organizations in which there was a perfect fit between the things they valued in the job and these being satisfied, this only accounted for 6 percent of variation in commitment. Cultural values have about twice as powerful an influence on behavior like commitment than does satisfaction with valued work features.

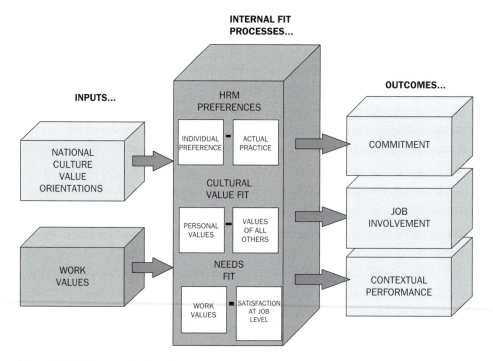

Figure 8.1 Different cultural pathways across antecedents, preferences for and outcomes from HRM
After Sparrow and Wu (1999)

The final and most sophisticated question is about the relative proximity of cultural values to the actual behavior that employees will exhibit, that is, do cultural values *work through* more immediate HR concerns (such as there being a fit between the individual's work goals and their job satisfaction) or do they have a direct (and independent or unmediated) influence?

This question actually gets at two important issues for the international HR director. First, if cultural values are mediated by other more immediate factors, then as an organization I might be able to mollify their influence by working on things like fit between the employee and the organization. If they impact on HRM independently of other factors, however, then I have to cope with the impact that these values will have regardless. The answer to this first question is as yet unclear. A study by Farh *et al.* (1997) found that the impact of cultural values could be mediated whilst a study by Wu and Sparrow (2000) found that cultural values have an independent and direct impact on commitment. A second follow-on question now being asked is "does organizational behavior work in the same way across all countries?" If, for example, US research shows me that perceptions of just procedures lessen the negative impact of downsizing on my US employees, if I create perceptions of just procedures in my Malaysian operations, will they have the same positive effect? In short, do values influence the same outcomes in a similar way across countries? This last question is now forming the basis of much work that will help provide international HR directors with more insight into delivering effective HR in different country contexts.

The above findings confirm that to assume that employees from around the world agree that there are obvious best practices is a little naive, and to expect these HR practices to have exactly the same effect on behaviors in different geographies is misguided.

Studies on the international HR function

Most of the literature examining the link between HRM and organizational performance focuses on HRM practices. However, a critical determinant of whether these practices deliver added value is the overall competence of the HR function. From the CIPD Benchmarking Study of sixty-four organizations (CIPD, 2001; Brewster *et al.*, 2002), it was clear that the majority of international HR directors did not feel that there was much difference between their role and domestic HR in terms of its ability to influence the business agenda. Only 37 percent considered that HRM on an international scale was more influential than on a domestic scale.

Problems of causality attribution, together with highly complex business structures, make this a daunting area of research. Identification of relevant respondents is another sticking point. Who would be appropriate to give meaningful comments on the impact of HR policies and practices throughout a global organization? Should it be HR professionals or line managers and from which locations? For instance, HQ HR professionals may be able to identify key components of policy and practice but may not have the information available to see how it influences at a local level.

Caligiuri and Stroh (1995) used HQ HR professionals as their respondents in a small-scale survey that examined both the relationship between MNCs' global management strategies and resulting IHR practices and the link between these strategies and economic success. Respondents were asked to indicate their overall positioning in terms of global management strategies using the Heenan and Perlmutter (1979) labels; ethnocentric, regiocentric, polycentric and geocentric. The authors argued that various human resource management practices were contingent on the MNC's international management strategy (Kobrin 1988; Adler and Ghadar 1990; Tung and Punnett 1993). Recruitment, selection and socialization were chosen as the HR practices most likely to reflect these differing international strategic orientations. For example, under an ethnocentric HRM perspective, subsidiaries will be staffed with expatriates in key management positions. These organizations will also expect their expatriate managers to transfer headquarters' cultures and philosophy by working with host nationals. In contrast, under a geocentric perspective, positions are staffed worldwide so that the best people are recruited for the positions, regardless of nationality. Since headquarters and the foreign subsidiaries of any geocentric MNC will view themselves as integrated parts of a global organization, the corporate culture will be highly unified – but not necessarily dictated by headquarters (p. 497). The results from the survey supported the hypothesis that HR practices (recruitment, selection and socialization) varied by global strategy. In particular, strategies varied between ethnocentric and geocentric companies, as would be expected. The authors then argued that geocentric MNCs, with their ability to recruit the best talent throughout the world, have a more strategic approach to IHR that would give them competitive advantage.

Efficiency: service level agreements (SLAs)

We noted at the beginning of the chapter that in order to assess the contribution of the International HR function, it is necessary to measure both *efficiency* and *effectiveness*. Effectiveness relates to the extent to which HR policy and practice contributes to the achievement of overall organizational goals. Efficiency looks at the processes by which the HR function achieves these goals. Typical indicators of international HR efficiency could include the ratio of the number of people in the international HR function to the total number of people employed, or full-time equivalents (FTEs); HR costs per FTE; cost per new recruit and so forth.

The need to deliver timely and cost-effective services to clients has become much more of an agenda item for global HR functions. Service-level agreements (SLAs) are increasingly being introduced in order to articulate performance standards at this level. The advantages of using SLAs are that they

- articulate the connection between the global HR function's vision, mission and strategic targets and the way in which it actually operates;
- establish a two-way accountability for service and impose a service management discipline on both parties;

- encourage the service provider to examine its service provision, bringing a sense of clarity to the relationships, support levels and commitments;
- build on the thought process behind total quality management and business process re-engineering by establishing critical levels of service and standardized expectations;
- remove levels of unpredictability and help foster more accurate levels of resource prediction; and
- define clear criteria for service evaluation.

Typically, they concentrate on three types of measures (Ulrich, 1995):

- *Customer value:* e.g., indicators of customer satisfaction with the quality of work conducted from surveys, focus groups, targeted interviews.
- *Cost of HR service:* e.g., productivity measures, overall measures of headcount, support ratios.
- *Cycle time:* e.g., time to transact services, accomplish work, meet key stages within a process.

In Chapter 4 we noted that the new HR operating model at Diageo will be evaluated by SLAs. At Shell this form of evaluation has long been practiced.

Evaluation at Shell People Services

Case Example

Shell People Services (SPS) is the HR Group Service. In 2001 it employed approximately 550 staff worldwide and had service delivery centers in Houston, London, the Hague, Melbourne, Wellington and Kuala Lumpur. With 250 people, the US was SPS's largest base, followed by Europe with around 125 people. The purpose of SPS is to provide common HR services to group companies and to participate in the setting of the Group's HR direction and policies. HR service provision in the past was done internally, supplemented by selective outsourcing. Service Companies provided global policy advice to the HR functions in Business Operating Units. In the early 1990s Shell experimented with Professional Service Units especially in the US. These early shared service attempts, in the IT area, faltered because the services focused too early on external customers ignoring the needs of Shell customers.

In 1998 the company decided to establish an internal shared HR service capability and to learn from its experience in the US. From the beginning this new shared-service initiative was looked upon as a global venture. More extensive outsourcing was not an option for the company because of worries about higher costs and a loss of organizational learning. By January 1999 SPS became a line of business in Shell Services International (SSI). Under SSI the prime importance for SPS was to build up a critical mass, to develop a commercial mindset and to work on their business model. SPS split away from SSI in January 2000 and was set up as a Global Shell Group Service to provide internal HR shared expertise and administrative services.

continued

SPS's mandate was to offer a market or benchmarking based discipline. This gives price transparency to customers. SPS offers its services to Joint Ventures and Shell affiliates where this fits the Shell business strategy. SPS only does business with external customers, charging a market rate, where they see an opportunity to reduce costs to Shell customers (reduced costs can be achieved through an increase in scale) or to bring in unique learning/benchmarking into Shell. The company is governed by Shell's HR Council, with quarterly reviews of performance. SPS's service provision is governed by a Global Framework Understanding signed with each business. This outlines Service Framework Agreements with parts of a business and provides detailed Service Level Agreements for specific areas of service. The organization reports through a Global Leadership Team (GLT) driving services to meet global customer requirements. This team has to continuously seek synergies and "connectivity" in SPS's activity. The services are delivered through a regional structure.

Evaluation of SPS's performance is achieved through a balanced scorecard system. This ensures that the company's services are customer-focused. As a rough proportion, 50 percent of the Scorecard metrics are linked to Group results (which themselves are customer-focused), 30 percent to customer measures, and 20 percent are people and financial metrics. In essence, 80 percent of the measures are aligned to customer needs tapping into how the customer feels and thinks about the services provided.

Service level agreements and the operation of shared services on a global basis can operate against a number of different business models. They might operate on a fully commercial model in which the unit lives or dies purely on the profits that it makes from its activities. This, however, can reduce the level of independence that the international HR function has in pricing its services. Another option is to operate on a full business-cost recovery model. In this mode the shared-service operations or international HR function charge the various constituent businesses at a level to cover their costs, including any investments that they wish to make in people and systems. Clearly, this is a more favorable model. It enables the international HR function to set targets which might give them a realistic chance of coming in below expected costs. When they do so, they can either give the savings back to the business through tariff reductions, credit notes or lump sum payments, or progress to a "profit neutral" position, where they can retain earnings to fund investments agreed with the client businesses.

Effectiveness: evaluating high-impact projects

Perhaps the most important assessment of the contribution of an international HR function is the measurement of effectiveness. In other words, how well does the IHR strategy inform and deliver the organizational objectives? An initial assessment of effectiveness can take the form of examining how well IHR strategy and policy and practices fit with the stated organizational strategy. How well these are implemented is another matter. Implementation can be assessed in a number of ways as can be seen in the following sections. We begin with the evaluation of high-impact projects that are undertaken by the IHR function.

The ability of global HR to deliver major organizational change is a key area of assessment of the effectiveness of the function. Global HR professionals are often engaged in projects which require them to help the organization design the structural, role and capability requirements to support major global business initiatives, such as moving to global lines of business.

The role of the global HR function in BOC Group's change process to pull its North and South Asian businesses into a global line of business (LOB) structure is introduced below. An extremely tight timescale highlighted the need for efficiency as well as effectiveness in delivering the project outcomes. A series of critical success factors was established at BOC by which its global HR intervention would be judged. The case study below demonstrates just why the approach of evaluating the international HR function against the high-impact projects that it is called upon to manage becomes such a central feature of global HRM. This is why we provide full details.

Critical success factors for a global HR organization development implementation at BOC

Case Example

In 2000 BOC embarked on a major change process to put all their North and South-East Asian operations into a global line of business (LOB) structure. The first phase of the proposed restructuring – putting the business units into place – was concluded by October 2002. The second phase – restructuring HR and the enabling service functions – was planned for completion in 2003. BOC used to manage through a standard regional structure. Highly autonomous country managing directors reported to regional directors. Results were collated in these regions and regional directors ran each one with immense autonomy. Four years ago they began a move towards a new business structure based on a global Line of Business model. By late 2001 BOC considered that it had made the transition from being essentially a regionally based organization to one that was structured around global lines of business. The majority of BOC activities fall within three global lines of business:

- Process Gas Solutions
- Industrial and Special Products
- BOC Edwards.

Process Gas Solutions (PGS) has a network of production plants for gases such as oxygen, nitrogen and air separation units serving key customers around the world. Industrial and Special Products (ISP) supplies services and cylinder gases to many businesses and service organizations. BOC Edwards represents about 17 percent of the business by turnover, but is a major source of long-term growth for BOC as it is linked to the semiconductor industry. BOC brought operations together around the whole world under these three LOBs in 1997 except for its activity in fifteen Asian countries. The Asian businesses only started to make

continued

this transition in October 2001 when the business unit heads were first appointed. BOC's reason for not integrating these countries in the initial restructuring was because of the level of economic and business system diversity. However, two geographies within Asia are now being merged into the global line of business structure (Latin America and Eastern European geographies will also eventually be brought into it):

- South-East Asia: e.g., Malaysia, Thailand, Philippines and Indonesia
- North Asia: e.g., China, Hong Kong and South Korea.

South Asia was not included in the initial alignment process but will ultimately be aligned. It was originally planned to include Japanese operations but these plans were superceded when management of BOC's Japanese business transferred to Air Liquide as a result of a merger. These geographies initially had a country-specific profit and loss structure but once the business unit structure was in place they were migrated into the three LOBs across all Asian operations. They moved away from country managers to a more mature matrix structure. BOC foresaw major cultural and HR challenges in doing this.

The challenge faced by the HR function was clear. The HR function had to display considerable insight into the realities of the organization design in order to gain the support of these managers. The people issues were really about the HR process in the broader sense, rather than the HR function itself. HR had to help the business manage the risk of taking out expatriates and putting local people into bigger positions, whilst also supporting the new managers and structures to help them succeed. The Asian organization had not been as "structurally evolved" as other geographic areas. Therefore, the organization capabilities in BOC were derived from "steady, stove-piped and seniority-driven" structures. The managing directors had been the only integrating point within the organization. The new global structure meant that even the country experience and insight of senior managers was not necessarily valuable. They could not apply what they had learned from similar jobs in countries because the jobs were now different. As a result of the LOB structure, those individuals below managing director level would now face real business management exposure, whilst also having global support and development. The country managing directors would slowly let go of control and would be gone within a couple of years. In the meantime, the country managers needed support from the HR function as the coach of new behaviors and as the manager of a wide number of individual transitions. HR acted both as a coach but also as a facilitator to ensure that other people – notably from within the business units – were doing this as well. This meant that the HR role was one of trust builders. They needed to create jobs and give responsibilities to managers that would help them to grow and flourish in a global structure. Paradoxically, it was the creation of global lines of business that had created the drive to enable the HR function to address the people development issues that it had long felt needed to be resolved.

Although several of the processes overlapped, BOC's HR strategy, pursued the following initiatives, in order of their centrality to the strategy over time:

- creating a sense of ownership amongst local management;
- developing a global HR model – identifying the structure in a perfect world and on an in-country basis, driven by the market and customer segmentation within the business;

- capability assessment of the current population of managers in the region, starting with the business unit heads;
- working with communications and values and using them to facilitate change in the region;
- one-to-one education within a cultural change agenda: trust and coaching with senior managers;
- selecting people for the new roles, putting people in place, and transitioning people out from their old roles;
- creation of common role definitions and structures in order to create knowledge transfer; and
- negotiating the gaps in the organization design: mixing and matching global process with local variation, building the design into a practical set of resources.

BOC's global HR professionals were now engaged in projects that required the HR function to help the organization design the structural role and capability requirements that followed on from its adoption of global lines of business.

The function evaluated itself against a range of "project success" metrics, which for BOC were considered as the set of principles that were essential to delivering HR across global lines of business:

- consistent with a global HR model where possible;
- compliant with global HR systems and processes;
- cost effective, with HR delivery against comparative benchmarks;
- able to deliver "best practice" HR functionality;
- able to share learning across Business Units;
- long-term efficiency through the use of HR systems and 'e'-enablement;
- sensitive to statutory and cultural requirements within geographies;
- developing a balance between local talent and home country resources/attraction of new regional HR talent.

Operating to this type of change process is ultimately, however, a matter of trust. In the eyes of the Chief Executive Asia, the change project initiator and sponsor, the final evaluation will be as follows: "The HR function needs to operate as an integral part of the business strategy and development process of the total organization and not have its own agenda. Success will depend on the degree to which HR has facilitated the filling of the new organizations with people who are competent, and provided training and development for them. Leadership needs to come from all managers within the company but HR needs to give the framework against which the organizations can flourish."

Source: Sparrow et al. (2003)

Balanced scorecards and HR scorecards

One direct way in which the effectiveness of both domestically based and international HR functions is assessed is through the balanced scorecard approach. HR lies at the heart of the method. Whilst the financial, internal and customer perspectives identify where the business stands now and where it needs to be in the future, learning and growth identify how it will get there. As we have seen throughout this book, a critical task for both HR and line managers in global organizations is the need to create an organizational infrastructure that empowers people to give their best. Developing people to be able to meet the challenges of the future is also a critical imperative. The discipline of a balanced scorecard approach also reinforces more sophisticated approaches to performance management, which helps align HR outcomes with strategic objectives. An alternative to the use of balanced scorecards is the adoption of high-level performance promises. This was seen, for example, in Diageo. A similar system based on a balanced scorecard approach exists within Ford of Europe.

Performance pledges at Diageo

Case Example

At Diageo, the performance of all businesses is measured against the business strategy, using an instrument called a "performance promise." These promises are written on one page but they create an implicit link between the business strategy and the focus of activity in the function and a metric for establishing whether the function has delivered against these linkages. The performance propositions are based around the linking activities. They identify the key result areas required from each business and the evidence of these particular actions. The promises therefore "bind" a senior leadership team into the strategy. They are backed up by an entrepreneurial reward system and are negotiated with the Diageo Executive Committee. HR is tied into a performance promise along with every other business function.

Source: after Braun *et al.* (2003a)

Recent work by several teams of researchers (Becker *et al.*, 2001; Phillips *et al.*, 2001) has led to the development of HR scorecards as a means of measuring return on investment (ROI) in HR programs. Becker *et al.* (2001) have produced a scorecard that has identification of HR deliverables, the use of the High-Performance Work System, HR system alignment and an HR efficiency measure as essential elements. They do so in order to reflect a balance between what they perceive as the twin HR imperatives of cost control and value creation. Cost control comes through measuring HR efficiency. Value creation comes through measuring HR deliverables.

Perceptions of effectiveness

Whereas the IHR function can set itself stringent performance criteria, true ratings of effectiveness need to come from the key stakeholders, namely employees and line managers in the various operating units throughout the world.

Stroh and Caligiuri (1998) adopted a "best practice" approach in their survey examining the effectiveness of the global HR function in sixty US MNCs. They asked global HR executives as well as managers of non-HR areas and the CEOs /business unit executives of the companies to rate the effectiveness of the HR function on the key delivery areas for global HR, (as ascertained previously through interviews with eighty-four HR executives from the sixty firms). These were split between principles that HR departments should implement on an *organization-wide* basis as follows:

1 position the human resource function as a strategic partner in global business;
2 develop global leadership through developmental cross-cultural assignments;
3 foster the global mindset of all employees through training and development;
4 implement formal systems that improve worldwide communication;
5 design and implement an IHR information system (HRIS);

and those that should be implemented within the *human resources function*:

1 ensure flexibility in all human resource programs and processes;
2 develop relationships with international HR counterparts to encourage information exchange;
3 have ability to express the relative worth of human resource programs in terms of their bottom-line contribution to the organization;
4 have ability to market HR globally as a source of strategic advantage;
5 encourage the relinquishing of domestic HR power to worldwide HR structure.

The survey findings demonstrated that the global HR executives and the CEO/business unit executives rated the global HR function relatively high, while the executives in the other functional areas rated its effectiveness somewhat low. The relationship between the effectiveness of the global HR function and firm performance was also examined through the development of a composite MNC Success Index of economic variables (return on capital, sales growth, return on equity, profit margin). This showed that three factors were related to bottom-line organizational performance measures. These were as follows:

1 developing global leadership through cross-cultural assignments;
2 making human resources a strategic partner in global business;
3 ensuring flexibility in all human resource programs and processes.

Whilst this is an interesting study, the limitations of the research include a lack of consideration of cross-cultural differences in perception (a problem faced by all evaluation techniques other than detailed 360-degree approaches), the lack of detail of actual HR practices and the extent to which these are localized or standardized in each subsidiary and an assumption of the universality of the "best practice" approach.

The CIPD survey of global HR directors in sixty-four MNCs (CIPD, 2001; Brewster *et al.*, 2002) addressed the issue of collecting more detail on HR practices and making an assessment of localization versus standardization (see, for example, Figure 3.2). It measured several different elements to assess the extent to which global HR functions were working as effective business partners. The elements measured were the link between business strategy and HR strategy and the key delivery areas. As outlined in Chapter 3, the findings revealed a close link between business strategy and HR strategy in the following areas:

- maximizing shareholder value
- creating core business processes
- building a global presence
- forging strategic partnerships.

There was also a close match between organizational and HR approaches in the variety of methods used to deliver global business strategies. The respondents were asked to rate the same key delivery areas as in the Stroh and Caligiuri (1998) study in terms of their importance for global HR effectiveness. We showed the factors that were considered to be the most important for the HR function to be effective at the global level in Table 3.2. In contrast to Stroh and Caligiuri's (1998) findings, where US companies reported this as their main motivation, our CIPD survey found that "developing global leadership through cross-cultural assignments" was seen to be important by only 30 percent of organizations.

Measuring the value of international assignments

Despite the expanding range of activity associated with IHR functions as organizations continue with their efforts to globalize HRM, one of the critical success factors for a global HR function remains the management of international assignments. Most organizations focus on ways of reducing the cost of international assignments and increasing the efficiency of administration. To deliver true effectiveness, however, organizations need to adopt a more sophisticated approach to assessing the overall contribution of an international assignment. The need to link objectives of international assignments and the profile of international workers with the strategic objectives of the organization has already been discussed in Chapter 7. Assessing the value of an international assignment constitutes another piece of the effectiveness mosaic.

Adopting a metrics-based approach, international assignments are seen as a value generation process, which contributes to the company's business performance improvement (Schiuma et al., 2002). As already noted in Chapter 7 international assignees are usually sent abroad for one of five main strategic reasons as follows: professional development; knowledge transfer; transfer of scarce skills; control; coordination. Each of these strategic reasons can add value to the organization in terms of either financial value or knowledge value (Edvinsson and Malone, 1997; Roos et al., 1997; Sveiby, 1997; Marr and Schiuma, 2001).

Figure 8.2 summarizes the framework. Financial value refers to the overall organization's assets that can be easily expressed in monetary terms. Knowledge value, on the other hand, includes all the company's intangible assets. Financial value can be split into two categories: monetary value and physical infrastructure. The former involves all financial

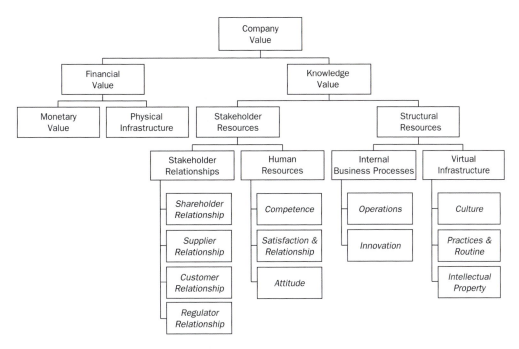

Figure 8.2 The expatriate value-added map
Source: Schiuma *et al.* 2002

values generated by the company. The latter corresponds to the value related to the overall tangible assets of an organization.

Knowledge value can also be split into two categories:

- stakeholder resources and
- structural resources.

Stakeholder resources are divided into stakeholder relationships and human resources. The first category identifies all external actors of a company. It is further subdivided into shareholder, customer, supplier and regulator relationships. The second category represents the internal actors of a company, that is, the employees and the assignees.

Structural resources are split into internal business processes and intangible infrastructure. The former refers to all values generated within the company in the form of performance improvement of the operations and of the innovation processes, related for example to both product development and research and development.

Intangible infrastructure represents the value related to the overall organizational intangible structure components of an organization. It is further subdivided into culture, routines and practices and intellectual property. Culture embraces corporate culture and management philosophies. Some important components are the organization's values, the networking practices of employees as well as the set of mission goals. Practices and routines include internal practices, virtual networks and routines, that is, tacit rules and procedures. Some key components are process manuals providing codified procedures and rules, databases, tacit rules of behavior as well as management style. Intellectual property is the sum of patents, copyrights, trademarks, brands, registered design, trade secrets and processes whose ownership is granted to the company by law.

Using this framework, a matrix can be derived which allows managers to plot where the value will be delivered for each assignment and also, the exact nature of the value to be delivered (see Figure 8.3).

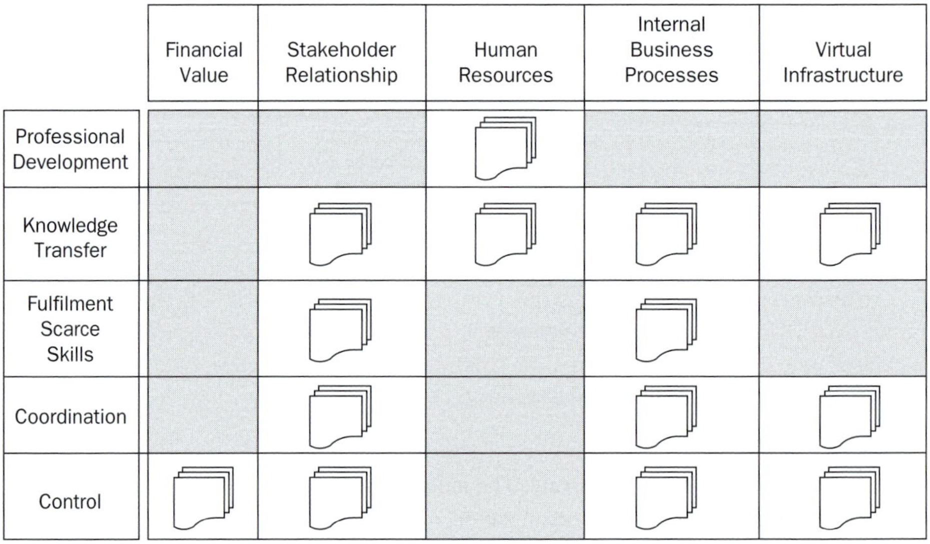

	Financial Value	Stakeholder Relationship	Human Resources	Internal Business Processes	Virtual Infrastructure
Professional Development			🗎		
Knowledge Transfer		🗎	🗎	🗎	🗎
Fulfilment Scarce Skills		🗎		🗎	
Coordination		🗎		🗎	🗎
Control	🗎	🗎		🗎	🗎

Figure 8.3 Matrix of the direct value-added contribution of an international assignment

For example, if an assignment is to be used primarily for knowledge transfer, this could be seen to deliver direct value to customers or suppliers and sometimes to regulators. It will also deliver direct value in the area of human resources in relation to employees. Improvement of internal business processes could also be seen as a direct value-added outcome, as would the more informal aspects of knowledge transfer, such as corporate culture transfer, within the virtual infrastructure box.

It should be pointed out, however, that the definition of these sorts of metrics requires considerable time and effort on the part of managers. A major issue for organizations will be whether these metrics can be operationalized and over what timescale: if, for example, the organization is using international working to develop a cadre of knowledgeable and internationally minded executives, at what point are the measures applied? It remains to be seen whether organizations will adopt the discipline of developing metrics in an area that is noticeable for its lack of sophistication in planning and measurement.

Audits for strategic aspects of global HRM

The need to combine both measures of efficiency and effectiveness is reinforced by Ulrich's (1997) multiple-role model for human resources, noted in Chapter 9 (see Figure 9.3). Florkowski and Schuler (1994) also combine measures of efficiency and effectiveness in their views of what a strategic audit of IHRM should include. In addition, they call for the need to examine both external and internal processes as shown in Figure 8.4.

External benchmarking includes examining the best practices of competitors in terms of HR from the perspective of both internal market structures and external market linkages. Items here would include the nationality mix of the board of directors, local and HQ HR systems linkages, use of international assignments and so forth. A strategic fit audit investigates whether international HRM policies collectively promote the cluster of behaviors dictated by an MNC's strategy. Key contingency factors in this area include the life stage of the MNC, the impact of national culture and the legal environment, all of which have been extensively discussed in this module.

Internal HRM audits have to take into account key stakeholders' interests, such as the MNC headquarters and host-country management, and external stakeholders, such as host governments and investors. Other issues for audit include the extent to which international HRM policies strengthen inter-unit linkages and support the strategic goals of overseas units. Key factors here are the international assignee staffing mix, universality and flexibility of strategic performance measures; global orientation of management development activities and unit-level alignments of HRM practices and competitive

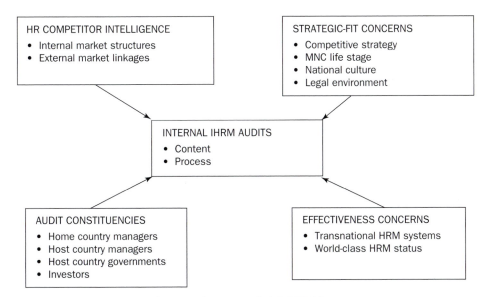

Figure 8.4 Designing audits for strategic aspects of global HRM
Source: Florkowski and Schuler (1994: 833)

strategy. Finally, as with the domestic literature on measuring the effectiveness of the HR function, the authors note the need to focus on capability of the international HR team to deliver global HRM initiatives that are transnational in scope, representation and process. Such an audit might include the characteristics identified by Schuler *et al.* (1993) that generally equate with "world-class" HRM departments as follows:

- extent of the global HRM function's inclusion in key business issues – both formulation and implementation;
- extent to which home management views HRM and organization issues as critical in strategy implementation;
- having a structure, organization and operation for global HRM activities that serve the strategic needs of the business and its individual units;
- facilitating or being capable of facilitating, major organizational change through the global HRM function;
- having competent, adaptive and flexible global HRM staff; and
- extent to which global HRM activities are being evaluated for value-added.

Diagnosing global HR positioning

As a result of our CIPD study (Brewster *et al.*, 2002), three key diagnostic frameworks were developed to allow global HR professionals (and other interested managers in the organization), to audit their current level of globalization and competence for delivering a global HR strategy. These frameworks include the following:

- the stage that the organization has reached in terms of the *Model of Processes Globalizing HRM* developed in Chapter 3 (set against the HR enablers, HR processes and global themes and organizational capability outcomes shown in Figure 3.3);
- the positioning of the organization on the three main roles of global HR professionals (these roles are outlined in the next chapter and shown in Figure 9.2); and
- an evaluation of the effectiveness of the global HR function.

Box 8.3 Key evaluation questions for the corporate HR function

1 *Stage reached on the Model of Processes Globalizing HRM*
   - How is the global HR function configured in order to maximize cost reductions and to provide the most efficient service delivery?
   - To what extent is it seen to be a knowledge management champion, not only for the HR function, but also as a support for broader organizational knowledge sharing?

2 *Positioning on the three main roles of global HR professionals*
- What percentage of HR resources are currently allocated to each of the three main roles?
- Is this the best model to deliver organizational capability in the most cost effective manner?

3 *Where does the global HR function fit on the model of Global HR?*

Probably the most effective way of assessing whether the HR function is delivering a truly global service is to ask its internal and external clients. Using a 360-degree approach, the function can be plotted against the following criteria:

- *Strategic Business Partner:* e.g., is the corporate HR function always a part of the organization's strategic planning team?
- *Networks:* e.g., to what extent has the corporate HR function developed networks with line managers in all countries in which the organization operates?
- *Competencies of global HR professionals:* e.g., what language skills do global HR professionals possess?
- *Cost benefit:* e.g., to what extent does the corporate HR function positively contribute to the bottom line of the organization?
- *Organizational relevance:* e.g., to what extent does the corporate HR function play a critical role in the development of the organization's values, mission and business planning?

© Brewster, Harris and Sparrow: Survey of Effectiveness of Corporate HR Function

We would argue that effectiveness should also be assessed through the 360-degree feedback techniques suggested above. Ultimately, this is the only way that cross-cultural differences in perception can be accommodated, let alone cross-functional perceptions. Such feedback, however, needs to ask clients to assess the performance of the HR function in all its major activities along various dimensions such as:

- effectiveness of service delivery
- insight into local market conditions
- relevance of policy
- quality of advice.

Using diagnostic techniques such as those outlined above will allow organizations to evaluate the reality of their current level of globalization within the HR function and identify the critical areas to address to move to their desired state.

Conclusion

It is apparent from the discussions in this chapter that there is no easy route to measuring the contribution of HRM, either at a domestic or particularly at an international level. Two distinct approaches were considered. The first examined attempts to prove a link between people management practices and organizational performance. From an international perspective, the need to take into account the impact of differing social, cultural, legal, political and economic contexts cautions against the acceptance of the universalist philosophy of both the best practice and configurational schools of thought. This chapter calls for a clear delineation of the impact of internal and external variables in studies of the impact of HRM on organizational performance. The second approach focused on methods of evaluation of the contribution of the HR function itself. The contextual nature of most of the methods to assess performance in this area helps prevent the problems associated with the universalistic approach but, once again, the criticality of taking into account the perspective of different stakeholders within an international context is highlighted. Despite the complexity inherent in this area, it is clear that organizations are requiring ever more explicit statements of the exact nature of the contribution of the global HRM function – a requirement that will push both the research agenda and practical organizational initiatives forward.

Developing global HR professionals

Introduction

We believe that we have covered much ground in this book and have shown the complex issues that face most IHR professionals. We began by defining what is meant by globalization and examining the debate surrounding its impact. We demonstrated that a universalist perspective within the field of IHRM is not appropriate. The field has to operate currently across highly nationalized contexts. Nonetheless, changes are afoot. We examined our survey data and developed a model of the processes involved in globalizing HRM. We analyzed the effect that technology is having on the delivery of HR services on a global basis through shared service models, e-enablement of HR and a series of other technical developments. Our review of the impact of technology and the automation of much of the transactional activity of HR professionals alongside shared service models highlighted a significant challenge, which is the need to re-professionalize the HR function. Moreover, we argued that this process has to happen within a fairly short time span. We then considered the challenges of global knowledge management and knowledge transfer within the IHR function, through such things as the role of expatriates, IJVs and mergers and acquisitions. We also considered the nature of HR knowledge that needs to be transferred from one IHR professional to another and concentrated on the role of global expertise networks and the development of centers of excellence within the HR community. We have considered a series of global themes that in practice have been used to provide a degree of consistency to organizations' people management worldwide through the use of global competencies or capabilities, initiatives in the area of employer branding, and talent management. We have addressed the pervasive problem of fostering heightened levels of international mobility and the need to manage the implications for individuals of various forms of mobility, including short-term and commuter assignments and frequent flying. Yet in delivering all of this, we have shown that IHR functions are under tight cost control and need to deliver strategically-relevant HR services. The evaluation of their function has become a central concern. So, what does all this mean for IHR professionals? In this last chapter we turn back to the IHR community and consider the challenges for their own development. We address a number of questions:

- What are the roles that they must now fulfil?
- What skills and competencies are coming to the fore?
- What are firms doing about the need to develop the global competence of their HR community?

The effects of globalization on HR roles and professionalism in HRM

What is the nature of professionalism in global HRM? To answer that question we have first to define the meaning of professionalism in HRM generally. We also need to understand the roles that HR specialists play in global HRM and the implications for their competencies. These issues form the framework of this chapter.

Losey (1997: 147), speaking as an official of the Society for Human Resource Management (SHRM – the personnel management association in the USA), stated, boldly, that "human resource management is a profession." This, he said, is because HRM has an established body of knowledge that can be taught, learned and tested and there is an ethical code of conduct. However, other US commentators, Ulrich and Eichinger (1998: 1), argued the following year that "HR must become more professional." It has not, in their view, reached that status yet; further study needs to be conducted into the body of knowledge that defines the discipline and into the definition and gaining of competencies. Ulrich (1997) also makes the point that the future of the HR profession lies in the definition of essential competencies and clear roles for practitioners. Gibb (1994) in the UK includes the requirement to be certified in order to practice as part of the definition of professionalism.

This is not uncontentious. Walker (1988) argued that HR people should stop conceptualizing their role as a professional, individual contributor and conceive their job more as providing organizations with leadership on HRM issues. Similarly, Boyatzis, being interviewed by Yeung (1996), states that HR practitioners have been trying to create a sense of being a profession since the 1960s, but that this is ultimately a damaging process, stifling creativity and innovation in the field. In a survey carried out by the Institute of Personnel Management in New Zealand, it is also argued that "it is irrelevant whether HR is a profession: what matters is whether HR practitioners behave in a professional manner" (Pajo and Cleland, 1997: 5).

The debate seems to be, in part, between different visions of professionalism (see, for example, Millerson, 1964; Johnson, 1972; Watson, 1977). If we look at the broader professionalization literature, we can see the importance of an expert body of knowledge and academic field to define the parameters of a profession (Abbott, 1988; Lounsbury, 2002). The role of the professional body is also instrumental in further enhancing professionalization of a field (Tolbert, 1991; Schneiberg, 1999), as well as creating and reproducing shared meanings (Greenwood et al., 2002). Van Hoy (1993: 90) highlights the fact that "the regulation of practitioners for the protection of the public is one of the most important functions professional associations claim to provide." In comparison to the debate around the characteristics of HR as a profession, it is suggested that: "professional communities such as law and accounting are highly organized as communities – association membership may be mandatory, association participation is extensive, and formal interaction and communication are highly developed" (Greenwood *et al.*, 2002: 74).

There is a dichotomy here for HR: if HRM is a profession, then its members should, like doctors and lawyers, serve an ideal of their role which may lead them to refuse to do what their employer wishes (the disclosure of privileged information, for example). If HRM practitioners see serving the interests of the employer as the only key to their role, then it is difficult to see HR as a profession. Of course, in most cases the two interests will not be incompatible, any more than they are for other professions, but it is the possibility of incompatibility that helps to define a profession.

Exploring the definitions presented above, the professionalism of HRM can be summarized as requiring the following traits:

- a community with a strong sense of identity;
- common standards of entry and performance and an ethical code of conduct;
- a distinct body of knowledge and a set of core competencies; and
- a requirement for training and certification.

This is an arena open to further conceptual and empirical research; in particular, to establish validity on an international scale. To date there has been limited empirical work on the role played by professional associations (Greenwood *et al.*, 2002; Van Hoy, 1993), particularly in relation to personnel management or HRM. Nevertheless, it is clear that the national personnel management associations are in a prime position to influence the professionalism of HR practitioners, regulating standards, education, training and certification (Johnson, 1972; Millerson, 1964). Whether they do so or not is a question that Brewster *et al.* (2000a, 2000b) attempted to answer on the basis of a survey of member associations of the World Federation of Personnel Management Associations by assessing current practice. We look now at each of the four traits noted above.

Professional community and sense of identity

One means of assessing the extent to which there is a sense of community is to examine evidence of HR practitioners' career paths. The longer individuals choose to remain within a work domain and the more often the senior specialists are drawn from current practitioners, the more that domain can be classed as a profession. Longer service and the restriction of senior positions to those with training and experience imply that the body of knowledge grows, and the sense of identity and distinctiveness increases. One study across Europe shows that senior HR practitioners have a mean of 13 years of experience (Brewster *et al.*, 2001). The same study also shows that over three-quarters of these senior HR managers have been HR specialists for a minimum of 5 years. By way of a further example, in the UK, over six out of ten employment relations' specialists have been in post for more than 10 years (Millward *et al.*, 2000).

Against the criteria of "professionalism," how does HRM around the world measure up (strictly, we should still also use the term "personnel management" here)? The World Federation of Personnel Management Associations has fifty-one member associations around the globe, and in the majority of countries there are additional personnel management associations representing HR specialists. The member associations are established organizations, largely employing staff rather than operating on a voluntary basis. Although the associations vary greatly in size, there are common features. Particularly, in general they have a mixture of individual and organizational membership statuses based on limited established criteria. Along with the evidence from studies of long-term careers in HR, this implies that HR practitioners do have a sense of common identity and a desire to be a part of a professional community. The professional associations are facilitating this identity and providing a framework for practitioners to come together under a single functional umbrella body. The professional bodies are also advocates for encouraging a highly qualified practitioner community, as we can see from their perception of the importance of practitioners holding a degree and a specialist HR qualification.

Common standards and codes of conduct

Standards of entry into the profession can be gauged by examining who is recruited to senior or other specialist HR positions. Across Europe, around six out of ten senior HR managers are recruited from amongst HRM specialists, either from internal or external sources (Brewster *et al.*, 2001). In New Zealand, a similar picture can be found, but it highlights the phenomenon that HR people having started their career in HRM is greatest amongst younger practitioners, indicating a changing trend over time (Pajo and Cleland, 1997). Despite the general trend of prolonged periods of time as HR specialists, and recruitment of HR practitioners being made mainly from those with HRM experience, it remains the case that in Europe HR directors and senior specialists are not exclusively promoted from within. Over three in ten are still appointed from outside the profession (Brewster *et al.*, 2001). The career paths of senior HR specialists are not uniform among countries. For example, HR specialists in the Philippines come from and move on into different management functions (PMAP, 1998).

In practice, associations have few restrictions on becoming a member. Many, though not all, are keen to have the largest possible membership, and then to divide their members into different categories according to achievements, status and location. This implies a lack of criteria for entry into professional membership; however, in order to achieve a specific category of membership, increasingly demanding standards are applied. These standards are not comparable across national boundaries due to differences in education and qualification systems in different countries.

The production of professional guidelines and standards on HRM activities is widespread across the world's personnel management associations, and covers the whole spectrum of HRM activities. However, a few areas of HRM are not covered by guidelines in some countries, which may indicate some gaps in the setting of standards. More significantly, although many guidelines are published, there is little follow-through in terms of performance management of members. Penalties for non-compliance with guidelines are very rare, and requirements for people to undergo a process of recertification once they have passed their initial examinations are few. Most countries have more than one personnel management association covering similar if not the same interests, so it is possible that standards for entry and performance vary within as well as between national contexts.

As with guidelines on general HR activities, the associations are enthusiastic publishers of codes of ethical conduct for their members, which is another indicator of the will to develop professionalism in HRM standards. However, again, few penalties are imposed for non-compliance. As noted earlier, criteria for entering the HR occupation vary greatly between organizations and between countries, reducing any potential for regulation. Professional associations cannot therefore be considered as true guardians of the occupation, preventing misconduct of practitioners in the public domain. Although they may have aspirations towards this end, the lack of performance management is indicative of the more relaxed approach being adopted in practice.

Body of knowledge and core competencies

The trait of professionalism that receives the greatest attention in the literature concerns the notion of a core set of competencies emanating from a generic body of knowledge. Again, an analysis of HRM competencies requires careful definition because of the considerable variance in the use of the terminology in the literature. For the purpose of this book, the numerous definitions of competency can be summarized effectively as a collection of technical and cultural capabilities (Brockbank, 1997).

A number of studies have already been carried out around the world to try to build a conceptual framework of HRM competencies within various single nations (Walker, 1988; Laabs, 1996; Lawson and Limbrick, 1996; Schoonover, 1998; Csoka and Hackett, 1998; Heneman *et al.*, 1998). These also include work done by companies and personnel management associations in a number of countries.

The roles of HR practitioners have also been extensively discussed in the literature and in textbooks of HRM (see, for example, Schuler and Huber, 1993; Purcell, 1995), with the emphasis on the extent to which these roles are changing due to both internal and external pressures such as lowering costs, enhancing quality, facilitating change and creating stronger business links (Bell *et al.*, 1999; Ulrich, 1997). This is affecting both the technical and strategic competency requirements of HR practitioners.

However, in defining HRM competencies, the specific job roles of HR practitioners may lead to variations in the nature or degree of the competencies required (Yeung, 1996). Irrespective of job role or job title, however, Ulrich *et al.* (1995: 487) argue that the elements of competence remain in the same order of importance, with any variation manifesting itself in weighting alone.

Education and training provision by associations is very wide-ranging, with courses and conferences that are well established and well attended in many countries. These courses and events cover very similar topics across national boundaries, reinforcing the idea that there is a generic body of knowledge and a core set of competencies from which all countries are drawing. This evidence is also supported by academic and practitioner literature. The body of knowledge is based on the principles of HRM, and covers personal, organizational, managerial and technical skills and knowledge sets, as identified in previous studies. The academic field of HRM is also widely accepted in universities globally. This is one of the least disputed traits of the professionalism of HRM.

Requirement for training and certification

As an example of practice in the early 1990s, in seven countries across Europe, only around one quarter of senior HR managers had specific HRM qualifications and/or was a member of their country's professional association (Brewster *et al.*, 2001). This would indicate that a need to be certified is not universal. In addition, many HRM activities can be implemented either by HRM specialists or by line managers, provided the individuals have the appropriate level of competence, or indeed through the use of information technology or outsourcing arrangements (Ulrich, 1997). On average across Europe, around a quarter of organizations have increased responsibilities of line management for HRM (Brewster *et al.*, 2001; Holt *et al.*, 2003). This should influence any analysis of future competency needs of HR practitioners.

Looking at the certification processes of the national personnel management associations, Wiley (1999) compared three major associations, in the UK, USA and Canada. She found similarities in the key criteria of stakeholders to the certification process across all three nations, but a large degree of variation in the way in which certification programs were established and implemented. Gray (1999) also considered the issue of certification in his study of HRD practitioners in New Zealand. He found both a lack of definition of common standards within the profession and a lack of nationally recognized qualifications for training HR practitioner trainers.

One of the most discriminating criterion of a profession is the need to be trained and certified in order to practice. The findings show that although there is a perceived need to be qualified in HRM in certain countries or more specifically, certain organizations, this is not a mandatory requirement in any country (with the exception of certain aspects of the role in some Canadian provinces). The need for a qualification in order to practice is not, for example, comparable to that in the medical, law or accounting professions.

The extent of certification amongst HR practitioners, who may or may not be association members, has also been shown to be limited.

There is a lack of empirical evidence in the literature of any variance in the effectiveness of certified and non-certified HR practitioners in the workplace. Indeed, in the USA, organizations are discouraged from stating that an HRM qualification is required in job advertisements, as it has not yet been proven to be a requirement related to performance and hence might fall foul of discrimination legislation. In short, HR as a profession falls at the hurdle of mandatory status, although in some instances this is actively being sought. For example, in the UK, the former Institute of Personnel and Development is now known as the Chartered Institute of Personnel and Development as steps have been taken to increase the expectations that HR practitioners are certified in order to practice.

Overall, then, many of the generic criteria for HRM to be classed as a professional occupation are being met on a global scale. The defined and established body of knowledge is being constructed. Professional associations exist which are keen to provide practitioners with education, training, guidelines for practice and codes of conduct for their activities. The areas of weakness center primarily on common standards of entry and performance in the profession, and a lack of requirement to be certified in the field.

Professionalism of global HRM?

If the jury is out on the question of HRM professionalism in general, what is the story on the professionalism of global HRM? Are there different requirements here? We noted in Chapter 1 that some of the early models of IHRM focused on the role of MNCs and argued that finding and nurturing the people able to implement international strategy is critical for such firms. IHRM was considered to have the same main dimensions as HRM in a national context but to operate on a larger scale, with more complex strategic considerations, more complex coordination and control demands and some additional HR functions. Additional HR functions were considered necessary to accommodate the need for greater operating unit diversity, more external stakeholder influence, higher levels of risk exposure and more personal insight into employee's lives and family situation (Dowling *et al.*, 1999). Their research focused on understanding those HR functions that changed when the firm went international and began to identify important contingencies that influenced the HR function as it became international. These included the following:

- the country that the MNC operated in
- the size and life cycle stage of the firm
- the type of employee.

The differences between domestic and IHRM have also been key issues for a number of authors, such as Morgan (1986), Dowling (1988), Adler and Bartholomew (1992) and Sundaram and Black (1992). These texts generally indicate the greater complexity and strategic importance of the international role. However, IHR professionals may be deemed "international" on a variety of bases. They may be involved in international work:

1 in the sense that the ownership of their employing firm is based outside their own country, so that they are reporting internationally;
2 because of the geographical coverage required from their own role ("HR Europe" or "HR Asia Pacific" for example);
3 because of the need for an international knowledge base in certain HR activities and topics; or
4 through an increasing internationalization of their client base (which indirectly requires them to be internationally aware).

We carried out a web-based questionnaire run in early 2001 covering HR specialists from all these international arenas. As noted in Chapter 1, it was a random sample of 732 HR practitioners from the UK whose organizations employed, in total, 2.4 million staff. Survey items covered: the HR functions engaged in domestically, internationally, or both; geographical boundaries to the role; type of employees covered by their role; and a series of demographic items about the employing organization. The main question we tried to address here was: Which functional activities in HR have more people with an international element involved in their role and their knowledge base?

Clearly, some HR functions are populated with professionals with higher levels of international role activity as shown in Figure 9.1. Communication, recruitment, pay, training, performance management and culture change functions were far more likely to be carried out by professionals on an international basis. There is an obvious logic here. In these cases the pressures on the organization to be as effective as possible across the whole of their operations is clear.

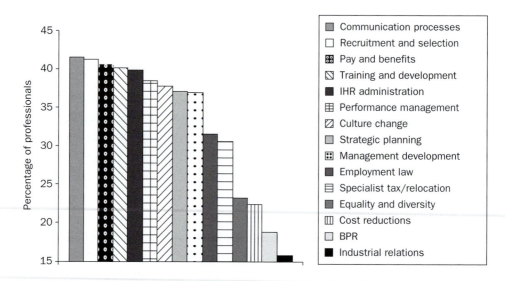

Figure 9.1 Internationalization of specific HR functions as engaged in by HR professionals

On the other hand, HR activity associated with equality and diversity, cost reductions, process re-engineering and employee voice activity associated with industrial relations were far more frequently domestic affairs. Again, some of the logic is obvious: there are, for example, in different countries very different trade union and regulatory regimes relating to the opportunities employees are given to have their voice heard in strategic issues within the organization. Some of this is less clear. Arguably issues such as equality and diversity, or cost reduction, are crucial policies at a worldwide level for international organizations. There are certainly different aspects of equality and diversity that come into play in international as opposed to domestic organizations. Furthermore, as we have shown elsewhere in this book, the drive for cost-reduction remains a key driver of global HRM. It may be that what we see here reflects no more than that the majority of operators in the IHRM field – still dominated by the management of international transferees – have not yet adjusted to the demands that are increasingly being placed upon them.

Some of the explanation for the tendency to think domestically on cost-reduction may be explained by the greater proportion of costs, and the greater visibility, of the home country operation. This still sits oddly with the need to deliver global business strategies in the most cost efficient manner possible identified in our survey of major international organizations and our case studies. This is not to be confused with "cheapest possible" – although it sometimes feels that way – because many of the firms we saw are making substantial investments in getting things right. But they are assessing their activities to cut out duplication and waste, to ensure added value and to move from purely *transactional* work, which can often be delivered directly by new technology towards those activities that deal with *capability* and *business development*. There is an increased interest in an organization's ability to measure the output of the HR function, reflecting the need to be able to deliver cost reductions and ensure HR affordability.

The substantial attention paid to communications in the role of the IHR specialist may be connected to the increased focus on knowledge management. So far, largely perhaps because much of this debate has been driven by the technical specialists, the possibilities of global HRM as the process which adds to and helps exploit the knowledge stock, and particularly the powerful intrinsic knowledge stock, have not been fully developed. But changes are happening. This is putting pressure on company intranets and on the technology, but the HR function also has to grapple with the intrinsic knowledge held in people's heads that is often the key to competitive advantage. Hence, HR departments are taking on responsibility for the conscious development of operating networks, both as practitioners within the HR community and as facilitators elsewhere in the organization.

As we noted in Chapter 4, the e-enablement of HRM has formed part of the response to these joint pressures and the pursuit of better ways to do things. A key challenge facing HRM is new information and communication technology. This applies across the board, but the impact on HRM in globally operating organizations could be immense. Many of those we spoke to had started down this path: none felt they were anywhere other than at the beginning of it; but most realized that it would change dramatically what HRM could do. The ability to get HRM information to and from, and support onto, line managers' desks without a formal HRM intervention opens up new possibilities, allowing HR to focus on its capability and business development roles. The e-enablement of HR is being engineered on a global basis. Organizations such as Diageo and Rolls-Royce find that they have different systems and software packages in many business functions – HR included. Over time these systems will have to integrate, often within the guise of centralized business services. Organizations such as Ford and Shell have global e-enablement programs, with their HR Online and Galaxy initiatives respectively.

Roles for global HR professionals

In order to identify whether there was a discernable pattern to this differential international role activity across the fifteen HR functions/role activities noted in Figure 9.1, we conducted an exploratory factor analysis.[1] The activities of the international experts fell into three main categories, as shown in Figure 9.2.

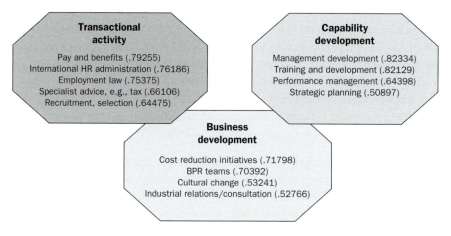

"In which of the following HR activities are you involved?" Items shown in order of item loading

Figure 9.2 Three dimensions to HR professionals' role activities

Figure 9.2 shows that the IHR roles fell into three (broadly equal) categories. The first category – *transactional activities* – are essentially those required for the administration of expatriate programs and packages (see Chapter 4 for an outline of transactional work). This might be thought of as the most traditional set of activities, although they only account for around a third of the items. Whilst we found little evidence in our case studies of any substantial move to outsource these functions, there was not only a widespread belief that they could be substantially streamlined through the use of information and communications technology, but several of the companies were investing heavily in making that happen.

The second and third categories indicate the way that the function is moving. *Capability development* encompasses in the international arena those activities that might be thought of as fulfilling the standard stock-in-trade of strategic HRM. This view has been expressed recently by Scullion and Starkey (2000: 1064): "the main role for corporate HR in the international firm concerns the management of senior managers and high-potential people who are identified as strategic human resources and seen as vital to the company's future and survival."

Other authors (see, for example, Sisson and Scullion 1985; Pucik, 1992; Hendry 1993; Margison *et al.*, 1993) have also emphasized the importance for strategic HRM of a focus on senior management planning and development. Against this received wisdom, however, there is already evidence here – as we have reported from other elements of our research, that the role of the global HRM specialist is becoming wider and more significant than this. Thus, this capability development role also includes wider training and development and performance management elements as applied to a global workforce.

The third category – *business development* – is in many ways the most interesting, focusing as it does directly upon this wider role. At first glance the elements of this role may seem an odd mixture, but a moment's thought shows the coherence of it. The cost reduction and business re-engineering elements are concerned with linking HRM activities as tightly as possible to the development of the organization. That is intrinsically inter-related to cultural change – and by extension to consultation with staff and, in many countries, that will include negotiations with trade unions.

These categories have considerable similarity with other modern outlines of potential HR roles such as that proposed by Ulrich (1997). Ulrich's model (see Figure 9.3) and questionnaire can be used at an international level; however, care needs to be exercised in defining the scope of responsibility for each HR professional's role.

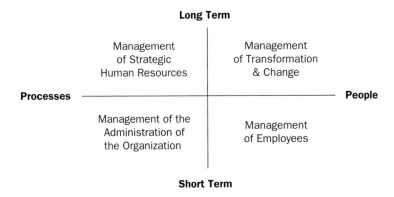

Figure 9.3 Ulrich's HR roles in building a competitive organization
Source: Ulrich (1997)

We have noted throughout this book that trends of globalization, market liberalization, deregulation and technical evolution are restructuring global markets and challenging traditional approaches to gaining competitive advantage (Hamel, 2000). Only the possession of specific capabilities and resources enables organizations to conceive and then implement global strategies. In order to make this diffuse concept of organizational capability more recognizable, Ulrich (2000) described the collection of attributes that it involves in terms of a series of *important outcomes that result from their existence*. The role of the HR professional is, it is argued, to help clarify these organizational capabilities and to craft the HR investments that are necessary to build them. Below, we summarize some of the outcomes articulated by Ulrich (2000) and some of the parallels and more detailed specifications of these in the context of global HR functions.

Box 9.1 How is organizational capability evidenced?

HR strategy writers find it easier to say what organizational capability looks like, rather than define exactly what it is. The following formula has become a commonplace explanation of capability in HR strategy:

- *Being able to move with speed and agility* into a new market in order to be the firm that sets the rules and then controls the future changes to these rules (in HR terms removing bureaucratic processes, establishing clarity of governance to enable rapid decision-making, building safeguarding disciplines into the organizational thought process and removing vestiges of old ways of doing things). We saw in Chapter 3 the importance of building rapid capability to organizations, and have seen practical examples of this requirement through various case studies such as Stepstone and Rolls-Royce.
- *Creating a brand for the firm*, such that its reputation draws consumers and the brand associated with the customer experience of the firm also becomes part of the experience or identity of the firm in the mind of all stakeholders (customers, employees, investors). Employee actions and HR policies are aligned with this identity. We outlined global developments in this area in Chapter 6 under the guise of employer branding.
- *A customer interface that captures and develops a more intimate relationship*, such that data on customers contains more insight into their actual behavior and needs, business processes are built around these needs as a priority, and customers also have involvement in or can comment on the design and practice of internal systems (for example, might be able to comment on the relevance of recruitment questions or provide feedback for performance management). Chapter 4, in its review of the impact of technology on the corporate HR function noted a number of developments surrounding shared-service structures, e-enablement of HR and the disintermediation of the HR service chain that involved this requirement.

- *Superior talent*, reflected in high levels of employee competence *and* commitment, such that there is an employee value proposition that makes the firm an attractive place to work, helps attract people into the right job, entices employees to give their discretionary energy to the firm and orients them towards effective performance very quickly. Again, this came to the fore in Chapter 6 as one of the global themes being pursued by corporate HR functions. It was evident in the strategies pursued at Shell, Rolls-Royce, Diageo.
- *Leveraged innovation and learning*, reflected in new and faster-developed services and products, a culture of inquisitiveness and risk taking, competencies of inventing and trying and an ability and willingness to learn from mistakes. Once the rhetoric is removed from this statement, then we would argue that the various developments described in Chapter 5 represent various attempts to both help the organization, and the corporate HR function, benefit from the transfer of knowledge on a global basis. However, as that chapter showed, "leveraging innovation and learning" within the HR community is easier said than done. Chapter 7, with its focus on the facilitation of greater levels of international mobility, provides another perspective on the development of this capability.
- *Resources sourced across alliances*, whereby firms can work across boundaries, marshal connections, share information and develop a sense of mutual dependency between a network of partners that means the best resources can be brought to bear on a situation, to everyone's benefit, without having to formally own or control them. This was evidenced through one of the organizational drivers identified in our model in Chapter 3.
- *Assigned accountability*, such that standards exist for employees and organizational decision-making (who makes them, how they are made and what processes are followed) is carried out with competence, authority and responsibility. This was seen in Chapter 6 under the use of global capabilities, and also highlighted in various case studies such as in Diageo's pursuit of a global performance management focus. Indirectly, the increased accountability being directed at the corporate HR function through the various forms of evaluation outlined in Chapter 8 reflects this requirement.

Source: Ulrich (2000)

Key competencies for global HR professionals

Our research, however, has highlighted a number of other key competencies and attributes that global HR professionals need to succeed in their new roles. These include the ability to think strategically, work virtually and tolerate the ambiguities and uncertainties typical of new business situations. They also need to be able to deal diplomatically with complex organizational politics and power struggles, and to respect

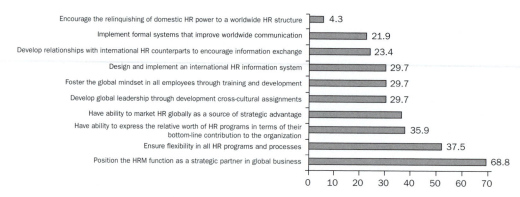

Figure 9.4 Competencies for the global HR function
Note: Data show percentage of companies performing item

cultural differences and a thorough grasp of the links between what they do and effective business performance across the world. (See Figure 9.4.)

The IHR specialists themselves see a need for the competencies outlined in Table 3.2. Interestingly, and in line with our argument throughout the book, the most frequently mentioned competence is not specific to IHRM, but is a more general HR issue: the need to position the HR function as a strategic partner. As we have mentioned several times, IHRM is most likely to be adding value – and is in a better position to add more value than HRM elsewhere – when it is closely aligned with the global business strategy and the specialists are working closely with those taking the key decisions in that arena. Equally, the need for competence in making visible the HR function's contribution to the organization's targets and the capability to market HR globally, were both mentioned by more than a third of the organizations.

Below these frequently mentioned "broad strategy" issues, Table 3.2 showed that between a fifth and a third of the organizations mentioned competencies which are more obviously international: worldwide communication; IHR systems; using training and development to foster a global mindset; and the ability to develop global leadership through cross-cultural assignments. There were similar numbers mentioning, perhaps somewhat ironically in this high-technology world, the important ability to network – to develop informal relationships with other IHR specialists in order to exchange information.

As we noted in Chapter 5, global networking has always been important within IHR. However, it is now considered to be critical because of the pace of organizational change. Historically global information, insight into local conditions and best practice have all tended to be shared through the process of IHR professionals just talking to each other – getting groups of people together within the organization to facilitate some transfer of learning. IHR professionals have to set up informal networks all the time – it is generally one of their key objectives. It is much easier to have a network in place working on a significant HR issue from the start. With a network, there is more chance of moving quickly, producing higher quality HR services and providing a better business focus. Networks also suit a more decentralized model of IHR. Within Diageo, for example, half a dozen global HR networks were established around strategically important initiatives such as recruitment and employee branding, performance and reward, organization development and international assignments. These global networks are not just put in place for the purpose of knowledge transfer. They are used increasingly to cut through bureaucracy and to act as important decision-making groups. Global HR networks are therefore being used more formally to

- provide and enable value-added cost-effective global, regional and local solutions in a series of core HR processes
- identify customer driven pan-national issues
- design solutions to meet specific customer needs and support the corporate people management strategy
- demonstrate to customers that global connectivity adds value by sharing knowledge and expertise
- ensure that knowledge and intellectual property that resides within HR silos is made freely available to all of the organization.

One of our case studies, Shell People Services, has been experimenting with global expertise networks that also serve a knowledge management role. The aims of SPS are to provide common HR services to group firms and to participate in the setting of the group's HR direction and policies. It was clear from the case study that a critical success factor in it being able to meet these goals is to maintain a repository of HR knowledge and expertise. Shell has developed several successful global communities that enable practitioners in a particular field to "meet" other practitioners and exchange ideas, problems and best practice. IHR staff are split over three continents and increasingly need to share information and work in virtual teams. In order that all HR staff, regardless of geographical location should be able to access an information store of best practice, agreed procedures and expertise, and to deploy this knowledge when working in collaborative and distributed teams, SPS has pursued a strategy based on selecting pilot IHR teams with a proven need for collaborative working and team sharing.

Clearly, a business-fostering role can befall the more capable IHR functions. This was clear in the development of the repair and overhaul business at Rolls-Royce, where even in a mature business, IHR professionals found themselves having to foster the development of organizational capability at a relatively rapid pace. It was seen in Chapter 3 where we noted the complexities involved for the IHR function in managing a business start-up situation at Stepstone. It was seen too in Chapter 8, where we explained the way in which BOC's change project to incorporate Asian operations into their global line-of-business structures was evaluated, on the basis of project evaluation metrics. We end this chapter by expanding on this case below. It provides a clear example of the capabilities needed by professionals within the IHR function.

Helping to globalize the last frontier at BOC

When BOC developed its Asia Pacific business in a serious way, the company's end-state Asian HR model comprised four constituencies: business unit heads, line of business Human Resource Directors, the Asia HR Director and County line of business General Managers. To be consistent with the global HR operating model, each business unit in Asia needed to have a Business Unit HR partner (BUHRP). This was a critically important role. The BUHRP reported to the Managing Director of the particular business unit and had a dotted line into central HRM. The BUHRP role was responsible for the interpretation of that business unit strategy into HR priorities.

The *HR leadership* for the service provision would come from the centralized HR services function, but the implementation would be done by country management. Initially, it was considered that the result of this would be that as the Asia HR service group was built up, the *calibre* and level of HR people that were employed locally at a country level would decline in seniority. This was envisaged to lead to cost reductions in the delivery of country HR services. Effectively, the introduction of the global LOB structure and an Asia HR services might have meant an upskilling of the regional service group and a deskilling of country-level HR functions. In fact this did not happen and the role of country-level HR management remained at a similar skill level.

The process of building up the Asia HR services operations meant sourcing HR professionals through various channels. The easiest option might have been to staff the entire Asia HR service group with expatriates and new recruits, but such a strategy would not have fitted in with BOC's commitments to Asia to develop existing talent into new and broader roles. Therefore in the initial change process, the transitional Asia HR services group comprised six people. None of these people had been in these roles six months prior. Two of them were expatriates. Two of them were new Asian recruits, both recruited in Singapore. Two of them were country HR managers that were moving into new roles.

The issue of capability became an important one for both the HR function and for the business as a whole. Looking at the HR function the message was clear. It was realized that the newly created Business Unit HR Partner (BUHRP) roles were particularly crucial for the success of the Global LOB structure. These new roles demanded HR people that had an understanding of the strategic direction of the Business Unit and that had a thorough business knowledge. They were a key element of the business unit. They needed to be able to translate business strategy into appropriate HR policies and practices. On the other hand, the job demanded particularly strong relationship management and influencing skills. Business Unit HR Partners needed to be able to challenge the Business Unit heads. At the same time, however, they needed to realize that it was the Business Unit head who ultimately made the decisions. So they needed to know when it was possible to challenge the Business Unit heads and when it was best to back down. A key question for BOC was whether they had sufficient people in the HR community who had developed enough in order to eventually fill the Business Unit HR Partner roles.

To BOC's Organizational Development Director for Asia, the people needed to manage the transitional HRM model would need considerable skills: "The person specification is for a change agent, someone who is able to deliver on their part and persuade Managing Directors to provide the resources . . . broker with the business unit head and influence the development of HR to make sure things are done . . . smart and not skinny."

The new HR role was a very individual role design, but would require the following:

- undertaking consultancy roles of uncertain duration and sustainability;
- hot-desking across geographic locations;
- learning about HR issues in a virtual environment;
- project management, communication skills and cross-country experience;
- flexible workloads managed across four or five different clients;
- a central focus on organizational learning and transfer of best practice; and
- bridging the social network within the organization back to the center, from where they could gain access to developing thinking on the LOB business model.

These roles needed to be filled fast. The global LOB structure was being put in place and Business Unit heads were increasing the pressure on HR. BOC decided that it would try to look for many of the Business Unit HR Partner roles outside BOC. A decision was made not to opt for expatriates because of the local development commitment the company had made towards local staff. BOC had relied heavily on expatriates in the past but it knew that it had not been successful in making these expatriates develop local staff. Given this background, the position taken on expatriates was understandable. Under the circumstances the question, however, was whether this view on expatriation was appropriate? It was acknowledged that it might be necessary for the company to revise and realign its expatriation policies in relation to expatriates within the HR function. It was very difficult to find the people for these roles – in fact it took 18 months to find four people – but in the final outcome BOC stuck rigidly to its plan and the key vacancies were filled with Asian managers.

Source: Sparrow *et al.* (2003)

We believe that the new roles for IHR professionals highlight the need for them to develop personal competencies that concern important process skills, political skills and technical knowledge. The attributes that were most frequently evident in the work of professionals that we studied were as follows:

- being a strategic thinker, articulating the benefits of having an effective HR process and capability and the risks to both personal and business objectives of not;
- possession of strong personal networks inside and outside the organization and the ability to build some structure into this collection of relationships;
- being a provider of information and advice within this business network, based on personal expertise and credibility;
- becoming a broker of appropriate knowledge, learning and ideas across a loose connection of people. Being seen as the owner of important new dialogues within the organization;

- capacity for and tolerance of the ambiguities and uncertainties inherent in new business situations, such as working through confused leadership;
- being a resource negotiator, persuading managers to invest and capturing unassigned resources;
- being a process facilitator, with diplomatic sensitivity to complex organizational politics and power struggles;
- mobilizing the energy and engagement behind ideas, maintaining pressure on people, managing the impact by under-promising but overachieving;
- having a respect for the countries and communities being dealt with. Insight into their needs both as consumers (as employees) and as clients (as global business functions);
- showing an appreciation of the ways in which culture influences core organizational behaviors; and
- the capacity to work virtually.

To deliver these competencies they need to be able to understand, develop an insight into and take an overview of the links between HR processes and effective business performance across the global network.

Conclusion

Overall, our research shows a function that, at the international level, is becoming more professional in its approach, even if it is not "professionalizing." It is a profession that is clear that its role is to work closely with the business, and to make a direct contribution to the organization's targets. These HR people are not employee champions. On the other hand, they are increasingly seeing their remit as the total staffing of the organization and not just limiting themselves to the senior management team.

This does not mean that IHR professionals are taking a narrow view: they understand that issues such as fostering a global mindset or developing global competencies through international assignments require a longer-term time horizon than organizations work with normally. Nor are the organizations that we spoke to in-depth sanguine about where they stand. They are conscious that they still need to work on their objectives, their own performance and contribution and on getting the rest of the organization to understand the contribution they can make. But they are thinking these issues through in detail and working hard to make sustainable progress in these areas. As one of them told us, "We are a long way from having reached our targets; but we are getting clearer about what they should be, and we are making real progress that the business can see in the way we are moving towards them."

In the final analysis, we believe that our study has provided a unique opportunity to grasp the nature of global HRM. We have tried to capture the essence of this approach to coherence and consistency in global HRM throughout this book. We have identified the key mechanisms by which global HRM can deliver organizational capability. The IHRM field is changing significantly and rapidly and there is a need for better understanding of these developments. The five distinct, but linked, organizational drivers of IHRM – an efficiency orientation, core business processes, building rapid global presence, information exchange, organizational learning and partnership and localization of decision making – are together creating a new set of pressures on HR professionals. Three distinct, but linked, enablers of high-performance IHRM are being developed by MNCs: HR affordability, a central HR philosophy and HR excellence and knowledge transfer. These enabling competencies in turn are being delivered through a series of important HR processes. Leading-edge global HR functions are acutely aware of the need to "position" themselves in order to deliver the enablers and processes which will lead to organizational capability.

Note

1 For the statisticians amongst our readers, this was done as follows. Responses were rescaled such that 0 meant that the HR professional did not engage in the activity, 1 meant that they engaged in the activity on a domestic basis and 2 meant that they engaged in the activity on an international basis. We used a principal components analysis with varimax rotation and accepted factors with eigenvalues greater than 1 and interpreted factor loadings greater than 0.5. The results of the factor analysis are shown in Table 9.1. Thirteen items loaded significantly onto three factors accounting for 58 per cent of the variance (the item loadings are shown in Figure 9.2).

Table 9.1 Factor analysis results for role types

Factor	Eigenvalue	Percentage of variance	Cumulative variance
Transactional activity	5.95	39.7	39.7
Capability development	1.70	11.3	51.0
Business development	1.09	7.3	58.3

Bibliography

Abbott, A. (1988) *The System of Professions*, Chicago: University of Chicago Press.

Adler, N.J. (1984) "Women do not want international careers: and other myths about international management," *Organizational Dynamics* 19 (3): 79–85.

Adler, N.J. (1986a) *International Dimensions of Organizational Behaviour*, 2nd edition, Boston, MA: PWS-Kent.

Adler, N.J. (1986b) "Do MBAs want international careers?," *International Journal of Intercultural Relations* 10: 277–300.

Adler, N.J. (1993a) "Competitive frontiers: Women managers in the Triad," *International Studies of Management and Organizations* 23: 3–23.

Adler, N.J. (1993b) "Women managers in a global economy," *HR Magazine* 38: 52–55.

Adler, N.J. and Bartholomew, S. (1992) "Managing globally competent people," *Academy of Management Executive* 6: 52–65.

Adler, N.J. and Ghadar, F. (1990a) "International strategy from the perspective of people and Culture: The North American context", in A. Rugman (ed.) *Research in Global Strategic Management*, vol. 1., Greenwood, CT: JAI Press.

Adler, N.J. and Ghadar, F. (1990b) "Strategic human resource management: A global perspective," in R. Pieper (ed.) *Human Resource Management in International Comparision*, Berlin: de Gruyter, pp. 235–260.

Adler, N.J., Doktor, R. and Redding, S.G. (1986) "From the Atlantic to the Pacific century," *Journal of Management* 12 (2): 295–318.

Albrecht M.H., Pagana, A.M. and Phoocharoon, P. (1996) "International joint ventures: An integrated conceptual model for human resource and business strategies," *Journal of Euro-Marketing* 4 (3): 89–127.

Ambos, B. and Reitsperer, W.D. (2002) *Governing knowledge processes in MNCs: The case of German R & D units abroad*. Paper presented at the 28th EIBA Conference, Athens, 8–10 December.

Applebaum, R.P. and Henderson, J. (1982) (eds) *States and Development in the Asia Pacific Rim*, Beverly Hills, CA Sage.

Arkin, A. (1999) "Return to the centre," *People Management* 6 May: 34.

Arthur, J. (1994) "Effects of human resource systems on manufacturing performance and turnover," *Academy of Management Journal* 37 (3): 670–687.

Arthur, M.B. and Rousseau, D.M. (1996) (eds) *Boundaryless Careers*, Oxford: Blackwell.

Aryee, S., Chay, Y. and Chew, J. (1996) "An investigation of the willingness of managerial employees to accept an expatriate assignment," *Journal of Organizational Behavior* 17: 267–284.

Ashkenas, R., Ulrich, D., Jick, T. and Kerr, S. (1995) *The Boundaryless Organization*, San Francisco, CA: Jossey-Bass.

Athanassiou, N. and Nigh, D. (2000) "Internationalization, tacit knowledge and the top management teams of MNCs," *Journal of International Business Studies* 31 (3): 471–488.

Baker J. and Ivancevich, J. (1971) "The assignment of American executives abroad: Systematic, haphazard or chaotic?" *California Management Review*, Spring, 13 (3): 39–44.

Barbash, J. (1987) "Like nature, industrial relations abhors a vacuum: The case of the union-free strategy," *Industrial Relations* 42 (1): 168–178.

Barber, B. (1996) *Jihad versus McWorld*. New York: Ballantine Books.

Barham K. and Wills, S. (1992) *Management Across Frontiers: Identifying the Competencies of Successful International Managers*, Berkhamsted: Ashridge Management Research Group and the Foundation for Management Education.

Barkema, H.G., Bell, J.H.J. and Pennings, J.M. (1996) "Foreign entry, cultural barriers, and learning," *Strategic Management Journal* 17: 151–166.

Barney, J. (1991) "Firm resources and sustained competitive advantage," *Journal of Management* 17 (1): 99–120.

Barry, D. and Elmes, M. (1997) "Strategy retold: Toward a narrative view of strategic discourse," *Academy of Management Review* 22 (2): 429–452.

Bartlett, C.A. and Ghoshal, S. (1989) *Managing Across Borders: The Transnational Solution*, Boston, MA: Harvard Business School Press.

Bartlett, C.A. and Ghoshal, S. (1995) *Transnational Management*, 2nd edition. Boston, MA: Irwin.

Bartlett, C.A. and Ghoshal, S. (1997) *International Management: Text, Cases and Readings in Cross-Border Management*, 2nd edition, Boston, MA: Irwin.

Becker, B, and Gerhart, B. (1996) "The impact of human resource practices on organizational performance: Progress and prospects," *Academy of Management Journal* 39: 779–801.

Becker, B.E., Huselid, M.A. and Ulrich, D. (2001) *The HR Scorecard: Linking People, Strategy and Performance*, Boston, MA: Harvard Business School Press.

Becker, B., Huselid, M., Pickus, P. and Spratt, M. (1997) "HR as a source of shareholder value: Research and recommendations," *Human Resource Management* 36 (1): 39–47.

Bell, D., Brewster, C., Croucher, R., Marshall, V., Parsons, D., Tregaskis O. and Waterhouse P. (1999) *Mapping the Employment Occupations*. UK: Employment NTO.

Berggren C. (1992) *Alternatives to Lean Production*, Ithaca, NY: ILR Press.

Berry, J.W. (1992) "Acculturation and adaptation in a new society," *International Migration Quarterly Review* 30: 69–87.

Berry, J.W. and Kim, U. (1988) "Acculturation and mental health," in P. Daasen and J.W. Berry (eds) *Health and Cross-Cultural Psychology*, Newbury Park, CA, Sage Publications, pp. 62–89.

Birkinshaw, J.M. and Hood, N. (1997) "An empirical study of development processes in foreign-owned subsidiaries in Scotland," *Management International Review* 37 (4): 339–364.

Birkinshaw, J.M. and Morrison, A.J. (1995) "Configurations of strategy and structure in subsidiaries of multinational corporations," *Journal of International Business Studies* 4: 729–753.

Black J.S. (1988) "Work role transitions: A study of American expatriate managers in Japan," *Journal of International Business Studies* 30 (2): 119–134.

Black J.S, and Gregersen H. (1991) "Antecedents to cross-cultural adjustment for expatriates in Pacific Rim assignments," *Human Relations* 44: 497–515.

Black, J.S., Gregersen, H.B., Mendenhall, M.E. and Stroh, L.K. (1999) *Globalizing People through International Assignments*, New York: Addison-Wesley, Longman.

Black J.S. and Stephens G.K. (1989) "The influence of the spouse on American expatriate adjustment in overseas assignments," *Journal Of Management* 15: 529–544.

Bochner, S., McLeod, B.M. and Lin, A. (1977) "Friendship patterns of overseas students: A functional model," *International Journal of Psychology* 12 (4): 277–294.

Bonache, J. and Brewster, C. (2001) "Knowledge transfer and the management of expatriation," *Thunderbird International Business Review* 43 (1): 145–168.

Bournois, F. (1991) *La Gestion Des Cadres En Europe*. Paris: Editions Liaisons.

Boxall, P. (1993) "The significance of human resource management: A reconsideration of the evidence," *International Journal of Human Resource Management* 4 (3): 645–664.

Boxall, P. (1995) "Building the theory of comparative HRM," *Human Resource Management Journal* 5 (5): 5–18.

Boxall, P. (1996) "The strategic HRM debate and the resource-based view of the firm," *Human Resource Management Journal* 6 (5): 5–17.

Boyer, R. and Hollingsworth, R. (1997) "How and why do social systems of production change?" in R. Hollingsworth and R. Boyer (eds) *Contemporary Capitalism: The Embeddedness of Institutions*, Cambridge: Cambridge University Press.

Braun, W., Sparrow, P.R., Brewster, C.B. and Harris, H. (2003a) *Diageo Case Study: Building Global HR Capability*. Manchester: Manchester Business School.

Braun, W., Sparrow, P.R., Brewster, C.B. and Harris, H. (2003b) *Stepstone Case Study: Managing Rapid Internationalization in the E-commerce Sector*. Manchester: Manchester Business School.

Brawley, M.R. (2003) *The Politics of Globalization: Gaining Perspective, Assessing Consequences*. Peterborough, Ontario: Broadview Press.

Brett, J.M. and Stroh, L.K. (1995) "Willingness to relocate internationally," *Human Resource Management* 34: 405–424.

Brewer, M.B., Dull, V. and Lui, L. (1981) "Perceptions of the elderly: Stereotypes as prototypes, *Journal of Personality and Social Psychology* 41: 656–670.

Brewster, C. (1995a) "Human resource management: The European dimension," in J. Storey (ed.) *Human Resource Management: A Critical Text*, London: Routledge.

Brewster, C. (1995b) "National cultures and international management," in Tyson (ed.) *Strategic Prospects for HRM*, Wimbledon: IPD.

Brewster, C. (1995c) "Effective expatriate training," in J. Selmer (ed.) *Expatriate Management: New Ideas for International Business*, Westport, CT: Quorum Books.

Brewster, C. (1999a) "Different paradigms in strategic HRM: Questions raised by comparative research," in P. Wright, L. Dyer, J. Boudreau and G. Milkovich (eds) *Research in Personnel and HRM*, Greenwich, CT: JAI Press Inc, pp. 213–238.

Brewster, C. (1999b) "Strategic human resource management: The value of different paradigms," *Management International Review Special Issue 1999/3* 39: 45–64.

Brewster, C. (2001) "HRM practices in multinational enterprises," in M.J. Gannon and K. Newman (eds) *Handbook of Cross-Cultural Management*, New York: Blackwell.

Brewster, C. and Harris, H. (1999) *International Human Resource Management: Contemporary Issues in Europe*, Routledge, London.

Brewster, C. and Hegewisch, A. (1994) *Policy and Practice in European Human Resource Management: The Price Waterhouse Cranfield Survey*, London: Routledge.

Brewster, C. and Scullion, H. (1997) "A review and an agenda for expatriate HRM," *Human Resource Management Journal* 7 (3): 32–41.

Brewster, C. and Tregaskis, O. (2003) "Convergence or divergence of contingent employment practices? Evidence of the role of MNCs in Europe," in W.M. Cooke (ed.) *Multinational Companies and Transnational Workplace Issues*, New York: Praeger.

Brewster, C., Farndale, E. and Whittaker, J. (2000a) HR competencies and professional standards. *Report to the World Federation of Personnel Management Associations*, Cranfield School of Management.

Brewster, C., Farndale, E. and Whittaker, J. (2000b) "Skills, knowledge and professional standards" *Worldlink* 10 (3): 4–5.

Brewster, C., Harris, H. and Sparrow, P.R (2001) "On top of the world," *People Management* 7 (21): 37–42.

Brewster, C., Harris, H. and Sparrow, P.R (2002) *Globalizing HR: Executive Brief*, London: Chartered Institute of Personnel and Development.

Brewster, C., Mayrhofer, W. and Morley, M. (2003) "Human resource management: A universal concept?," in *Human Resource Management in Europe: Evidence of Convergence?* London: Butterworth Heinemann.

Brewster, C., Sparrow, P. and Harris, H. (2001) *Globalization and HR: A Literature Review*, London: Chartered Institute of Personnel and Development.

Brewster, C., Tregaskis, O., Hegewisch, A. and Mayne, L. (1996) "Comparative Research in Human Resource Management: a review and an example," *International Journal of Human Resource Management* 7 (3): 585–604.

Brewster, C., Communal, C., Farndale, E., Hegewisch, A., Johnson, G. and Van Ommeren, J. (2001) *The HR Healthcheck. Benchmarking HRM Practice across the UK and Europe.* London: Financial Times/Prentice Hall.

Brewster, C.J., Mayrhofer, W. and Morley, M. (eds) (2000) *New Challenges for European Human Resource Management*, London: Macmillan.

Brislin, R. (1981) *Cross-Cultural Encounters*, New York: Pergamon Press.

Brockbank, W. (1997) "HR's future on the way to a presence". *Human Resource Management* 36: 65–69.

Brown, J.S. and Duguid, P. (1991) "Organizational learning and communities-of-practice: towards a unified view of working, learning and innovating," *Organization Science* 2 (1): 40–57.

Budwhar, P.S. and Sparrow, P.R. (2002) "An integrative framework for understanding cross national human resource management principles," *Human Resource Management Review* 10 (7): 1–28.

Budwhar, P.S. and Sparrow, P.R. (2003) "Strategic HRM through the cultural looking glass: mapping the cognition of British and Indian managers," *Organization Studies* 23 (4): 599–638.

Buller, P.F. and McEvoy, G.M. (1999) "Creating and sustaining ethical capability in the multinational corporation," in R.S. Schuler and S.E. Jackson (eds) *Strategic Human Resource Management*. Oxford: Blackwell.

Business Week (2003a) "Brands in an age of anti-Americanism," August 4th, 45–51.

Business Week (2003b) "Outsourcing jobs: Is it bad?" August 18th–25th, pp. 26–28.

Caligiuri, P. (2000) "The Big Five Personality Characteristics as predictors of expatriate success," *Personnel Psychology* 53: 67–88.

Caligiuri, P. and Cascio (1998) "Can we send her there? Maximising the success of western women on global assignments," *Journal of World Business* 33 (4): 394–416.

Caligiuri, P. and Stroh, L.K. (1995) "Multinational corporation management strategies and international human resource practices: Bringing international HR to the bottom line," *International Journal of Human Resource Management* 6 (3): 494–507.

Caligiuri, P.M. and Tung, R.L. (1998) "Are masculine cultures female friendly? Male and female expatriates success in countries differing in work value orientations," in G. Hofstede (Chair), *Masculinity/Femininity as a Cultural Dimension*. Paper presented at the International Congress of the International Association for Cross-Cultural Psychology, The Silver Jubilee Congress, Bellingham, WA.

Caligiuri, P.M., Joshi, A. and Lazarova, M. (1999) "Factors influencing the adjustment of women on global assignments," *International Journal of Human Resource Management* 10 (2): 163–179.

Caligiuri, P.M., Hymand, M.A., Joshi, A. and Bross, A. (1998) "Testing a theoretical model for examining the relationship of family adjustment and expatriate's work adjustment," *Journal of Applied Psychology* 83 (4): 598–614.

Cappelli, P. (1999) *The New Deal at Work*, Boston, MA: Harvard Business School Press.

Carnoy, M. and Castells, M. (1997) *Sustainable Flexibility: A Prospective Study on Work, Family and Society in the Information Age*, Paris: OECD.

Carr, C. (1993) "Global, national and resource-based strategies: An examination of strategic choice and performance in the vehicle components industry," *Strategic Management Journal* 14 (7): 551–568.

Carrington, L. (2002) "Oiling the wheels," *People Management* 8 (13): 31–32.

Carter A. and Robinson D. (2000) *Employee Returns: Linking HR Performance Indicators to Business Strategy*, IES Report 365.

Caves, R.E. (1996) *Multinational Enterprise and Economic Analysis*, Cambridge University Press: Cambridge.

Cavusgil, S.T. and Godiwalla, Y.M. (1982) "Decision-making for international marketing," *Management Decision* 20: 48–57.

Cerdin, J.-L. (2003) "International diffusion of HRM practices: The role of expatriates," *Beta: Scandinavian Journal of Business Research* 17 (1): 48–58.

Chandler, A.D. (1962) *Strategy and Structure*, Cambridge: MIT Press.

Chandler, A.D. (1977) *The Visible Hand: The Managerial Revolution in American Business*, Cambridge: Harvard University Press.

Chandler, A.D. and Daems, H. (eds) (1980) *Managerial Hierarchies: Comparative Perspectives on the Rise of the Modern Industrial Enterprise*, Cambridge, MA: Harvard University Press.

Chiesa, V. and Manzini, R. (1996) "Managing knowledge transfer within multinational firms," *International Journal of Technology Management* 12 (4): 462–476.

Cianni, M. and Tharenou, P. (2000) "A cross-cultural study of the willingness of graduating students to accept expatriate assignments," in R. Edwards, C. Nyland and M. Coulthard (eds) *Readings in International Business*, Victoria: Prentice Hall, pp. 337–360.

CIPD (2001) "Global human resource management practice survey," *Chartered Institute of Personnel and Development*, London: CIPD.

Clegg, S.R., Ibarra-Colado, E. and Bueno-Rodriquez, L. (eds) (1999) *Global Management: Universal Theories and Local Realities*, London: Sage.

Clugston, M., Howell, J.P. and Dorfman, P.W. (2000) "Does Cultural Socialization Predict Multiple Bases and Foci of Commitment?" *Journal of Management* 26: 5–30.

Collis, D.J. (1991) "A resource-based analysis of global competition: The case of the bearings industry," *Strategic Management Journal* 12: 49–68.

Conner, K.R. and Prahalad, C.K. (1996) "A resourced-based theory of the firm: knowledge versus opportunism," *Organizational Science* 7: 477–501.

Conrad, P. and Pieper, R. (1990) "HRM in the Federal Republic of Germany," in R. Pieper (ed.) *Human Resource Management: An International Comparison*, Berlin: Walter de Gruyter.

Crabb, S. (2003) "High expectations," *People Management*, 26th June, p. 59.

Csoka, L.S. and Hackett, B. (1998) *Transforming The HR Function For Global Business Success*. US: The Conference Board, William M. Mercer.

Cyr, D. (1995) *The Human Resource Challenge of International Joint Ventures*, Westport, CT: Quorum Books.

Cyr, D. and Schneider, S. (1996) "Implications for learning: human resource management in East–West joint ventures," *Organization Studies* 17 (2): 201–226.

Dacin, M.T., Ventresca, M. and Beal, B. (1999) "The embeddedness of organizations: dialogues and directions," *Journal of Management* 25 (3): 317–357.

Daniels, J.D. and Bracker, J. (1989) "Profit performance: do foreign operations make a difference?," *Management International Review* 29 (1): 46–56.

Davenport, T.H. (1999) *Human Capital: What It Is and Why People Invest in It*, San Francisco: Jossey-Bass.

Davenport, T.H. and Prusak, L. (1998) *Working Knowledge: How Organizations Manage What They Know*, Boston, MA: Harvard Business School Press.

Davenport, T.H., Jarvenpaa, S.L. and Beers, M.C. (1996) "Successful knowledge management projects," *Sloan Management Review* 39 (2): 43–57.

Davies, G., Chun, R., Da Silva, R.V. and Roper, S. (2003) *Corporate Reputation and Competitiveness*, London: Routledge.

D'Avini, R.A.I. (1994) *Hypercompetition*, New York: Free Press.

de Chernatony, L. (2001) *From Brand Vision to Brand Evaluation*, Oxford: Butterworth-Heinemann.

DeFidelto, C. and Slater, I. (2001) "Web-based HR in an international setting," in A.J. Walker (ed.) *Web-based human resources: the technologies that are transforming HR*. London: McGraw-Hill.

De Saá-Pérez, P. and García-Falcón, J.M.. (2002) "A resource-based view of human resource management and organisational capabilities development," *International Journal of Human Resource Management* 13 (1): 123–140.

Delaney, J. and Huselid, M. (1996) "The impact of human resource management practices on perceptions of organizational performance," *Academy of Management Journal* 39: 349–369.

Dell, D. and Ainspan, N. (2001) "Engaging employees through your brand," *Conference Board Report, Number R.1288-01-RR*, April, Washington, D.C: Conference Board.

Desouza, K.C. (2003) "Knowledge management barriers: Why the technology imperative seldom works," *Business Horizons*, January–February, 25–29.

Desouza, K.C. and Evaristo, R. (2003) "Global knowledge management strategies," *European Management Journal* 21 (1): 62–67.

DiMaggio, P. and Powell, W. (1983) "The iron cage revisited: Institutional isomorphism and collective rationality in organizational fields," *American Sociological Review* 48: 147–160.

DiMaggio, P. and Powell, W. (1991) *The New Institutionalism in Organizational Analysis*, Chicago: University of Chicago Press.

Doremus, P., Keller, H., Pauly, L. and Reich, S. (1998) *The Myth of the Global Corporation*, Princeton, N J: Princeton University Press.

Dowling, P. (1988) "International human resource management," in L.D. Dyer (ed.) *Human Resource Management: Evolving Roles And Responsibilities*. Washington DC: BNA Books

Dowling, P., Schuler, R. and Welch, D. (1994) *International Dimensions of Human Resource Management*, 2nd edition, Belmont, CA: Wadsworth.

Dowling, P.J., Welch, D. and Schuler, R.S. (1999) *International Human Resource Management: Managing People in a Multinational Context*, 3rd edition, London: South Western College Publishing.

Doz, Y. and Prahalad, P.K. (1981) "Headquarters influence and strategic control in MNCs," *Sloan Management Review* 23: 15–29.

Doz, Y. and Prahalad, P.K. (1986) "Controlled variety: A challenge for human resource management in the MNC," *Human Resource Management* 25 (1): 55–71.

Due, J., Madsen, J. and Jensen, C. (1991) "The social dimension: convergence or diversification of industrial relations in the single European market?" *Industrial Relations Journal* 22 (2): 85–102.

Dunning, J.H. (1993) *Multinational Enterprises and the Global Economy*. Reading, MA: Addison-Wesley.

Dunning, J.H. (1997) (ed.) *Governments, Globalization and International Business*, Oxford: Oxford University Press.

Dyer, L. (1985) "Strategic human resources management and planning," in K.M. Rowland and G.R. Ferris (eds) *Research In Personnel And Human Resources Management*, vol. 3, Greenwich, CT: JAI Press.

Dyer, L. and Kochan, T. (1995) "Is there a new HRM? Contemporary evidence and future directions," in B. Downie, P. Kumar and M.L. Coates (eds) *Managing Human Resources in the 1990s and Beyond: Is the Workplace Being Transformed?* Kingston, Ontario: Industrial Relations Centre Press, Queen's University.

Earley, P.C. and Mosakowski, E. (1995) "A framework for understanding experimental research in international and intercultural context," in B.J. Punnett and O. Shenkar (eds) *Handbook of International Management Research*, London: Blackwell, pp. 83–114.

Earley, P.C. and Singh, H. (1995) "International and inter-cultural research: what's next?," *Academy of Management Journal* 38: 1–14.

Earley, P.C. and Singh, H. (2000) (eds) *Innovations in International and Cross-Cultural Management*, Thousand Oaks, CA: Sage.

Easterby-Smith, M., Malina, D. and Yuan, L. (1995) "How culture-sensitive is HRM? A comparative analysis of practice in Chinese and UK companies," *International Journal of Human Resource Management* 6 (1): 31–59.

Economist, The (2000a) "The world's view of multinationals," 354 (8155): 21–22.

Economist, The (2000b) "Special Report: A survey of globalization and tax," 354 (8155): 1–18.

Economist, The (2002a) "E-commerce: Profits at last," 365 (8304): 95–96.

Economist, The (2002b) "Defence companies: the war dividend," 364 (8290): 31.

Economist, The (2003a) "The new geography of the IT industry," 368 (8353): 53–55.

Economist, The (2003b) "They cost plenty. Are they worth it?," 368 (8356): 24.

Edvinsson, L. and Malone, M.S. (1997) *Intellectual Capital: Realizing Your Company's True Value by Finding its Hidden Brainpower*, New York, Harper Business.

Edwards, T. (1998) "Multinationals, labour management and the processes of reverse diffusion: A case study," *International Journal of Human Resource Management*, 9 (4): 696–709.

Edwards, T. and Ferner, A. (2004, forthcoming) "Multinationals, reverse diffusion and national business systems," *Management International Review*.

Eisenstat, R.A. (1996) "What corporate human resources brings to the picnic: Four models for functional management," *Organisational Dynamics* 25 (2): 6–14.

Elkjaer, B. (1999) "In search of a social learning theory," in M. Easterby-Smith, J. Burgoyne and L. Araujo (eds), *Organizational Learning and the Learning Organization: Developments in Theory and Practice*, London: Sage.

Engardio, P., Bernstein, A. and Kripalani, M. (2003) "The new global job shift," *Business Week*, February 3.

Epstein, M. and Schnietz, K. (2002) "Measuring the cost of environmental and labor protests to globalisation: an event study of the failed 1999 Seattle WTO talks," *The International Trade Journal* 16 (2): 19.

Evans, J. (2003) "Out in the open," *People Management*, 29th May: 32–33, p. 32

Evans, P., Pucik, V. and Barsoux, J.L. (2002) *The Global Challenge: Frameworks for International Human Resource Management*, London: McGraw-Hill.

Falk, R. (1993) "The making of global citizenship," in J. Brecher, J.B. Childs and J. Cutler (eds) *Global Visions*, Boston, MA: South End Press.

Farh, J.L., Earley, P.C. and Lin, S.C. (1997) "Impetus for action: A cultural analysis of justice and organizational citizenship behavior in Chinese society," *Administrative Science Quarterly* 42: 421–444.

Farnham, A. (1994) "Global – or just globaloney?" *Fortune*, June 27th: pp. 97–100.

Feldman, D.C. (2001) "Domestic and international relocation for work," in C.L. Cooper and I.T. Robertson (eds) *International Review of Industrial and Organizational Psychology*, New York: Wiley, pp. 215–244.

Fenton-O'Creevy, M. (2003) "The diffusion of HR practices within the multinational firm: towards a research agenda," *Beta: Scandinavian Journal of Business Research* 17 (1): 36–47.

Fenwick, M., DeCieri, H. and Welch, D.E. (1999) "Cultural and bureaucratic control in MNC s: the role of expatriate performance management," *Management International Review* 39 (3): 107–124.

Ferguson, D. (2001) "Euro varsity farce," *Trends International Belgium* April, 3: 5.

Ferner, A. and Quintanilla, J. (1998) "Multinational, national business systems and HRM: the enduring influence of national identity or a process of 'Anglo Saxonization'?", *International Journal of Human Resource Management* 9 (4): 710–731.

Fladmoe-Lindquist, K. and Tallman, S. (1994) "Resource-based strategy and competitive advantage among multinationals," in P. Shrivastava, A. Huff and J. Dutton (eds) *Advances in Strategic Management*, vol. 10. Greenwich, CT: JAI Press.

Flood, P.C., Ramamoorthy, N. and Liu, W. (2003) "Knowledge and innovation: diffusion of HRM systems," *Beta: Scandinavian Journal of Business Research* 17 (1): 59–68.

Florkowski, G.W. and Schuler R.S. (1994) "Auditing human resources management in the global environment," *International Journal of Human Resource Management* 5 (4): 827–851.

Fombrun, C.J., Tichy, N. and Devanna, M.A. (1984) *Strategic Human Resource Management*, New York: John Wiley.

Ford, J.D. and Ford, L.W. (1995) "The role of conversations in producing intentional organizational change," *Academy of Management Review* 20 (3): 541–570.

Forster, N. (1997): "The persistent myth of high expatriate failure rates: A reappraisal" *International Journal of Human Resource Management* 8 (4): 414–431.

Forster, N. and Johnsen, M. (1996) "Expatriate management policies in UK companies new to the international scene," *International Journal of Human Resource Management* 7: 179–205.

Foss, N.J. (1997) "On the rationales of corporate headquarters," *Industrial and Corporate Change* 6 (2): 313–337.

Gereffi, G. (1994a) "The organization of Buyer-driven global commodity chains: How U.S. retailers shape overseas production networks," in G. Gereffi and M. Korzeniewicz (eds) *Commodity Chains and Global Capitalism*, Westport, CT: Greenwood Press.

Gereffi, G. (1994b) "Capitalism, development and global commodity chains," in L. Sklair (ed.) *Capitalism and Development*, London: Routledge.

Gereffi, G. (1997) "The reorganization of Production on a world scale: States, markets and networks in the apparel and electronics commodity chains," in D. Campbell, A. Parisotto, A. Verma and A. Lateef (eds) *Regionalization and Labour Market Interdependence in East and Southeast Asia*, Geneva: MacMillan Press in association with International Institute for Labour Studies.

Gereffi, G. and Korzeniewicz, M. (eds) (1994) *Commodity Chains and Global Capitalism*. Westport, CT: Greenwood Press.

Gerhart, B. (1999) "Human resource management and firm performance: Challenges in making causal inferences," in P.M. Wright, L.D. Dyer and J.W. Boudreau (eds) *Research in Personnel and Human Resources Management*, Supplement 4: *Strategic Human Resources Management in the Twenty First Century*, Oxford: Elsevier, pp. 31–74.

Ghoshal, S. and Bartlett, C.A. (1988) "Creation, adoption, and diffusion of innovations by subsidiaries of multinational corporations," *Journal of International Business Studies*, 29: 365–388.

Ghoshal, S. and Bartlett, C.A. (1995) "Building the entrepreneurial organization: the new organizational processes, the new organizational tasks," *European Management Journal*, 13 (2): 139–155.

Ghoshal, S. and Gratton, L. (2002) "Integrating the enterprise," *Sloan Management Review* 44 (1): 31–38.

Ghoshal, S. and Nohria, N. (1989) "Internal differentiation within multinational corporations," *Strategic Management Journal* 10: 323–337.

Ghoshal, S. and Nohria, N. (1993) "Horses for courses: Organizational forms for multinational corporations," *Sloan Management Review* 35: 23–35.

Gibb, S. (1994) *A big step forward or a giant leap back? An evaluation of the personnel standards lead body (PSLB) model of personnel management*, Occasional paper 6, Department of HRM, University of Strathclyde, Glasgow.

Glaister, K.W. and Buckley, P.J. (1996) "Strategic motives for international alliance formation," *Journal of Management Studies* 33: 301–332.

GMAC Global Relocation Services / Windham International (2000), *Global Relocation Trends 2000 Survey Report*, GMAC Global Relocation Services / Windham International, New York.

Gomez-Mejia, L.R. and Balkin, D.B. (1992) "Determinants of faculty pay: An agency theory perspective ," *Academy of Management Journal* 35: 921–955.

Gonzales, B., Ellis, Y.M., Riffel, P.J. and Yager, D. (1999) "Training at IBM's Human Resource Service Center: Linking People, Technology, and HR processes," *Human Resource Management* 38 (2): 135–142.

Gordon, E.E. (2000) *Skill Wars*, Boston, MA: Butterworth-Heinemann.

Goss, D. (1994) *Principles of Human Resource Management*, London: Routledge.

Grant, R.M. (1991) "The resource-based theory of competitive advantage: implications for strategy formulation," *California Management Review* 33 (3): 114–135.

Grant, R.M. (1996) "Toward a knowledge-based theory of the firm," *Strategic Management Journal* 17: 109–122.

Grant, R.M., Almeida, P. and Song, J. (2000) "Knowledge and the Multi-national Enterprise," in C.J.M. Millar, R.M. Grant and C.J. Choi (eds) *International Business: Emerging Issues and Emerging Markets*, Basingstoke: Macmillan, pp. 102–114.

Gratton, L. (2003) "The humpty dumpty effect: A view of a fragmented HR function," *People Management* 9 (9): 18.

Gray, J. (1998) *False Dawn: The Delusions of Global Capitalism*, London: Granta Books.

Gray, L. (1999) "New Zealand HRD practitioner competencies: Application of the ASTD competency model", *International Journal of Human Resource Management* 10: 1046–1059.

Greenwood, R., Suddaby, R. and Hinings, C.R. (2002) "Theorizing change: The role of professional associations in the transformation of institutionalized fields," *Academy of Management Journal* 45 (1): 58–80.

Gregersen, H.B. and Black, J.S. (1990) "A multi-faceted approach to expatriate retention in international assignments," *Group and Organization Studies* 15 (4): 461–485.

Greider, W. (1997) *One World Ready Or Not*, New York: Simon and Schuster.

Guest, D. (1990) "Human Resource Management and the American Dream," *Journal of Management Studies* 27 (4): 377–397.

Guest, D. (1992) "Right enough to be dangerously wrong: an analysis of the In Search of Excellence," in G. Salaman (ed.) *Human Resource Strategies*, London: Sage.

Guest, D. (1997) "Human Resource Management and performance: A review and research agenda," *The International Journal of Human Resource Management* 8 (3): 263–276.

Guest, D., Michie, J., Conway, N. and Sheehan, M. (2003) "Human resource management and corporate performance in the UK," *British Journal of Industrial Relations* 41 (2): 291–314.

Gupta, A. and Govindarajan, V. (1991) "Knowledge flows and the structure of control within multinational corporations," *Academy of Management Review*, 16: 768–792.

Hall P.A. and Soskice D. (2001) *Varieties of Capitalism*, Oxford: Oxford University Press.

Hamel, G. (2000) *Leading the Revolution*, Boston, MA: Harvard Business School Press.

Hamel, G. and Prahalad, C.K. (1985) "Do you really have a global strategy?" *Harvard Business Review*, July/August, 139–148.

Hamel, G. and Prahalad, C.K. (1994) *Competing For the Future*, Boston, MA: Harvard Business School Press.

Hansen, M.T. (1999) "The search-transfer problem: The role of weak ties in sharing knowledge across organization subunits," *Administrative Science Quarterly* 44: 82–111.

Hansen, M.T. and Haas, M.R. (2001) "Competing for attention in knowledge markets: Electronic document dissemination in a management consulting company," *Administrative Science Quarterly* 46 (1): 1–28.

Hansen, M.T., Nohria, N. and Tierney, T. (1999) "What is your strategy for managing knowledge?," *Harvard Business Review* 77(2): 106–116.

Harding, J. (2001) "Capitalism under siege: Globalization's children strike back," *Financial Times*, September 11th, p. 14.

Harris, F. and de Chernatony, L. (2001) "Corporate branding and corporate brand performance," *European Marketing Journal* 35 (3/4): 441–456.

Harris, H. (1995) "Organisational influences on women's career opportunities in international management," *Women in Management Review* 10 (3): 26–31.

Harris, H. (1999) "Women in international management," in C. Brewster and H. Harris (eds) *International HRM: Contemporary Issues in Europe*. Routledge, London.

Harris, H. and Brewster, C. (1999) "An integrative framework for pre-departure preparation," in C. Brewster and H. Harris (eds) *International HRM: Contemporary Issues in Europe*, London: Routledge.

Harris, H., Brewster, C. and Sparrow, P.R. (2003) *International Human Resource Management*, London: CIPD Publishing.

Harvey, M. (1995) "The impact of dual-career families on international relocations," *Human Resources Management Review* 5 (3): 223–244

Harvey, M. (1996) "The selection of managers for foreign assignments: A planning perspective," *Columbia Journal of World Business*, 31(4): 102–118.

Harvey, M (1997) "Dual-career expatriates: Expectations, adjustment and satisfaction with international relocation," *Journal of International Business Studies*. 28(3): 627–657.

Harvey, M. (1998) "Dual-career couples during international relocation: The trailing spouse," *International Journal of Human Resource Management*. 9 (2): 309–322.

Harvey, M. and Novicevic, M.H. (2002) "The co-ordination of strategic initiatives within global organizations: The role of global teams," *International Journal of Human Resource Management*, 13 (4): 660–676.

Harzing, A.-W.K. (1999) *Managing the Multinationals*. Northampton: Elgar.

Haslberger, A. (1999) *The measurement of cross-cultural adaptation*. Unpublished dissertation.

Haspeslagh, G. and Jemison, D.B. (1991) *Managing Acquisitions: Creating Value Through Corporate Renewal*, New York: Free Press.

Hatch, M.J. and Schultz, M. (2001) "Are the strategic starts aligned for your corporate brand?," *Harvard Business Review*, February: 129–134.

Hechanova, R., Beehr, T.A. and Christiansen, N.D. (2003) "Antecedents and consequences of employees' adjustment to overseas assignment: A meta-analytic review," *Applied Psychology: An International Review*, 52(2): 213–236.

Hedlund, G. (1986) "The hypermodern MNC – A heterarchy?" *Human Resource Management* 25 (1): 9–35.

Hedlund, G. (1986) "The hypermodern MNC – A heterarchy?" *Human Resource Management* 25 (1): 9–35.

Hedlund, G. and Ridderstråle, J. (1997) "Toward a theory of self-renewing MNCs," in B. Toyne and D. Nigh (eds) *International Business: An Emerging Vision*, Columbia, SC: University of South Carolina Press.

Heenan, D.A. and Perlmutter, H.V. (1979) *Multinational Organizational Development: A Social Architectural Approach*, Reading, MA, Addison-Wesley.

Hegewisch, A., Harris, H., Brewster, C.B. and Sparrow, P.R. (2003) *ActionAid Case Study: A Values Based Approach to HR*. Cranfield: Cranfield University Business School.

Held, D., McGrew, A., Goldblatt, D. and Perraton, J. (1999) *Global Transfomations*, Cambridge: Polity Press.

Henderson, J. (1986) "The new international division of labour and urban development in the contemporary world-system," in D. Drakakis-Smith (ed.) *Urbanization in the Developing World*, London: Routledge.

Henderson, J. (1989) *The Globalization of High Technology Production*, London and New York: Routledge.

Henderson, J. (1997) "The changing international division of labour in the electronics industry," in D. Campbell, A. Parisotto, A. Verma and A. Lateef (eds) *Regionalization and Labour Market Interdependence in East and Southeast Asia*, Geneva: Macmillan Press in association with International Institute for Labour Studies.

Hendry, C. (1993) *Human Resource Strategies For International Growth*, London: Routledge.

Heneman, H.G., Metzler, C.A., Roosevelt, T.R.J. and Donohue, T.J. (1998) "Future challenges and opportunities for the HR profession," *HRMagazine* 43: 68–75.

Hepple, B. (2001) "Equality and empowerment for decent work," *International Labour Review*, Spring.

Heskett, J.L., Earl, W. and Schlesinger, L. (1997) *The Service Profit Chain*. New York: New York Free Press.

Hirst, P. and Thompson, G. (1999) *Globalization in Question: The International Economy and the Possibilities of Governance*, 2nd edition, Cambridge: Policy Press.

Hitt, M.A., Hoskisson, R.E., Johnson, R.A. and Moesel, D.D. (1996) "The market for corporate control and firm innovation," *Academy of Management Journal* 39: 1084–1119.

Hodgkinson, G.P. and Sparrow, P.R. (2002) *The Competent Organization: A Psychological Analysis of the Strategic Management Process*. Milton Keynes: Open University.

Hofstede, G. (1980) *Culture's Consequences: International Differences in Work-Related Values.*, Beverly Hills, CA: Sage Publications.

Hofstede, G. (1991) *Cultures and Organizations: Software of the Mind*, New York: McGraw-Hill.

Hofstede, G. (1993) "Cultural constraints in management theories," *Academy of Management Executive* 7 (1): 81–94.

Holden, N.J. (2002) *Cross-Cultural Management: A Knowledge Management Perspective.* Harlow: Pearson Education.

Hollingworth, J.R. and Boyer, R. (1997) *Contemporary Capitalism: The Embeddedness of Instituions*, Cambridge: Cambridge University Press.

Holm, U. and Pedersen, T. (eds) (2000) *Managing Centres of Excellence*, Basingstoke, Macmillan.

Holmes, S. and Ostrovsky, S. (2003) "The new cold war at Boeing," *Business Week*, 3 February.

Holt Larsen, H. and Brewster, C. (2003) "Line management responsibility for HRM: what's happening in Europe?", *Employee Relations* 25 (3): 228–244.

Hu, Y-S. (1992) "Global or stateless corporations are national firms with international operations," *California Management Review* 34 (2):107–126.

Hugo, G., Rudd, D. and Harris, K. (2001) *Emigration from Australia*. CEDA: Melbourne.

Humes, S. (1993) *Managing the Multinational: Confronting the Global–Local Dilemma*. Hemel Hempstead: Prentice Hall.

Huselid, M. (1995) "The impact of human resource management practices on turnover, productivity and corporate financial performance," *Academy of Management Journal* 38 (3): 635–672.

Huselid, M. and Becker, B. (1996) "Methodological issues in cross-sectional and panel estimates of the human resource–firm performance link," *Industrial Relations* 35 (3): 400–422

Ichniowski, C., Kochan, T., Levin, D., Olson, C. and Strauss, G. (1996) "What works at work: Overview and assessment," *Industrial Relations* 35 (3): 299–333.

Iles, P. and Yolles, M. (2002) "International joint ventures, HRM and viable knowledge migration," *International Journal of Human Resource Management* 13 (4): 624–641.

ILO (1998a) "Impact of flexible labour market arrangements in the machinery, electrical and electronic industries," Geneva: ILO Sectoral Activities Programme, ILO.

ILO (1998b) Bureau for Multinational Enterprise Activities (MULTI), "Export Processing Zones: addressing the social and labour issues," Geneva: ILO publications.

ILO (1999a) "Impact of flexible labour market arrangements in the machinery electrical and electronic industries," part 9, Geneva: ILO.

ILO (1999b) "Decent Work in the Global Economy," Discussion Paper No.1, Geneva: International Policy Group, ILO.

ILO (2000) "Labour Practices in the Footwear, Leather, Textiles and Clothing Industries," Geneva: ILO.

Industrial Relations Services (1999) "IBM delivers international HR," *Employment Trends* no. 689, October. London: IRS.

Inkpen, A. (1996) "Creating knowledge through collaboration," *California Management Review* 39: 123–140.

Inkson, K., Arthur, M.B., Pringle, J. and Barry, S. (1997) "Expatriate assignment versus overseas experience," *Journal of World Business* 32:351–368.

International Herald Tribune (1998) "France sets out to educate future world leaders," *International Herald Tribune*, 12 November, p. 1.

Ireland, R. and Hitt, M. (1999) "Achieving and maintaining strategic competitiveness in the 21st century: the role of strategic leadership," *Academy of Management Executive* 13 (1): 43–57.

Ivancevich, J.M. (1969) "Selection of American managers for overseas assignments," *Personnel Journal* 18 (3): 189–200.

Ives, B. and Jarvenpaa, S.L. (1991) "Applications of global information technology: key issues for management," *MIS Quarterly* 15 (1): 32–49.

Janssens, M. and Brett, J.M. (1994) "Co-ordinating global companies: The effects of electronic communication, organizational commitment, and a multi-cultural managerial workforce," *Trends in Organizational Behavior* 1.31–46.

Jelinek, M. and Adler, N.J. (1988) "Women: World-class managers for global competition," *Academy of Management Executive* 2 (1): 11–19.

Johansson, J.K. and Yip, G.S. (1994) "Exploiting globalization potential: U.S. and Japanese strategies," *Strategic Management Journal* 15 (8): 579–601.

Johnson, J.L. and Podsakoff, P.M. (1994) "Journal influence in the field of management: An analysis using Salancik's index in a dependency network," *Academy of Management Journal* 37: 1392–1407.

Johnson, T.J. (1972) *Professions and Power*, Basingstoke/London: Macmillan.

Johnston, J. (1991) "An empirical study of repatriation of managers in UK multinationals," *Human Resource Management Journal* 1 (4): 102–108.

Kaplan, R. and Norton, D. (1996) *The Balanced Scorecard: Translating Strategy Into Action.* Boston, MA, Harvard Business School Press.

Kay, J. (1993) *Foundations of Corporate Success*. Oxford: Oxford University Press.

Keenoy, T. (1990) "HRM: A case of the wolf in sheep's clothing," *Personnel Review* 19 (2): 3–9.

Kern, H. and Schumann, M. (1984) "New concepts of production in German plants," in P.J. Katzenstein (ed) *Industry and Politics in West Germany: Toward the Third West German Republic*, Cornell, Cornell University Press.

Kerr, C. (1983) *The Future of Industrial Societies*, Cambridge: Harvard University Press.

Kim, K., Park, J-H. and Prescott, J.E. (2003) "The global integration of business functions: A study of multinational businesses in integrated global industries," *Journal of International Business Studies* 34: 327–344.

Kirkman, B.L. and Shapiro, D.L. (2000) "The impact of cultural values on job satisfaction and organizational commitment in self-managing work teams: The mediating role of employee resistance," *Academy of Management Journal* 44: 557–569.

Klaas, B.S., McClendon, J.A. and Gainey, T.W. (2001) "Outsourcing HR: The impact of organizational characteristics," *Human Resource Management* 40 (2): 125–138.

Klein, J., Edge, G. and Kass, T. (1991) "Skill-based competition," *Journal of General Management* 16(4): 1–15.

Kobrin S.J. (1988) "Expatriate reduction and strategic control in American multinational corporations," *Human Resource Management* 27 (1): 63–75.

Kobrin, S.J. (1994) "Is there a relationship between a geocentric mind-set and multinational strategy?," *Journal of International Business Studies* 25 (3): 493–511.

Koch, M.J. and McGrath, R.G. (1996) "Improving labor productivity: Human resource management policies do matter," *Strategic Management Journal* 17: 335–354.

Kochan, T. (1998) "Strategic human resource management in the twenty-first century," in P.M. Wright, L.D. Dyer, J.W. Boudreau and G.T. Milkovich (eds) *Research in Personnel and Human Resource Management Volume 4*, Stamford, CT: JAI Press.

Kochan, T., Katz, H. and McKersie, R. (1986) *The Transformation of American Industrial Relations*, New York: Basic Books.

Kogut, B. (1997) "The evolutionary theory of the multinational corporation: Within and across country options," in B. Toyne and D. Nigh (eds) *International Business: An Emerging Vision*. Columbia, SC: University of South Carolina Press.

Korten, D. (1995) *When Corporations Rule The World*, San Francisco: Berrett-Kochler.

Kostova, T. (1999) "Transnational transfer of strategic organizational practices: A contextual perspective," *Academy of Management Review* 24 (2): 308–324.

Kostova, T. and Roth, K. (2002) "Adoption of an organizational practice by subsidiaries of multinational corporations: Institutional and relational effects," *Academy of Management Journal* 45 (1): 215–233.

Kostova, T. and Roth, K. (2003) "Social capital in multinational corporations and a micro-macro model of its formation," *Academy of Management Review* 28 (2): 297–317.

Krishnan, H.A., Miller, A. and Judge, W.Q. (1997) "Diversification and top management team complementarity: Is performance improved by merging similar or dissimilar teams?" *Strategic Management Journal* 18: 361–374.

Kuchinad, C. (2003) "Crafting an international HRM research agenda for the Asian context" *US Academy of Management Conference*, Seattle, 1–6 August.

Kuemmerle, W. (1999) "Building effective R & D capabilities abroad," *Harvard Business Review* March–April: 61–69.

Kuhn, T. (1970) *The Structure of Scientific Revolutions*, Chicago: University of Chicago Press.

Kunda, Z. and Thagard, P.F. (1996) "Forming impressions from stereotypes, traits and behaviours: A parallel-constraint-satisfaction theory," *Psychological Review* 103: 284–308.

Laabs, J.J. (1996) "Must-have global HR competencies: know-how for a successful international HR career," *Personnel Journal* 1: 13.

Lado, A. and Wilson, M. (1994) "Human resource systems and sustained competitive advantage: A competency based perspective," *Academy of Management Review* 19: 699–727.

Lane, C. (1998) "Theories and issues in the study of trust," in C. Lane and R. Bachmann (eds) *Trust Within and Between Organizations*, Oxford: Oxford University Press.

Laurent, A. (1981) "Matrix organizations and Latin cultures," *International Studies of Management and Organization* 10 (4): 101–114.

Laurent, A. (1986) "The cross-cultural puzzle of international human resource management," *Human Resource Management* 25 (1): 91–102.

Lawler, E.E. (1997) *From the Ground Up*. San Francisco: Jossey-Bass.

Lawson, T.E. and Limbrick, V. (1996) "Critical competencies and developmental experiences for top HR executives," *Human Resource Management* 35: 67–85.

Legge, K. (1995) "HRM: rhetoric, reality and hidden agendas," in J. Storey (ed.) *Human Resource Management: A Critical Text*, London: Routledge.

Lentz, S. (1996) "Hybrid organisation structures: A path to cost savings and customer responsiveness," *Human Resource Management* 35 (4): 453–469.

Levitt, T. (1983) "The globalization of markets," *Harvard Business Review* May/June: 92–102.

Liebeskind, J.P. (1996) "Knowledge strategy, and the theory of the firm," *Strategic Management Journal* 17: 93–107.

Linehan, M. and Scullion, H. (2002) "Repatriation of European female corporate executives: An empirical study," *International Journal of Human Resource Management* 13 (2): 254–267.

Locke, R., Kochan, T. and Piore, M. (eds) (1995) *Employment Relations in a Changing World Economy*, Cambridge: MIT Press, pp. 359–384.

Losey, M.R. (1997) "The future HR professional: competency buttressed by advocacy," *Human Resource Management*, 36: 147–150.

Lounsbury, M. (2002) "Institutional transformation and status mobility: The professionalization of the field of finance," *Academy of Management Journal* 45 (1): 255–266.

Lowe, K.B., Downes, M. and Kroeck, K. (1999) "The impact of gender and location on the willingness to accept overseas assignments," *International Journal of Human Resource Management* 10: 223–234.

Lu, Y. and Björkman, I. (1997) "HRM practices in China–Western joint ventures: MNC standardization versus localization," *International Journal of Human Resource Management* 8: 614–628.

Mabert, V.A., Soni, A. and Venkataraman, M.A. (2003) "The impact of organization size on enterprise resource planning (ERP) implementations in the US manufacturing sector," *Omega, International Journal of Management Science* 31 (3): 235–246.

MacDuffie, J.P. (1995) "Human resource bundles and manufacturing performance: Organizational logic and flexible production systems in the world auto industry," *Industrial and Labor Relations Review* 48: 197–221.

McKenzie, A. and Glynn, S. (2001) "Effective employment branding," *Strategic Communications Management* 5 (4): 22–26.

Madani, D. (1999) "Review of the role and impact of export processing zones," *Policy Research Working Paper*, The World Bank Development Research Group, Trade, November 1999.

Makhija, M.V., Kim, K. and Williamson, S.D. (1997) "Measuring globalization of industries using a national industry approach: empirical evidence across five countries and over time," *Journal of International Business Studies* 28 (4): 679–710.

Malbright, T. (1995) "Globalization of an ethnographic firm," *Strategic Management Journal* 16: 119–141.

Marchington, M. and Grugulis, I. (2000) "'Best practice' human resource management: Perfect opportunity or dangerous illusion?' *International Journal of Human Resource Management* 11 (4): 905–925.

Margison, P., Buitendam, A., Deutschmann, C. and Perulli, P. (1993) "The emergence of the euro-company: Towards a European industrial relations," *Industrial Relations Journal* 24 (3): 182–190.

Margison, P., Sisson, K., Martin, R. and Edwards, P. (1988) *Beyond the Work-Place: The Management of Industrial Relations in Large Enterprises*, Oxford: Blackwell.

Marr, B. and Schiuma, G. (2001) "Measuring and managing intellectual capital and knowledge assets in new economy organisations," in M. Bourne (ed.) *Handbook of Performance Measurement*, Gee: London.

Martell, K. and Caroll, S.J. (1995) "How strategic is HRM?" *Human Resource Management* 34: 253–267.

Martin, G. and Beaumont, P. (1998) "HRM and the diffusion of best practice," *International Journal of Human Resource Management* 9 (4): 671–695.

Martin, G. and Beaumont, P. (2001) "Transforming multinational enterprises: Towards a process model of strategic human resource management change," *International Journal of Human Resource Management* 12 (8): 1234–1250.

Martin, G. and Beaumont, P. (2003) *Branding and People Management: What's in a Name?* London: Chartered Institute of Personnel and Development.

Martin, X. and Salomon, R. (2003) "Knowledge transfer capacity and its implications for the theory of the multinational corporation," *Journal of International Business Studies* 34: 356–373.

Maurice, M., Sellier, F. and Silvestre, J. (1986) *The Social Foundations of Industrial Power*. Cambridge, MA: The MIT Press.

Mayrhofer, W. and Brewster, C. (1996) "In praise of ethnocentricity: Expatriate policies in European MNCs," *International Executive* 38 (6): 749–778

Mayrhofer, W. and Scullion, H. (2002) "Female expatriates in international business: Empirical evidence from the German clothing industry," *International Journal of Human Resource Management* 13 (5): 815–836.

Maznevski, M. L., DiStefano, J.J., Gomez, C.B., Noorderhaven, N.G. and Wu, P.C. (2002) "Cultural dimensions at the individual level of analysis: The cultural orientation framework," *International Journal of Cross-Cultural Management* 2 (3): 275–295.

Mendenhall, M. and Oddou G. (1985) "The dimensions of expatriate acculturation," *Academy of Management Review* 10: 39–47.

Meyer, J.W. and Rowan, B. (1983) "The structure of educational organizations," in J.W. Meyer and W.R. Scott (eds) *Organizational Environments: Ritual and Rationality*, Beverly Hills, CA: Sage, pp. 179–197.

Michaels, E., Handfield-Jones, H. and Axelrod, B. (2001) *The War for Talent*. Boston, MA: Harvard Business School Press.

Miller, D. (1993) "The architecture of simplicity," *Academy of Management Review* 18: 116–138.

Millerson, G. (1964) *The Qualifying Associations: A Study in Professionalization*. London: Routledge and Kegan Paul.

Millward, N., Bryson, A. and Forth, J. (2000) *All Change at Work?* London: Routledge.

Mitter, S. (1994) "On organising women in casualised work: A global overview," in S. Rowbotham and S. Mitter (eds) *Dignity and Daily Bread*, London and New York: Routledge.

Mittleman, J. (1994) "The globalization challenge: Surviving at the margins," *Third World Quarterly* 15 (3): 427–434.

Mohrman, S., Cohen, S. and Mohrman, A. (1995) *Designing Team-Based Organizations*, San Francisco: Jossey-Bass.

Montealegre, R. (2002) "A process model of capability development: lessons from the electronic commerce strategy at Bolsa de Valores de Guayaquil," *Organization Science* 13 (5): 514–531.

Moore, K. and Lewis, D. (1999) *Birth of the Multinationals: 2000 Years of Ancient British History – From Ashur to Augustus*, Copenhagen: Copenhagen Business Press.

Morgan, G. (1986) *Images of Organization*, Beverly Hills, CA: Sage.

Morrison, A.J. and Roth, K. (1992) "A taxonomy of business-led strategies in global industries," *Strategic Management Journal* 13 (6): 399–418.

Murtha, T.P., Lenway, S.A. and Bagozzi, R.P. (1998) "Global mind-sets and cognitive shift in a complex multinational corporation," *Strategic Management Journal*, 19: 97–114.

Myloni, B. (2002) "Transferability of Human Resource Management across Borders," in F. Analoui (ed.) *The Changing Pattern of human Resource Management*, Aldershot: Ashgate.

Mytelka, L.K. (1987) "Knowledge-intensive production and the changing internationalization strategies of multinational firms," in J.A. Caporoso (ed.) *International Economy Yearbook*, vol. 2, London: Francis Pinter.

Napier, N., Tibau, J., Jenssens, M. and Pilenzo, R. (1995) "Juggling on a high-wire: the role of the international human resources manager," in G. Ferris, S. Rosen and D. Barnum (eds) *Handbook of Human Resource Management*. Oxford: Blackwell, pp. 217–242.

Nohria, N. and Ghoshal, S. (1997) *The Differentiated Network: Organizing Multinational Corporations For Value Creation*. San Francisco, CA: Jossey-Bass Inc.

North D. (1990) *Institutions, Institutional Change and Economic Performance*, Cambridge, MA: Harvard University Press.

Novicevic, M.M. and Harvey, M. (2001) "The changing role of the corporate HR function in global organizations of the twenty-first century," *International Journal of Human Resource Management* 12 (8): 1251–1268.

Nyambegera, S., Daniels, K. and Sparrow, P.R. (2001) "Why fit doesn't always matter: The impact of HRM and cultural fit on job involvement of Kenyan employees," *Applied Psychology: an International Review* 50 (1): 109–140.

Nyambegera, S., Sparrow, P.R. and Daniels, K. (2000) "The impact of cultural value orientations on individual HRM preferences in developing countries: Lessons from Kenyan organizations," *International Journal of Human Resource Management* 11 (4): 639–663.

OECD (1996) *Measuring What People Know: Human Capital Accounting for the Knowledge Economy*. Paris: OECD.

OECD (2001) *Knowledge and Skills For Life. First Results from PISA 2000*. Paris: OECD.

Ohmae, K. (1990) *The Borderless World*, New York: HarperCollins.

Ohmae, K. (1996) *The End of the Nation State*, Cambridge, MA: Free Press.

Oliver, C. (1991) "Strategic responses to institutional processes," *Academy of Management Review* 16 (1): 145–179.

ORC (2001) "Worldwide survey of international assignment policies and practices," London and New York: Organization Resources Counselors.

Orr, J.E. (1990) "Sharing knowledge, celebrating identity: community memory in a service culture," in D. Middleton and D. Edwards (eds) *Collective Remembering*. London: Sage.

Ouchi, W.G. (1981) *Theory Z: How American Business Can Meet the Japanese Challenge*. New York, Avon Books.

Oviatt, B. and McDougall, P.P. (1995) "Global start-ups: Entrepreneurs on a worldwide stage," *Academy of Management Executive* 9 (2): 30–43.

Pajo, K. and Cleland, J. (1997) *Professionalism in Personnel. The 1997 Survey of the HR Profession*. New Zealand: Massey University.

Parker, B. (1998) *Globalization and Business Practice: Managing Across Boundaries*, London: Sage.

Parker, P. and Inkson, J. (1999) "New forms of career: The challenge of human resource management," *Asia Pacific Journal of Human Resources* 37: 76–85.

Pascale R. T. and Athos A. G. (1982) *The Art of Japanese Management*. London, Allen Lane.

Patterson, M.G., West, M.A., Lawthom, R. and Nickell, S. (1998) *Impact of People Management Practices on Business Performance*, London: Institute of Personnel and Development.

Perlmutter, M.V. (1969) "The tortuous evolution of the multinational corporation," *Columbia Journal of World Business* 4 (1): 9–18.

Peters, T. and Waterman, R. (1982) *In Search of Excellence*. New York: Harper Row.

Petrovic, J., Harris, H. and Brewster, C. (2000) "New forms of international working," *Centre for Research into the Management of Expatriation*, Cranfield: Cranfield School of Management.

Pettigrew, A.M. (1995) "Longitudinal field research on change: Theory and practice," in Huber, G.P. and Van de ven, A. (eds) *Longitudinal Field Research Methods: Studying the Processes of Organizational Change*. London: Sage.

Pfeffer, J. (1994) *Competitive Advantage Through People*, Boston, MA: Harvard Business School Press.

Pfeffer, J. (1998) *The Human Equation*. Boston, MA: Harvard Business School Press.

Phillips, J.J., Stone, R.D. and Phillips, P.P. (2001) *The Human Resources Scorecard: Measuring The Return On Investment*. Woburn, MA: Butterworth-Heinemann.

Pickard J. (1999) *Successful Repatriation: Organisational and Individual Perspectives*. Ph.D. Thesis, Cranfield University, UK.

Pieper, R. (1990) (ed.) *Human Resource Management: An International Comparison*, Berlin: Walter de Gruyter.

Pilkington, A. (1996) "Learning from joint ventures: the Rover – Honda relationship," *Business History* 38: 90–116.

PMAP (Personnel Management Association of the Philippines) (1998) *HR Competencies: The Total Picture*. Philippines: WFPMA.

Poole, M. (1986) *Industrial Relations – Origins and Patterns of National Diversity*. London: RKP.

Poole, M. (1990) "Human resource management in an international perspective," *International Journal of Human Resource Management* 1 (1): 1–15.

Porter, M.E. (1986a) "Changing patterns of international competition," *California Management Review* 28 (2): 29–40.

Porter, M.E. (1986b) "Competition in global industries: A conceptual framework," in M. Porter (ed.) *Competition in Global Industries*. Boston: Harvard Business School Press.

Porter, M.E. (1990) *The Competitive Advantage of Nations*, London: Macmillan.

Prahalad C.K. and Doz Y. (1987) *The Multinational Mission: Balancing Local Demands and Global Vision*, New York: The Free Press.

Prahalad, C.K. and Hamel, G. (1990) "The core competence of the corporation," *Harvard Business Review* 68 (3): 79–91.

Prakash, A. and Hart, J.A. (2000) (eds) *Coping With Globalization*. London: Routledge.

Pricewaterhouse Coopers (1999) *International Assignments: European Policy and Practice 1999/2000*. London: Pricewaterhouse Coopers.

Pricewaterhouse Coopers (2000) *Managing a Virtual World: Key Trends 2000/2001*. London: Pricewaterhouse Coopers.

Pucik, V. (1992) *Globalizing Management*, London: John Wiley.

Pucik, V. (1998) "Selecting and developing the global versus the expatriate manager: A review of the state-of-the-art," *Human Resource Planning* 21 (4): 40–54.

Pucik, V. (2003) "Crafting an international HRM research agenda for the Asian context," *US Academy of Management Conference*, Seattle, 1–6 August.

Purcell, J. (1995) "Corporate strategy and its link with human resource management strategy," in J. Storey (ed.) *Human Resource Management: A Critical Text*. London: Routledge, pp. 63–86.

Purcell, J. (1999) "The search for best practice and best fit in human resource management: chimera or cul-de-sac?" *Human Resource Management Journal* 9 (3): 26–41.

Purcell, J. and Ahlstrand, B. (1994) *Human Resource Management in the Multi-Divisional Firm*, Oxford: Oxford University Press.

Radice, H. (1995) "Organizing markets in Central and Eastern Europe: Competition, governance and the role of foreign capital," in J. Eckhard, G. Dittrich, G. Schmidt and R.Whitley (eds) *Industrial Transformation in Europe*, Sage Publications.

Ramaswamy, K. (1992) "Multinationality and performance: A synthesis and redirection," *Advances in International and Comparative Management*, 7: 241–267.

Ramaswamy, K., Kroeck, K.G. and Renforth, W. (1996) "Measuring the degree of internationalization of a firm: A comment," *Journal of International Business Studies* 27 (1): 167–177.

Reed, R. and DeFillippi, R.J. (1990) "Causing ambiguity, barriers to imitation, and sustainable competitive advantage," *Academy of Management Review* 15 (1): 88–102.

Reich, R. (1994) *The Work of Nations*, New York: Alfred Knopf.

Reich, R. (2000) *The Future of Success*, New York: Alfred Knopf.

Reilly, P. (2000) "HR shared services and the realignment of HR," *Institute of Employment Studies Report 368*, Brighton: IES.

Ronen, S. and Shenkar, O. (1985) "Clustering countries on attitudinal dimensions: A review and synthesis," *Academy of Management Review* 10 (3): 435–454.

Roos, J., Roos, G., Dragoneeti, N.C. and Edvinsson, L. (1997) *Intellectual Capital: Navigating in the New Business Landscape*, London, Macmillan.

Rosenzweig, P.M. and Nohria, N. (1994) "Influences of human resource management practices in multinational firms," *Journal of International Business Studies* 20 (2): 229–252.

Rousseau, D.M. (1995) *Psychological Contracts in Organizations: Understanding Written and Unwritten Agreements*. Newbury Park, CA: Sage.

Ruggles, R. (1998) "State of the notion: Knowledge management in perspective," *California Management Review* 40 (3): 80–89.

Rugman, A. (2001) *The End Of Globalization*, London: Random House Business Books.

Sackmann, S.A. (1991) *Cultural knowledge in organizations: Exploring the collective mind.* Newbury Park, CA: Sage.

Sackmann, S.A. (1992) "Culture and sub-cultures: an analysis of organizational knowledge," *Administrative Science Quarterly* 37: 140–161.

Sanchez, R. and Heene, A. (1997) *Strategic Learning and Knowledge Management*. New York: John Wiley.

Sanders, W. and Carpenter, M. (1998) "Internationalization and firm governance: The roles of CEO compensation, top team composition, and board structure," *Academy of Management Journal* 41: 158–178.

Scarbrough. H. and Elias, J. (2002) *Evaluating Human Capital*. London: Chartered Institute of Personnel and Development.

Schackwell, S. (2002) "Brand champions will be rewarded," *Personnel Today* 3 December, pp. 22–24.

Schein, V.E. (1996) "Career anchors revisited: Implications for career development in the 21st century," *Academy of Management Executive* 10 (4): 80–88.

Schein, V.E., Mueller, R., Lituchy, T. and Liu, J. (1996) "Think manager – think male: a global phenomenon?" *Journal of Organizational Behavior* 17 (1): 33–41.

Schiuma, G., Harris, H. and Bourne, M. (2002) "Assessing the value of international assignments," *Centre for Business Performance/Centre for Research into the Management of Expatriation*, Cranfield School of Management.

Schiuma, G., Bourne, M., Neely, A. and Harris, H. (2001) "Assessing the value of international assignments, *Cranfield School of Management Report*, Cranfield.

Schneiberg, M. (1999) "Political and institutional conditions for governance by association: Private order and price controls in American fire insurance," *Politics and Society* 27: 67–103.

Schneider, S.C. (1989) "Strategy formulation: The impact of national culture," *Organization Studies* 10 (2): 149–168.

Schneider, S.C. and Barsoux, J-L. (2003) *Managing Across Cultures*, 2nd edition, Harlow: Pearson Education.

Scholz, C. (1993) *Personalmanagement. Informationsorientierte und Verhaltenstheoretische*, Munchen: Franz Vahlen.

Schoonover, S.C. (1998) *Human Resource Competencies For The Year 2000*. US: SHRM Foundation.

Schuler, R.S. (1992) "Linking the people with the strategic needs of the business," *Organizational Dynamics*, Summer: 18–32.

Schuler, R.S. (2001) "Human resource issues and activities in international joint ventures," *International Journal of Human Resource Management* 12 (1): 1–52.

Schuler, R.S. and Huber, C.H. (1993) *Personnel and Human Resource Management*, 5th edition, Minneapolis/St. Paul: West Publishing Company.

Schuler, R.S. and Jackson, S. (1987) "Linking competitive strategies with human resource management practices," *Academy of Management Executive* 1 (3): 207–219.

Schuler, R.S. and Jackson, S.E. (2001) "HR issues and activities in mergers and acquisitions," *European Management Journal* June: 253–287.

Schuler, R.S., Dowling, P. and De Cieri, H. (1993) "An integrative framework of strategic international human resource management," *Journal of Management* 19 (2): 419–459.

Schuler, R.S., Jackson, S.E. and Luo, Y. (2003) *Managing Human Resources in Cross-Border Alliances*, London: Routledge.

Schwarz, S.H (1990) "Individualism-collectivism: critique and proposed refinements" *Journal of Cross-Cultural Psychology* 21: 139–157.

Schwarz, S.H (1992) "Universals in the content and structure of values: Theoretical advances and empirical tests in 20 countries," in M. Zanna (ed.) *Advances in Experimental Psychology* 25: 1–66.

Schwarz, S.H. (1994) "Beyond individualism/collectivism: New cultural dimensions of values," in U. Kim, H.C. Triandis, C. Kagitcibasi, S.C. Choi and G. Yoon (eds) *Individualism and Collectivism*, London: Sage.

Scott, W.R (1995) *Institutions and Organizations*, Thousand Oaks, CA: Sage.

Scullion, H. (1992) "Strategic recruitment and development of the international manager," *Human Resource Management Journal* 3 (1): 57–69.

Scullion, H. and Brewster, C. (2001) "The management of expatriates: Messages from Europe," *Journal of World Business* 36 (4): 346–365.

Scullion, H. and Starkey, K. (2000) "In search of the changing role of the corporate human resource function in the international firm," *International Journal of Human Resource Management* 11 (6): 1061–1081.

Sera, K. (1992) "Corporate globalization: A new trend," *Academy of Management Executive* 6 (1): 89–96.

Shackwell, S. (2002) "Brand champions will be rewarded," *Personnel Today* 3 December: 22–24.

Singh, R. (1992) "Human resource management: A sceptical look," in B. Towers (ed.) *Handbook of Human Resource Management*, Oxford: Blackwell.

Sisson, K. and Scullion, H. (1985) "Putting the corporate personnel department in its place," *Personnel Management* 17 (12): 36–40.

Solomon, C.M. (1994) "Staff selection impacts global success," *Personnel Journal* 73 (1): 88–101.

Spar, D.L. and La Mure, L.T. (2003) "The power of activism: Assessing the impact of NGOs on global business," *California Management Review* 45 (3): 78–101.

Sparrow, P.R. (1995) "Integrating HRM strategy using culturally-defined competencies at British Petroleum: Cross-cultural implementation issues," in J.M. Hiltrop and P.R. Sparrow (eds) *European Casebook on Human Resource and Change Management*, London: Prentice-Hall.

Sparrow, P.R. (1997) "Organizational competencies: creating a strategic behavioural framework for selection and assessment," in N. Anderson and P. Herriot (eds) *International Handbook of Selection and Assessment*, Chichester: John Wiley, pp. 343–368.

Sparrow, P.R. (1998) "Re-appraising psychological contracting: Lessons for employee development from cross-cultural and occupational psychology research," *International Studies of Management and Organization* 28: 30–63.

Sparrow, P.R. (1999) *The CIPD Guide on International Recruitment, Selection and Assessment.* London: Chartered Institute of Personnel and Development.

Sparrow, P.R. (2000) "International reward management," in G. White and J. Drucker (eds) *Reward Management – A Critical Text*, London: Routledge.

Sparrow, P.R. (2001) "Limited 'window' for HR's global influence," *Worldlink* 11 (4): 1–3.

Sparrow, P.R. (2002) "Globalization as an uncoupling force: Internationalization of the HR Process?" in P. Gunnigle (ed.) *The John Lovett Lectures: A Decade of Development of Human Resource Management in Ireland*, Dublin: Liffey Press, pp. 245–278.

Sparrow, P.R. and Budwhar, P. (1997) "Competition and change in India: Mapping transitions in HRM," *Journal of World Business* 32 (3): 224–242.

Sparrow, P.R. and Cooper, C.L. (2003) *The Employment Relationship: Key Challenges for HR*, London: Butterworth-Heinemann.

Sparrow, P.R. and Hiltrop, J.M. (1994) *European Human Resource Management in Transition*, London: Prentice-Hall.

Sparrow, P.R. and Hiltrop, J.M. (1997) "Redefining the field of European human resource management: A battle between national mindsets and forces of business transition," *Human Resource Management* 36 (2): 1–19.

Sparrow, P.R. and Wu, P.C. (1998) "How much do national value orientations really matter? Predicting HRM preferences of Taiwanese employees," *Employee Relations: The International Journal* 20 (1): 26–56.

Sparrow, P.R. and Wu, P.C. (1999) "How much do national value orientations really matter?" Predicting HRM preferences of Taiwanese employees," in S. Lähteenmäki, L. Holden and I. Roberts (eds) *HRM and the Learning Organization.* Turun Kauppakorkeakoulun Julkaisuja: Turku.

Sparrow, P.R., Schuler, R.S. and Jackson, S. (1994) "Convergence or divergence: Human resource practices and policies for competitive advantage worldwide," *International Journal of Human Resource Management* 5 (2): 267–299.

Sparrow, P.R., Braun, W., Brewster, C.B. and Harris, H. (2003) *BOC Case Study: Globalizing The Last Frontier.* Manchester Business School.

Sparrow, P.R., Braun, W., Harris, H. and Brewster, C.B. (2003) *Shell People Service Case Study: Engineering International HR Knowledge.* Manchester Business School.

Spender, J.-C. (1998) "The dynamics of individual and organizational knowledge," in C. Eden and

J.-C. Spender (eds) *Managerial and Organizational Cognition: Theory, Methods and Research.* London: Sage.

Stahl, G. and Cerdin, J-L. (forthcoming) "Global careers in French and German MNCs," *Journal of Management Development.*

Stevens, T. (2002) *The IBM Case Study*, Paper presented at E&P International Seminar on New International Structures of the HR Function, Paris, 11–12 April, 2002.

Stone, R.M. (1991) "Expatriate selection and failure," *Human Resource Planning* 14 (1): 8–9.

Stonehouse, G., Hamill, J., Campbell, D. and Purdie, T. (2000) *Global and Transnational Business: Strategy and Management.* Chichester: Wiley.

Stopford, J.M. and Dunning, J.H. (1983) *The World Directory of the Multinational Enterprises 1982–83.* Detroit, MI: Gale Research Company.

Stopford, J.M. and Wells, L.T. (1972) *Managing the Multinational Enterprise.* New York: Basic Books.

Stopper, W.G. (2003) "Point-Counterpoint: How does HR outsourcing impact the power and influence of the function?" *Human Resource Planning* 26 (1): 9–11.

Storey, J. (1992) "HRM in Action: the truth is out at last," *Personnel Management* April: 28–31.

Strange, S. (1998) *Mad Money.* Manchester: Manchester University Press.

Stroh L.K. and Caligiuri P. (1998) "Increasing Global Effectiveness Through Effective People Management," *Journal of World Business* 33 (1): 1–17.

Stroh, L.K., Gregerson, H.B. and Black, J.S. (1998) "Closing the gap: expectations versus reality among expatriates," *Journal of World Business* 33 (2): 11–124.

Sullivan, D. (1994) "Measuring the degree of internationalization of a firm," *Journal of International Business Studies* 25 (2): 325–342.

Sullivan, D. (1996) "Measuring the degree of internationalization of a firm: A reply," *Journal of International Business Studies* 27 (1): 179–192.

Sullivan, D. and Bauerschmidt, A. (1989) "Common factors underlying barriers to exports: a comparative study in the European and US paper industry," *Management International Review* 29 (2): 46–63.

Sundaram, A.K. and Black, J.S. (1992) "The environment and internal organization of multinational enterprises," *Academy of Management Review* 17: 729–757.

Suutari, V. and Brewster, C. (1999) "International assignments across European borders: No problems?" in C. Brewster and H. Harris *International Human Resource Management: Contemporary Issues in Europe*, Routledge, London.

Suutari, V. and Brewster, C. (2000) "Making their own way," *Journal of World Business* 35: 417–436.

Suutari, V. and Brewster, C. (2001) "Expatriate management practices and perceived relevance: Evidence from Finnish expatriates," *Personnel Review* 30 (5): 554–577.

Suutari, V. and Brewster, C. (2003) "Repatriation: Empirical evidence from a longitudinal study of careers and expectations among Finnish expatriates," *International Journal of Human Resource Management* 14 (7): 1132–1151.

Sveiby, K.E. (1997) *The New Organizational Wealth – Managing and Measuring Knowledge Based Assets*, San Francisco, CA: Berrett-Koehler.

Tallman, S. and Fladmoe-Lindquist, K. (2002) "Internationalization, globalization and capability-based strategy," *California Management Review* 45 (1): 116–135.

Tayeb, M. (2003) *International Management: Theories and Practices*, Harlow: Pearson Education.

Taylor, S., Beechler, S. and Napier, N. (1996) "Toward an integrative model of strategic international human resource management," *Academy of Management Review* 21 (4): 959–985.

Teece, D.J., Pisano, G. and Shuen, A. (1997) "Dynamic capabilities and strategic management," *Strategic Management Journal* 18 (7): 509–533.

Tharenou, P. (2004) "The initial development of receptivity to working abroad: self-initiated international work opportunities in young graduate employees," *Journal of Occupational and Organizational Psychology.*

Tichy, N., Fombrun, C.J. and Devanna, M.A. (1982) "Strategic human resource management," *Sloan Management Review* 23 (2): 47–60.

Tolbert, P.S. (1991) "Occupations, organizations, and boundaryless careers", in M.B. Arthur and D.M. Rousseau (eds) *The Boundaryless Career.* New York: Oxford University Press, pp. 331–349.

Tolbert, P.S. and Zucker, L.G. (1996) "The institutionalization of institutional theory," in S.R. Clegg, C. Hardy and W.W. Nord (eds) *Handbook of Organizational Studies*, London: Sage, pp. 175–90.

Torbiorn, I. (1982) *Living Abroad: Personal Adjustment and Personnel Policy in the Overseas Setting*, New York: Wiley.

Trends International (2001) "Foreign investment: Belgium favourite," *Trends International Belgium* April (3):42.

Trompenaars, F. (1993) *Riding the Waves of Culture: Understanding Cultural Diversity in Business*, London: Economist Books.

Tung, R.L. (1993) "International human resource management practices of multinationals in transition: The case of Australia," in P.D. Frub and D. Khambata (eds) *The Multinational Enterprise in Transition*, 4th edition, Princeton, NJ: The Darwin Press, pp. 343–351.

Tung, R.L. (1995) "Strategic human resource challenge: Managing diversity," *International Journal of Human Resource Management* 6 (3): 482–493.

Tung R.L. (1998) "American expatriates abroad: From neophytes to cosmopolitans," *Journal of World Business* 33 (2): 125–144.

Tung, R.L. (1981) "Selection and training of personnel for overseas assignments," *Columbia Journal of World Business* 23: 129–143.

Tung, R.L. and Punnett, B.J. (1993) "Research in international human resource management," in D. Wong-Rieger and F. Rieger (eds) *International Management Research: Looking to the Future*, Berlin: De Gruyter, pp. 35–53.

Turner, T. and Morley, M. (1995) *Industrial Relations and the New Order: Case Studies in Conflict and Co-Operation*, Dublin: Oak Tree Press.

Ulrich, D. (1987) "Organizational capability as competitive advantage: Human resource professionals as strategic partners," *Human Resource Planning* 10: 169–184.

Ulrich, D. (1989) "Tie the corporate knot: Gaining complete customer commitment," *Sloan Management Review* 32: 19–28.

Ulrich, D. (1995) "Shared services: From vogue to value," *Human Resource Planning* 18 (3): 12–23.

Ulrich, D. (1997) *Human Resource Champions: The Next Agenda for Adding Value to HR Practices*, Boston: Harvard Business School Press.

Ulrich, D. (1998) "Intellectual capital = Competence $\times$ Commitment," *Sloan Management Review* 41: 15–26.

Ulrich, D. (2000) "From eBusiness to eHR," *Human Resource Planning* 20 (3): 12–21.

Ulrich, D. and Eichinger, R.W. (1998) "Delivering HR with an attitude," *HRMagazine*, June, accessed via www.shrm.org/hrmagazine/articles/0698ulrich.htm

Ulrich, D. and Lake, D. (1990) *Organization Capability: Competing From the Inside Out*, New York: Wiley.

Ulrich, D., Brockbank, W., Yeung, A.K. and Lake, D.G. (1995) "Human resource competencies and empirical assessment," *Human Resource Management* 34: 473–495.

United Nations Development Programme (UNDP) (1999) *"Human Development in this age of Globalization,"* New York and Oxford: Oxford University Press.

Van Fleet, D.D., McWilliams, A. and Siegel, D.S. (2000) "A theoretical and empirical analysis of journal rankings: The case of formal lists," *Journal of Management* 26: 839–861.

Van Hoy, J. (1993) "Intraprofessional politics and professional regulation," *Work and Occupations* 20 (1): 90–110.

Vermuelen, F. and Barkema, H. (2001) "Learning through acquisitions," *Academy of Management Journal* 44 (3): 457–476.

Vernadat, F.B. (1996) *Enterprise Modelling and Integration: Principles and Applications*, London: Chapman and Hall.

Vernon, R. (1971) *Sovereignty at Bay: The Multinational Spread of U.S. Enterprises*. New York: Basic Books.

Vernon, R. (1998) *In the Hurricane's Eye: The Troubled Prospects of Multinational Enterprises*, Cambridge, MA: Harvard University Press.

Viatsos, C. (1989) "Radical technological changes and the new 'order' in the world economy," in R. Kaplinsky and C. Cooper (eds) *Technology and Development in the Third Industrial Revolution*, Newbury Park: Frank Cass.

Walker, J. (1988) *Defining Requirements for Human Resource Staff Effectiveness*. Working paper, The Walker Group.

Wanniski, J. (1995) The New American Imperialism. *Wall Street Journal*, 6 July, p. 8.

Watson, T J. (1977) *The Personnel Managers. A Study in the Sociology of Work and Employment.* London: Routledge and Kegan Paul.

Weick, K.E. and Van Orden, P. (1990) "Organizing on a global scale," *Human Resource Management* 29: 49–62.

Welch, D. (1998) *The Psychological Contract and Expatriation: A Disturbing Issue for HRM?*, Paper presented at the 6th Conference on International Human Resource Management, University of Paderborn, 22–25 June, 1998.

Werner, S. (2002) "Recent developments in international management research: A review of 20 top management journals," *Journal of Management* 28 (3): 277–305.

Westwood, R.I. and Leung, S.M. (1994) "The female expatriate manager experience: Coping with gender and culture," *International Studies of Management and Organization* 24: 64–85.

Whipp, R. (1991) "Human resource management, strategic change and competition: The role of learning," *International Journal of Human Resource Management* 2 (2): 165–191.

Whitley, R.D. (1999) *Divergent Capitalisms: The Social Structuring and Change of Business Systems*, Oxford University Press, Oxford.

Whitley, R.D. (ed.) (1992) *European Business Systems: Firms and Markets in their National Contexts*, London: Sage.

Wild, A. (2003) "Pressure point," *People Management* 9 (14): 34–35.

Wiley, C. (1999) "A comparative analysis of certification in human resource management," *International Journal of Human Resource Management* 10: 737–762.

Williams, B. (1985) *Ethics and the Limits of Philosophy*, Fontana Press/Collins.

Williamson, J.G. (1996) "Globalization and inequality: Then and now," *Working Paper 5491*, March. Cambridge, MA: National Bureau of Economic Research.

Williamson, O.E (1975) *Markets and Hierarchies*, New York: Free Press.

Williamson, O.E. (1985) *The Economic Institutions of Capitalism*, New York: Free Press.

World Bank (1995) "Workers in an integrating World," *World Development Report*, New York: Oxford University Press.

Wright, P.M. and Dyer, L. (2001) "People in the e-business: New challenges and solutions," *US Human Resource Planning Society State-of-the-Art Report*, Cornell University: Cornell Center for Advanced Human Resource Studies.

Wright, P.M. and Gardner, T.M. (2003) "The human resource-firm performance relationship: methodological and theoretical challenges," in D. Holman, T. Wall, C. Clegg, P. Sparrow and A. Howard (eds) *The New Workplace: A Guide to the Human Impact of Modern Working Practices*, Chichester: Wiley.

Wright, P.M. and McMahan, G.C. (1992) "Theoretical perspectives for strategic human resource management," *Journal of Management* 18 (2): 295–320.

Wright, P.M. and Snell, S.A. (1991) "Toward an Integrative view of strategic human resource management," *Human Resource Management Review* 1: 203–225.

Wright, P.M., McMahan, G.C. and McWilliams, A. (1994) "Human resources and sustained competitive advantage: A resource-based perspective," *International Journal of Human Resource Management* 5: 301–326.

Wright, P.M., Gerhart, B.A., Snell, S.A. and McMahan, G.C. (1997) "Strategic human resource management: Building human capital and organizational capacity," *Technical report, SHRM Foundation and Human Resource Planning Society*.

Wu, P.C. and Sparrow, P.R. (2002) "Influence of cultural values and work value/job satisfaction fit on organizational commitment," Paper presented at US Academy of Management Conference, Denver, CO.

Yeung, A.K. (1996) "Competencies for HR professionals: An interview with Richard E. Boyatzis," *Human Resource Management* 35: 119–31.

Yip, G.S. (1992) *Total Global Strategy*, Englewood Cliffs, NJ: Prentice-Hall.

Yu, E. and Mylopoulos, J. (1997) "Modelling organizational issues for enterprise integration," in *Proceedings of International Conference on Enterprise Integration and Modelling Technology*, London: Springer-Verlag.

Index